GREAT CHEFS OF THE CARIBBEAN

GREAT CHEFS
OF THE CARIBBEAN

From the television series
Great Chefs of the Caribbean

Edited by

JULIA M. PITKIN

A CUMBERLAND HOUSE HEARTHSIDE BOOK

CUMBERLAND HOUSE
Nashville, Tennessee

Copyright © 2000 by Great Chefs® Publishing, Division of GCI, Inc.

Great Chefs® is a registered trademark of Great Chefs® Television/Publishing,
a division of G.C.I. Inc. Great Chefs® Trademark
Reg. U.S. Pat. Off. and in other countries.

A free catalog of other Great Chefs products is available.
Call 1-800-321-1499, or contact www.greatchefs.com.

Published by Cumberland House Publishing, Inc.
431 Harding Industrial Drive
Nashville, Tennessee 37211

Design by Bruce Gore, Gore Studio, Inc., Nashville, Tennessee.

Library of Congress Cataloging-in-Publication Data

Great chefs of the Caribbean : from the television series Great Chefs of the Caribbean /
edited by Julia M. Pitkin.
   p.   cm.
  "A Cumberland House hearthside book."
  ISBN 1-58182-019-4 (hardcover : alk. paper)
  1. Cookery, Caribbean.   I. Pitkin, Julia M.
TX716.A1 G76 1999
641.5'09729—dc21   90–050054

Printed in the United States of America
1 2 3 4 5 6 7 — 03 02 01 00 99

CONTENTS

CREDITS

TELEVISION SERIES

Producer/Director/Writer	John Beyer
Presenter	Mary Lou Conroy
Announcer	Al Smith
Camera	Dave Landry
	Jo Ann Newhart
Lighting	Dave Landry
Editor/Animation	George Matulik
Assistant Editor	Nick Maucele
Post-Production Audio	Nick Maucele
Theme Music composed by	Edwin Yearwood
performed by	Tony Prescott, courtesy
	of Atlantik Records
Original Music	The Charlie Byrd Sextet
	Charlie Byrd, guitar
	Chuck Redd, percussion
	Derek Dicenzo, steel
	drum
	Ken Peplowski, clarinet
	Dave Easly, clarinet
	Bill Huntington, bass
Recording Engineer	Steve Reynolds
Transportation Crew	Gen. Denny Banner
	Col. Tom Dietrich
	Capt. Mark McNab
Additional Footage	Fast Cat, St. Croix
	Atlantis Submarines
	Casa de Campo,
	Dominican Republic
Official Hotels	Casa de Campo,
	Dominican Republic

Official Airline	
Executive Administrative	
Assistant to	
the Executive Producer	Cybil W. Curtis
Executive Producer	John Shoup

BOOK

For Great Chefs	
Photography	Eric Futran
Recipe Development	Karen Levin
	Sarah Labensky,
	Mississippi University
	for Women
	Linda Anne Nix
	Alison Winter

FOR CUMBERLAND HOUSE HEARTHSIDE PUBLISHING

Editor-in-Chief	Julia M. Pitkin
Book Design	Bruce Gore

Cinnamon Reef Resort,
Anguilla
El Conquistador,
Puerto Rico
The Four Seasons Nevis
Half Moon Resort,
Jamaica
La Samanna, St. Martin
The Ritz-Carlton
Cancun
The Ritz-Carlton
St. Thomas
American Airlines

MAIL ORDER SOURCES

BALDUCCI'S
P.O. Box 10373
NEWARK, NJ 07193-0373
1-800-225-3822

The mail order division of the famed New York gourmet market, with everything from fresh pastas and excellent sauces to prime meats, desserts, and such foods as pâté de foie gras, capon, pheasant, squab, venison, and imported and domestic caviars.

CHICKORY FARMS
723 HILARY STREET
NEW ORLEANS, LA 70118
1-800-605-4550

All manner of mushrooms, both cultivated and wild.

D'ARTAGNON
399-419 ST. PAUL AVENUE
JERSEY CITY, NJ 07306
1-800-327-8246

Fresh foie gras, plus sausages, ducks and duck fat, and other specialty items.

LEGAL SEAFOOD
33 EVERETT STREET
ALLSTON, MA 02134
800-343-5804

This firm gained regional fame by offering the finest quality of seafood in its restaurants. In addition to shipping clambakes, they ship many varieties of fish and shellfish.

LEONARD SOLOMON'S WINES AND SPIRITS
L&L DISTRIBUTING
1456 NORTH DAYTON
CHICAGO, IL 60622
312-915-5911
312-915-0466 FAX

Grains, including spelt; rattlesnake and other beans, vinegars, crème fraîche, smoked fish, pâtés, caviars, special sausages, smoked duck breast, pastrami, imported cheeses, Amazon spices, frozen purées, and vanilla beans.

L'ESPRIT DE CAMPAGNE
P.O. Box 3130
WINCHESTER, VA 22604
703-955-1014

Dried vine-ripened tomatoes in various forms, including halves marinated in extra-virgin olive oil with herbs, purées, and sprinkles. The company also offers dried apples, cherries, blueberries, and cranberries, all with no preservatives.

MO HOTTA, MO BETTA
P.O. Box 4136
SAN LUIS OBISPO, CA 93403
800-462-3220
805-545-8389 FAX

Write for a catalog of hot sauces, Asian, Latin American, Indian, African, and Caribbean spices and sauces; wasabi powder, dried mushrooms, barbecue sauces, jerk sauces, and condiments.

MORE THAN GOURMET
115 W. BARTGES STREET
AKRON, OH 44311
1-800-860-9392

Demi-Glace Gold® and Glace de Poulet Gold®, two classic French sauces of four-star quality that are made in the classic manner of Escoffier. An ultimate shortcut for the home cook.

PAPAYA ORCHARDS OF HAWAII, INC.
800 LEILANI STREET
HILO, HI 96720
800-678-6248

Frozen passion fruit, papaya, and guava purées, fresh papaya.

PENZEYS, LTD.
P.O. BOX 1448
WAUKESHA, WI 53187
414-574-0277
414-574-0278 FAX

A wonderful source of spices and herbs by mail. A mail order catalog is available.

SWEET CELEBRATIONS
P.O. BOX 39426
EDINA, MN 55439
1-800-328-6722
612-943-1688

A complete catalog of confectioners' supplies, including chocolate and other ingredients, and equipment.

TAKE HOME MAUI, INC.
121 DICKENSON STREET
LAHAINA, HI 96761
808-661-8067
808-661-1550 FAX

A mail-order source for fresh pineapple, papaya, and macadamia nut products.

ALBERT USTER IMPORTS, INC.
9211 GAITHER ROAD
GAITHERSBURG, MD 20877
1-800-231-8154

A professional source for confectionery and bakery supplies and tools, including edible gold dust.

WILTON ENTERPRISES, INC.
2240 WEST 75TH STREET
WOODRIDGE, IL 60515
708-963-7100, EXT. 320

Pastry and cake decorating supples, paste food colors, and icing ingredients.

Soups and Salads

Cucumber Soup

Bent Rasmussen

Top Hat
St. Croix, U.S. Virgin Islands

SERVES 6

3	medium cucumbers
1	stalk celery
1	large leek
3	cups Chicken Stock (see page 235) or canned chicken broth
1	bay leaf
2	tablespoons all-purpose flour
2	tablespoons butter, softened (start with half)
½	cup sour cream (or crème fraîche), plus additional for garnish

¼	cup heavy cream (or additional sour cream or crème fraîche)
2	tablespoons chopped fresh dill, plus additional for garnish
1	tablespoon fresh lime juice
1	teaspoon sugar
¾	teaspoon salt
½	teaspoon ground white pepper
	Black caviar

❀ Peel, seed and dice two of the cucumbers. Place in a food processor and process until puréed. Transfer the purée to a large saucepan. Chop the celery stalk and white part of the leek. Place in the food processor and process until very finely chopped. Add to the saucepan. Add the chicken stock and bay leaf to the saucepan, and bring to a simmer. Simmer uncovered for 20 minutes.

❀ In a small bowl combine the flour and butter, mixing until well blended. Add to the soup and simmer for 2 minutes or until thickened. Remove from the heat and cool to room temperature. Cover and chill at least 2 hours or overnight.

❀ Discard the bay leaf. Stir the sour cream and cream into the soup. Peel, seed, and coarsely shred the remaining cucumber. Stir the cucumber into the soup. Stir in the dill, lime juice, sugar, salt and pepper. Cover and chill until cold.

❀ To serve: Ladle the soup into bowls. Top each serving with a spoonful of sour cream and caviar. Sprinkle with additional dill.

SHRIMP ASOPAO

ALFREDO AYALA

Chayote Restaurant
San Juan, Puerto Rico

SERVES 6

Asopao is a simple home-style soup/stew. Chef Alfredo Ayala dresses his for company with shrimp, capers, olives, and a garnish of roasted red pepper.

SOUP

1	cup short-grain or basmati rice
1	tablespoon olive oil
1	small onion, finely chopped
2	garlic cloves, minced
1	small banana pepper or other mild chili pepper, seeded, deribbed, and finely chopped
1	small tomato, seeded and finely chopped
2	ounces smoked ham, minced
¼	cup pitted green olives
1	tablespoon drained capers
6	cups Fish Stock (see page 236) and/or shellfish stock or bottled clam broth
1	cup coarsely chopped green beans
1	cup diced, peeled winter-style squash (butternut, pumpkin, or Hubbard)
1	clove garlic, peeled
1	tablespoon fresh oregano leaves
½	teaspoon salt
½	teaspoon freshly ground black pepper
2	pounds medium or large shrimp, cleaned and deveined
¼	cup cilantro, finely chopped
2	tablespoons culantro, finely chopped (optional)

GARNISH

1	red bell pepper, roasted, peeled, and cut into thin strips (see page 235)
1	lime, cut into 6 wedges

❈ In a medium bowl cover the rice with cold water and set aside. In a very large sauté pan or Dutch oven heat the olive oil over medium-high heat and sauté the onion, garlic, chili pepper, tomato, and ham for 1 minute. Add the olives and capers. Pour in the fish stock. Bring to a simmer. Cook at medium heat for 5 minutes. Add the green beans and squash and continue cooking for 5 minutes. Strain the rice and add to the pot. Reduce the heat to low and cook uncovered for 15 minutes or until the rice is tender.

❈ In a mortar or small bowl mash together the garlic clove, oregano, salt, and black pepper. Stir this mixture and the shrimp into the soup. Add the cilantro and culantro and cook for 3 minutes or until shrimp are opaque. Adjust the seasoning to taste.

❈ TO SERVE: Ladle the soup into large, shallow bowls. Top with strips of roasted red pepper, and serve each with a wedge of lime.

LANGOUSTINE COURT BOUILLON WITH WILD MUSHROOMS, LEEKS, AND CITRONELLA

THIERRY ALIX
La Samanna
St. Martin

SERVES 4

12	medium langoustines, or jumbo prawns	4	baby leeks
		12	wild mushrooms
	Juice of 3 lemons		
1¾	cups (3½ sticks) unsalted butter, cut into	4	sprigs chervil
	tablespoon-size pieces	4	stalks lemongrass (citronella)
4	stalks lemongrass (citronella)		
	Sea salt and freshly ground black pepper to taste		

❀| Twist the tails from the langoustines (if using prawns, remove the shells and heads). Twist the middle of the tail fins and carefully remove the black intestinal vein. Set the tail meat aside.

❀| In a large saucepan over medium-high heat bring 8 cups of water with the lemon juice and 8 tablespoons of the butter to a boil. Add the langoustine heads and shells and cook 5 minutes. Strain through a fine-mesh sieve and add the lemongrass. Return the broth to the heat and cook 8 more minutes to reduce in volume. Whisk in 8 more tablespoons of butter, sea salt, and pepper. Whisk in 4 more tablespoons of butter. Place on low heat to keep warm.

❀| Cut off the base and tips of the leeks. Clean the leeks carefully, removing all sand. Bring a pan of water to a boil, plunge the leeks into the water, return the water to a boil, and remove from heat. Drain and plunge the leeks into cold water, then drain again.

❀| Cut off the base of the mushroom stalks and scrape the stems and caps with a small knife to clean; wash briefly only if dirt is visible. In a large sauté or frying pan melt 8 tablespoons of butter over medium-high heat and sear the langoustine tails on all sides. Add the mushrooms and sear for 1 minute, rolling them gently about in the pan.

❀| TO SERVE: Place 3 langoustine tails and 3 mushrooms in each warmed serving bowl. Add 1 leek. Pour the court bouillon over them and garnish with chervil and lemongrass.

Mixed Vegetable Salad with Sweet and Sour Pan-fried Scallops

Thierry Alix
La Samanna
St. Martin

SERVES 4

Thierry Alix stresses that the vegetables must be fresh for the best salad. His spicy dressing adds an unusual "island" taste. This recipe uses nutmeg jelly; you can substitute a little apple or apricot jelly flavored with nutmeg if you can't find it in a specialty market. On the television program Chef Alix uses scallops with the coral (roe) still attached; the dish may also be made with scallops without the coral.

12	green string beans		2	teaspoons tamarind
4	baby string beans		4	teaspoons nutmeg jelly
12	snow peas		8	fresh coriander leaves
8	green peas		8	fresh mint leaves, sliced into narrow strips
1	broccoli head			
½	cauliflower head			
8	baby turnips		**Pan-fried Scallops**	
4	baby leeks		12	medium sea scallops
8	stalks white asparagus			Sea salt and freshly ground black pepper
			¼	cup olive oil
¼	cup olive oil			
8	shiitake mushroom pieces		4	red cherry tomatoes
			4	orange cherry tomatoes
			8	radishes
Ginger Vinaigrette Dressing			¼	cup grain, cooked and cooled (whole wheat-berries, quinoa, or other natural grain)
12	tablespoons ginger juice			
1	cup grapeseed oil		4	sprigs cilantro
4	teaspoons soy sauce			

❀ ❘ Snap the tips of the large green beans, wash, and drain. Bring 2 quarts of salted water to a rolling boil over high heat. Plunge the large green beans and baby green beans into the water and cook, uncovered, for 2 minutes. With a slotted spoon, remove the beans from the boiling water and plunge them into a bowl of ice water. Leave until completely cold, then drain and pat dry with paper towels. Repeat the operation with the peas, broccoli, cauliflower, turnips, leeks, and asparagus. Refrigerate until needed. Heat the oil in a sauté pan and sauté the mushrooms over medium-high heat for 2 to 3 minutes, until golden. Set aside to cool.

❀ ❘ To make the ginger vinaigrette dressing: In a deep small bowl, whisk all ingredients together.

❀ ❘ To prepare the pan-fried scallops: Season the scallops on each side with salt and pepper. Heat 1 tablespoon of olive oil in a medium skillet until it ripples; sear three scallops in the oil until they color. Turn to sear all sides; do not let them touch one another. Set aside and keep warm; repeat the operation with the remaining olive oil and scallops, three at a time.

🐢 | To serve: Slice the cauliflower into quarters, then slice each quarter into ¼-inch slices. Fan them in the center of the plates. Place the other cooked vegetables around the cauliflower. Divide the tomatoes and radishes among the plates. Drizzle with ginger vinaigrette. Sprinkle the dishes with grain. Place 3 scallops on each plate, and garnish with cilantro sprigs.

SALAD OF SAPOTE, MANGO, AVOCADO, PAPAYA, AND JICAMA WITH KEY LIME-GUAVA VINAIGRETTE

ROY KHOO
The Ritz-Carlton St. Thomas
St. Thomas, U.S. Virgin Islands

SERVES 4

A simple fruit salad mixture is tossed in a dressing that combines key lime and guava for a tropical taste. The sapote used in the recipe is a tropical fruit that has peach, avocado, and vanilla notes in its flavor. Many large markets will carry it; if you can't find it, peach or nectarine may be substituted.

GUAVA COULIS

2	teaspoons unsalted butter
3	guavas, peeled and roughly chopped
2	teaspoons sugar
¼	cup water

KEY LIME, GUAVA, AND POPPY SEED VINAIGRETTE

3	tablespoons key lime juice
7	tablespoons grapeseed oil
	Salt and freshly ground black pepper to taste
1	teaspoon poppy seeds
1	tablespoon guava coulis

SALAD

1	sapote, peeled and diced
1	mango, peeled, pitted, and diced
1	avocado, peeled, pitted, and diced
¼	papaya, peeled and julienned
1	jicama, peeled and julienned

GARNISH

2	cups coconut shavings, loosely packed
1	sprig mint, stemmed and julienned

❋| To MAKE THE COULIS: In a small skillet melt the butter over medium heat and toss the guava pieces in the butter to coat. Cook 1 minute, tossing to prevent the guava from sticking. Add the sugar and one-half of the water and cook for 3 to 4 minutes, until the guava is soft. In a blender or food processor purée with the remaining water and strain through a fine-mesh sieve into a small bowl. Put in a squeeze bottle and set aside.

❋| To MAKE THE VINAIGRETTE: Place the lime juice in a small glass or stainless steel bowl and gradually add the grapeseed oil, whisking constantly to incorporate. Whisk in the salt and pepper. Add the poppy seeds and whisk again. Set aside.

❋| To PREPARE THE GARNISH: Preheat the broiler. Spread the coconut shavings on a baking sheet and toast until slightly browned, about 1 minute. Remove and set aside to cool.

❋| To SERVE: Whisk 1 tablespoon of the guava coulis into the vinaigrette. Toss the sapote, mango, and avocado with two tablespoons of the vinaigrette. Place a 2-inch ring mold on each plate and fill with diced fruit, pressing down slightly. Lift the molds. Place the julienned papaya and jicama around the plates and drizzle with the remaining vinaigrette. Drizzle the plates with guava coulis. Top the fruit with toasted coconut and garnish each plate with mint.

CRAYFISH SALAD WITH VANILLA DRESSING

ALAIN LAURENT
Malliouhana Hotel
Anguilla

SERVES 6

¾	cup corn oil	12	large crayfish or colossal or jumbo shrimp
2	whole vanilla beans		Cajun or Creole seasoning mix (optional)
¼	cup fresh lemon juice	1	tablespoon olive oil
	Salt and freshly ground black pepper	6	cups mesclun or gourmet mixed salad
2	ripe papayas		greens
1	ripe mango		

❀| If time permits, infuse the oil by placing one vanilla bean in the oil; cover and let stand 3 days or up to 3 weeks. If desired, dry a second vanilla bean and grind to a powder in a spice or coffee grinder.

❀| Split open 1 vanilla bean (or use the drained bean from the infused oil) and scrape the pulp into the corn oil. Reserve the split bean. In a small bowl combine the oil and lemon juice. Season the dressing with salt and pepper to taste.

❀| Peel the papayas and mango. Dice one-third of each fruit, and stir into the dressing. Cut the remaining fruit lengthwise into thin slices.

❀| If using crayfish, separate the head portion from the tails. If desired, boil the head portion until bright red and reserve for plate garnish. Cut the crayfish tails (or shrimp) in half lengthwise, remove from the shell, and discard the vein. Sprinkle lightly with salt and freshly ground black pepper or with Cajun seasoning, if desired. Sprinkle with ground vanilla bean, if desired. In a large nonstick skillet heat the olive oil. Add the reserved vanilla bean. Sauté the crayfish or shrimp 2 to 3 minutes per side until golden brown and opaque.

❀| Toss the salad greens with ½ cup of the dressing. Arrange in the center of 6 serving plates. With a slotted spoon, drain and arrange the marinated diced fruit around the salad. Arrange 4 pieces of crayfish and some of the sliced fruit attractively over greens. Garnish each plate with crayfish heads, if desired.

Shrimp Salad Pionono with Calabaza Seed Vinaigrette

Jeremie Cruz

El Conquistador
Fajardo, Puerto Rico

SERVES 4

This shrimp salad gets its depth from the grilling of the shrimp and toasting of the calabaza, or pumpkin, seeds. This dish has many parts that can be used for other dishes: The pionono shells could contain any salad or even fresh fruit; the oils and glaze can accent fish or poultry. Everything can be made earlier in the day and assembled at the last minute, a real bonus!

CILANTRO OIL

1	bunch cilantro
½	cup vegetable oil
	Pinch of salt
	Pinch of freshly ground black pepper

ANNATTO OIL

½	cup grapeseed oil
¼	cup annatto (achiote) seeds

BALSAMIC GLAZE

1	cup balsamic vinegar
⅓	cup sugar

PIONONO SHELLS

2	large plantains
¼	potato, peeled
	Oil for frying

SHRIMP SALAD

18	16- to 20-count raw shrimp, shelled and deveined
4	tablespoons Cajun-style seasoning
½	head frisee lettuce
3	cups assorted greens
1	cup Calabaza Seed Vinaigrette (recipe follows)
12	Plantain Chips (see page 239)

❀ | TO MAKE THE CILANTRO OIL: Finely chop the cilantro, then whisk with the oil, salt, and pepper until blended. Put in a squeeze bottle.

❀ | TO MAKE THE ANNATTO OIL: In a saucepan heat the oil and seeds together over low heat until the oil just begins to bubble, 8 to 10 minutes. Remove from the heat and set aside for 1 hour. Strain out the seeds and put the oil in a squeeze bottle.

❀ | TO MAKE THE GLAZE: In a saucepan mix the vinegar and sugar together and cook over medium-low heat until the mixture is reduced by one-fourth. Set aside to cool. Place in a squeeze bottle.

❀ | TO MAKE THE PIONONO SHELLS: Cut the plantain lengthwise into ⅛-inch-thick strips. Cut the potato into matchsticks, ⅛ inch by 1 inch. Fold a plantain strip into a teardrop shape and pin the ends together with a potato stick; you may need to cut small slits in the plantain strip to let the potato stick pass through. Repeat with the other plantain strips to make 12. Preheat the oil to 350°F in a deep fryer. Fry the plantain circles for 1 to 2 minutes, until crisp. Drain on paper towels, open them out, and set aside.

❁| TO MAKE THE SALAD: In a small mixing bowl combine the raw shrimp and Cajun-style seasoning. Sear the shrimp in a Teflon-lined sauté pan until opaque, about 30 seconds per side. Set aside to cool, then chop coarsely. Fill a large mixing bowl with ice water, clean the lettuce, and let the leaves sit in the ice water for 2 minutes. Rinse and drain on paper towels or in a salad spinner.

❁| TO SERVE: Toss the shrimp and greens with the vinaigrette until coated. Place 3 pionono shells on each serving plate, circular parts together, and fill with the salad. Drizzle the oils and glaze around the plates. Garnish with plantain chips.

CALABAZA SEED VINAIGRETTE

MAKES 1 CUP

2	tablespoons calabaza or pumpkin seeds	2	sprigs cilantro, stemmed and minced
1	shallot, minced	8	chives, minced
2	large garlic cloves, minced	¼	cup white vinegar
¼	small red onion, minced	¾	cup olive oil

❁| Preheat the oven to 350°F. Spread the seeds in a single layer on a baking sheet and toast for 5 minutes. Place all ingredients except the oil in a mixing bowl and mix well. Slowly whisk in the oil until blended.

Appetizers

❁

ESCARGOT-STUFFED MUSHROOMS

CECILE BRIAUD

Le Chanticlair
St. Martin

SERVES 4

MUSHROOMS

12	large stuffing mushrooms
¼	cup bottled clam juice
2	tablespoons fresh lemon juice

LEEK SAUTÉ

1	tablespoon extra-virgin olive oil or unsalted butter
1	large leek, white and light green parts julienned
¾	cup fresh or rehydrated wakame seaweed (If seaweed is not available, use two leeks.)
¼	cup bottled clam juice
	Salt and freshly ground black pepper

MUSHROOM FILLING AND SAUCE

½	ounce dried morel mushrooms
1	cup boiling water
1	tablespoon unsalted butter
¼	cup minced shallots
¼	cup bottled clam juice
1	cup heavy cream
	Salt, freshly ground black pepper, and freshly grated nutmeg

ESCARGOT

1	tablespoon unsalted butter
36	drained canned escargot
1	log (7 to 8 ounces) goat cheese
2	cups packed baby spinach leaves, stems discarded

OPTIONAL GARNISHES

Deep-fried julienned leeks, parsley sprigs, and tomato skins

❁ | FOR THE MUSHROOMS: Heat the oven to 350°F. Clean the mushrooms; remove and reserve the stems. Place the mushrooms hollow side down in a shallow baking dish in one layer. Pour clam juice and lemon juice over the mushrooms. Cover the dish with foil and bake for about 30 minutes until the mushrooms are tender. Drain the mushrooms, reserving the juices. Keep warm.

❁ | FOR THE LEEK SAUTÉ: In a large nonstick skillet heat the olive oil over medium-high heat. Add the leek(s) and cook for 5 minutes or until golden brown, stirring occasionally. Add the seaweed and sauté for 1 minute. Add the clam juice and simmer for 1 minute. Season with salt and pepper to taste. Keep warm.

❁ | FOR THE MUSHROOM SAUCE: Cover the dried morel mushrooms with boiling water. Let stand for 30 minutes or until the mushrooms are hydrated and tender. Chop the reserved fresh mushroom stems. Drain and chop the morel mushrooms. In a large saucepan melt the butter over medium heat. Add the chopped mushrooms and shallots and sauté about 5 minutes until tender. Add the reserved baked mushroom juices and clam juice and simmer for 5 minutes. Add the cream and simmer for 5 minutes. Season with salt, pepper, and nutmeg to taste. Strain the mixture, reserving the solids and liquid. Reheat the liquid in the same saucepan.

❀| FOR THE ESCARGOTS AND ASSEMBLY: In a large skillet melt the butter over medium heat. Add the escargot and sauté for 3 minutes or until hot.

❀| TO SERVE: Spoon the leek mixture into 4 warmed shallow serving bowls. Place 3 mushrooms hollow sides up in each dish. Spoon the reserved chopped mushroom mixture into the mushroom caps. Top each mushroom cap with 3 escargot. Cut the goat cheese into 12 slices; place 1 slice over each mushroom cap. (Alternately, goat cheese may be crumbled and sprinkled over the mushrooms.) Place the bowls on a large baking sheet. Broil 3 to 5 inches from the heat source about 3 minutes, just until the cheese is golden brown. Add the spinach leaves to the cream mixture in the saucepan. Cook 1 minute or until the spinach is slightly wilted. Spoon the sauce and spinach around the mushrooms. Garnish as desired.

HONDURAN SCALLOP CEVICHE

DOUGLAS RODRIGUEZ

El San Juan Hotel & Casino
San Juan, Puerto Rico

This ceviche is a quick and easy dish to prepare that speaks of the Caribbean. The sweetness of the scallops and coconut is balanced by the heat of the garnish. The fish sauce may be found in many markets and in Asian groceries.

SERVES 4

SCALLOP CEVICHE

2	pounds bay scallops
1	cup lime juice
1	teaspoon salt
2	cans coconut milk
3	ounces fresh ginger
2	tablespoons fish sauce (nam pla)
1	tablespoon sugar

GARNISH

	Rock salt for serving
4	coconuts, halved (see page 240)
2	scallions, chopped
1	bunch chives, chopped
1	small onion, julienned
1	bunch cilantro, chopped
1	jalapeño pepper, seeded and chopped (see page 235)

❀ | TO MAKE THE CEVICHE: Place the scallops in a nonreactive bowl with the lime juice and salt. Marinate for 5 minutes. Strain the scallops into a bowl and set aside. Add the marinade to a blender with the coconut milk, ginger, fish sauce, and sugar. Purée. Pour over the scallops again and refrigerate for at least 4 hours.

❀ | TO SERVE: Place a mound of rock salt on each serving plate. Place one coconut half on each mound to stabilize for service. Divide the scallops and marinade among the coconut shells. Surround the shells with crushed ice. Sprinkle with various chopped and julienned garnishes.

Ecuadorian Shrimp Ceviche

Douglas Rodriguez

El San Juan Hotel & Casino
San Juan, Puerto Rico

This fresh-tasting ceviche starts with blanched shrimp. The lime juice is added as close as possible to serving time. The dish gets its spicy heat from jalapeños and Tabasco; roasting the vegetables adds depth to the flavor. The chef adds a whimsical touch with a garnish of cornnuts and popcorn.

SERVES 4

1	pound shrimp, peeled and cleaned
1	large tomato, roasted and seeded
2	red bell peppers, roasted and seeded
2	green bell peppers, roasted and seeded
2	jalapeño peppers, roasted
½	medium onion, roasted
¾	cup fresh lime juice
½	cup fresh orange juice
¼	cup ketchup
	Tabasco or other hot pepper sauce to taste
	Salt to taste
2	scallions, white and green parts, chopped

1	small whole red onion, sliced into thin rings
4	whole cilantro leaves or 2 culantro leaves, cut into chiffonade

GARNISH

1	avocado
1	large tomato, peeled, seeded, and chopped
½	cup cornnuts
1	cup popcorn, popped
4	chives, chopped
4	cilantro or culantro leaves

❊ Bring a large pot of water to a rolling boil and add the shrimp all at once. Let the water return to a rolling boil; the shrimp will begin to curl. Immediately drain into a colander, then plunge the shrimp into ice water. Let chill. Remove and pat dry.

❊ In a blender place the tomato, peppers, onion, lime juice, orange juice, ketchup, and hot pepper sauce, and purée. Season to taste with salt. Place the shrimp in a large bowl and pour the sauce over them. Toss to cover. Add the chopped scallions, one-half of the sliced onion rings, and cilantro or culantro.

❊ To serve: Remove the pit from the avocado, remove the skin, and cut into 4 long wedges. Slice each wedge into thin pieces, keeping the pieces together. Lift one of the sliced wedges, holding it together with your hands, and place it to one side of the plate. With your hands, slide the pieces apart slightly, creating a wall of sliced avocado. Repeat with the remaining plates. Spoon the ceviche in the center of the plates and pour extra sauce over each plate. Top the ceviche with the remaining onion rings. Sprinkle tomato cubes, cornnuts, and popcorn around the plate. Top with chives and a cilantro or culantro leaf.

TURMERIC COCO-YUCA WITH DUCK CONFIT AND TAMARIND GLAZE

RAMESH PILLAI

El Conquistador
Fajardo, Puerto Rico

Richly spiced, this duck confit is crisped just before serving. The turmeric coco-yuca blends the mild yuca with browned coconut and ginger, and serves as a Caribbean-flavored base for the dish. The duck is salted and refrigerated for 24 hours before being cooked; the cilantro oil and tamarind paste can both be made ahead of time.

SERVES 4

CILANTRO OIL

1	bunch cilantro
8	ounces (1 cup) grapeseed oil

TAMARIND GLAZE

2	teaspoons tamarind paste
2	teaspoons sugar
½	cup water
	Pinch of salt

DUCK CONFIT

	Kosher salt
2	duck legs and 2 duck thighs
1	tablespoon olive oil
3	cinnamon sticks
1	tablespoon cinnamon
6	whole cloves
12	black peppercorns

12	coriander seeds
12	juniper berries
3	bay leaves
1	pound duck fat
½	bunch fresh thyme, stemmed and crushed
½	carrot, minced
½	medium onion, minced
½	stalk celery, minced
1	garlic clove, minced

TURMERIC COCO-YUCA

2	cups yuca, peeled and diced
1	teaspoon turmeric
	Pinch of salt
2	teaspoons butter
2	teaspoons chopped shallots
½	cup coconut, grated
½	teaspoon chopped gingerroot
½	jalapeño pepper, seeded and deribbed

❈ | TO PREPARE THE CILANTRO OIL: Blanch the cilantro by plunging into boiling water for 30 seconds, then plunging into ice water to cool. Dry with paper towels. In a blender purée the cilantro with the grapeseed oil. Strain through a fine-mesh sieve and store in a covered glass jar.

❈ | TO PREPARE THE TAMARIND GLAZE: In a medium saucepan mix all ingredients and reduce over medium heat to a syrupy consistency, about 10 minutes. Store in a covered glass jar; if refrigerated, rewarm before using.

❈ | TO PREPARE THE CONFIT: Using about 1 teaspoon kosher salt per pound of duck, thoroughly coat the duck legs and thighs with salt and refrigerate for 24 hours.

❀ | Rinse off the salt and pat the duck dry with paper towels. In a medium skillet heat the olive oil over medium-high heat and sear the duck legs and thighs on both sides to brown. Add the cinnamon, cloves, peppercorns, coriander seeds, juniper berries, and bay leaves to the pan and reduce the heat to medium. Cook for 3 minutes. Remove from the heat and set aside.

❀ | Preheat the oven to 225°F. In a Dutch oven melt the duck fat over medium heat. Add the thyme, carrot, onion, celery, and garlic. Stir in the duck and spices from the skillet; the fat should just cover the duck pieces. Cover and bake for 2 hours, or until the meat falls off the bones.

❀ | Take out of the oven, remove the duck skin, and trim off the fat. Pull the meat off the bones and shred.

❀ | To PREPARE THE COCO-YUCA: Bring a pot of water to a boil over medium-high heat. Add the yuca, half of the turmeric, and a pinch of salt, and boil until fork-tender. Drain and set aside. In a small sauté pan or skillet melt the butter and sauté the shallots, coconut, ginger, and pepper for about 2 minutes until the coconut is lightly toasted. Add the yuca and remaining turmeric. Sauté 2 minutes, then remove from the heat.

❀ | To SERVE: Preheat the broiler to high. Spread the duck on a baking sheet and lightly crisp under the broiler. Divide the coco-yuca among the plates. Top with the duck confit. Garnish with cilantro oil and tamarind glaze.

CARIBBEAN TUNA TARTARE

MARK EHRLER

The Ritz-Carlton Cancun
Cancun, Mexico

SERVES 4

DRIED MANGOES

    Corn oil
1   ripe mango, peeled
    Freshly ground black pepper

TARTARE

⅓   cup plus 1 tablespoon corn oil, divided
½   cup chopped onion
2   tablespoons adobo paste or powder*
½   cup diced banana
½   cup diced mango
⅓   cup chicken stock or canned chicken broth

1   egg yolk**
1   pound sushi-quality ahi tuna, cut into small
       dice
    Salt
    Lime juice

GARNISH

    Shaved celery root or fennel bulb
    Chicken stock or canned chicken broth
    Baked masa dough spoons or wafers
      (optional)

❀ | TO PREPARE THE DRIED MANGOES: Heat the oven to 200°F. Using a mandolin, cut thin (⅛ inch thick) lengthwise slices of peeled mango. Place a sheet of parchment paper in a jelly roll pan. Spread a thin film of oil over the parchment. Arrange the mango slices in one layer over the parchment; sprinkle with pepper. Bake for 1 hour to 1 hour and 15 minutes or until dry, but not brown. Cool and cut any large slices in half lengthwise.

❀ | TO PREPARE THE TARTARE: In a large skillet heat 1 tablespoon of the oil over medium-high heat. Add the onion and sauté for 5 minutes. Add the adobo paste or powder and cook 1 minute. Add the banana and mango, and mix well. Add the chicken stock, and simmer uncovered for 5 minutes or until the mixture is thickened. Cool. Purée in a blender or food processor. Chill the mixture until cold.

❀ | Reserve ¼ cup of the chilled mixture for the sauce; transfer the remaining mixture to a food processor. Add the egg yolk. With the motor running, add the remaining ⅓ cup of oil in a stream through the feed tube. Process until the mixture is the consistency of mayonnaise. Season to taste with salt. Combine 3 tablespoons of this mixture with the tuna and mix well. Add just enough additional mixture to bind and season the tuna. Season to taste with salt and lime juice.

❀ | For each serving, arrange a 4 x 3-inch rectangle of dried mango slices over a banana leaf or piece of plastic wrap. Spoon one-fourth of the tuna mixture down one short side of the rectangle. Roll the mixture tightly into a cylinder. Repeat with the remaining ingredients to make 4 cylinders; chill until cold.

❀ | TO SERVE: Unwrap the tuna cylinders and stand upright on 4 serving plates. Arrange shaved celery root around the tuna. Stir chicken stock into the ¼ cup of reserved adobo mixture until the desired sauce consistency; spoon over the celery root. Garnish with masa spoons, if desired.

*If adobo paste or powder is not available, substitute 1 tablespoon of Mexican seasoning blend plus ½ teaspoon of crushed saffron threads or paprika.

**The egg yolk in this recipe is not cooked; if you are concerned about possible salmonella contamination in the eggs you buy, heavy cream may be substituted.

ARTICHOKE TERRINE WITH SMOKED SALMON AND GOAT CHEESE

ALAIN LAURENT
Malliouhana Hotel
Anguilla

SERVES 4

4	large artichokes, trimmed	4	ounces thinly sliced smoked salmon
8	ounces goat cheese (chèvre)	½	cup extra-virgin olive oil
½	cup whipping cream	3	tablespoons balsamic vinegar
6	tablespoons chopped fresh chives, divided		Garnish: yellow teardrop tomato and red
	Salt and freshly ground black pepper to taste		cherry tomatoes

❀ | In a large pot cook the artichokes in boiling salted water about 45 minutes until tender. Drain and cool to room temperature. Discard the tough outer leaves, and reserve softer inner leaves and "cap" of the artichoke leaves. Pull off and discard the fuzzy choke from the artichoke heart. Slice each heart horizontally into thirds.

❀ | In a medium bowl combine the goat cheese, whipping cream, and 4 tablespoons of the chives, and mix well. Season with salt and pepper. For each serving, arrange one slice of artichoke on a work surface. Spread a layer of goat cheese over the artichoke; top with a slice of salmon, folding or cutting to fit. Repeat layering with the remaining 2 slices of artichoke heart, goat cheese, and salmon. Spread a layer of goat cheese around the edges of the terrines. Arrange the reserved artichoke leaves and "cap" over the layered mixture attractively. Place a ring mold around each artichoke terrine to hold it in place as it chills. Chill at least 2 hours or overnight. In a medium bowl combine the oil, vinegar, and remaining 2 tablespoons of chives. Whisk well and season to taste with salt and pepper. Cover and chill until serving time.

❀ | TO SERVE: Unmold the artichoke terrines onto 4 serving plates. Arrange the tomatoes and additional reserved artichoke leaves attractively around the terrines. Drizzle the oil mixture over and around the terrines.

Barbuda Langouste Risotto with Sun-dried Tomatoes and Beet and Curry Oils

Keith Scheible

St. James's Club
Antigua

Creamy risotto is flavored with langouste and tomato, with colorful bits of spinach chiffonade.

SERVES 2

Beet Oil		1	tablespoon olive oil
½	cup beet juice	⅔	cup Arborio rice
¼	cup olive oil	½	cup dry white wine
		2	cups lobster broth
Curry Oil		2	tablespoons tomato paste
½	cup olive oil	2	tablespoons chopped sun-dried tomatoes
1	tablespoon Madras curry powder	1	small tomato, diced
		4	large spinach leaves, stemmed and cut in chiffonade
1	langouste, or spiny lobster		Salt and freshly ground black pepper
		1	tablespoon unsalted butter
1	small onion, minced	¼	cup freshly grated Parmesan cheese
4	garlic cloves, minced		

❦ | To make the beet oil: In a small saucepan over medium heat, stir together the beet juice and olive oil. Cook until the mixture is reduced by one-fourth. Remove from heat and set aside to cool. When cool, put in a squeeze bottle.

❦ | To make the curry oil: In a small saucepan over medium heat, warm 2 tablespoons of the oil and stir in the curry powder. Cook, stirring gently, for 30 seconds. Add the remaining oil and heat until bubbles form. Remove from the heat and set aside to cool. When cool, put in a squeeze bottle.

❦ | Bring a large saucepan of lightly salted water to a boil over high heat and add the langouste. Cover and cook for 6 to 8 minutes until opaque throughout. Remove the langouste and drain, reserving the cooking broth. Cool the langouste, twist off the tail, and remove the tail meat. Cut two medallions from the tail and reserve. Roughly chop the remaining tail meat.

❦ | In a large saucepan over medium heat combine the onion, garlic, and olive oil, and sauté until the vegetables are translucent, stirring occasionally to keep them from sticking. Stir in the rice, toss to coat, and cook for 5 minutes. Combine the wine and lobster broth. Add ½ cup of the wine-broth mixture to the rice, stirring constantly until it is absorbed. Add a second half cup of wine-broth mixture and stir until absorbed. Stir in the tomato paste and dried tomato. Continue adding the liquid ½ cup at a time, stirring between additions until the liquid is absorbed. The process takes about 15 minutes. When the rice has absorbed all the liquid and is creamy, fold in the diced tomato, three-fourths of the spinach chiffonade, and the langouste meat. Stir in the butter and cheese until they are melted and the rice is slightly bound together by the cheese.

❀| To SERVE: Place a 3-inch ring mold in the center of a serving plate and fill with risotto, packing it slightly with the back of a spoon. Gently lift the mold. Place a medallion of langouste meat on top of the risotto. Repeat with the remaining plate. Sprinkle the plates with spinach chiffonade and top each risotto with a few pieces of leek. Drizzle the plate with beet and curry oils.

Fresh Red Tuna Tartare

PATRICK GATEAU
The Carl Gustav Hotel
St.-Barthélemy

Perfect, sushi-grade tuna is the basis for this dish, and it must be fresh. The lovely presentation creates a torte, iced with sour cream and topped with a cherry tomato. The dish may be made ahead of time and set to chill; when ready, lift the molds and add the garnish.

SERVES 4

1½	pounds fresh red tuna, cut into ½-inch dice	1	tomato, diced
	Salt and freshly ground white pepper to	1	bunch scallions, minced
	taste	1	tablespoon extra-virgin olive oil
	Juice of 12 limes		Salt and freshly ground black pepper to taste
¼	cup capers, chopped		
12	cornichons or other tiny dill pickles, chopped	½	cup sour cream
2	shallots, minced	8	to 10 chives, minced
1	tablespoon ketchup		
¼	cup mayonnaise	4	cherry tomatoes
		4	sprigs fresh fennel

❀| In a large bowl mix the tuna, salt and pepper, lime juice, capers, pickles, shallots, ketchup, and mayonnaise, and refrigerate. In a separate bowl mix together the tomato, scallions, olive oil, and salt and pepper, and chill.

❀| Place a 5-inch steel ring or piece of PVC pipe about 1½ inches tall in the center of each serving plate. Divide the tuna mixture among the rings and press down slightly. Top the tuna with sour cream and spread to the edges. Chill.

❀| To SERVE: Lift the molds off the tuna. Place a cherry tomato in the center of each. Place tablespoonfuls of the tomato mixture around the plates. Garnish the plates with fennel sprigs.

ONION PIE

PIERRE CASTAGNE
Le Perroquet
St. Maarten

You need to start a day ahead, as the onion purée must be cold for the final preparation.

SERVES 8

ONION PURÉE

5   jumbo onions, cut into rings
1   tablespoon butter

PIE SHELL

¾   pound puff pastry

⅔   cup heavy (whipping) cream
5   whole eggs
     Salt and freshly ground black pepper to taste
1   sprig parsley, stemmed and chopped

1   head Bibb lettuce, cleaned
1   large tomato, stemmed and cut into thin
     vertical slices

❀| TO MAKE THE ONION PURÉE: Place the onions and butter in a covered saucepan and put over medium heat. Cook for 15 minutes, remove the cover, and turn the heat to medium-high to reduce the liquid. Cook for 10 minutes until the onions are the color of blond caramel and the liquid has cooked away. Remove from the heat and cool completely. Cover and chill overnight.

❀| TO MAKE THE PIE SHELL: Roll the puff pastry out on a floured board until it is ⅛ inch thick and 11 to 12 inches across. Roll up on the rolling pin, place on a 9-inch fluted tart pan with a removable bottom, and unroll across the pan. Press into the pan, then press the sides into place, and trim flat across the top. Trim any excess from the rim. Prick the crust lightly with the tip of a knife or a fork.

❀| TO FINISH: Preheat the oven to 450°F. In a medium bowl blend the cold onion purée with the heavy cream and eggs. Stir in the seasonings and parsley. Pour the mixture into the pie shell and place the oven. Cook for 10 to 15 minutes, until the top is golden brown and a knife inserted in the center comes out clean. Remove from the oven and let cool. Remove the pan and cut into 8 slices. Serve each with Bibb lettuce leaves and a thin slice of tomato.

CUCUMBER SOUP (PAGE 2)

SHRIMP ASOPAO (PAGE 3)

MIXED VEGETABLE SALAD
WITH SWEET AND SOUR PAN-FRIED SCALLOPS (PAGE 5)

SALAD OF SAPOTE, MANGO, AVOCADO, PAPAYA, AND JICAMA WITH KEY LIME-GUAVA VINAIGRETTE
(PAGE 6)

CARIBBEAN TUNA TARTARE (PAGE 18)

CRAYFISH SALAD WITH VANILLA DRESSING (PAGE 8)

HONDURAN SCALLOP SEVICHE (PAGE 14)

ARTICHOKE TERRINE WITH SMOKED SALMON
AND GOAT CHEESE (PAGE 19)

BARBUDA LANGOUSTE RISOTTO WITH SUN-DRIED TOMATOES
AND BEET AND CURRY OILS (PAGE 20)

COLOMBO OF BLACK MUSSELS WITH LEEKS (PAGE 39)

CALABAZA RISOTTO (PAGE 40)

PARMESAN BASKET WITH POLENTA AND ROASTED VEGETABLES (PAGE 42)

BONITO TARTARE (PAGE 44)

CARIBBEAN LOBSTER SPRING ROLLS
WITH CRISP LEEKS AND RED CURRY-HONEY
DIPPING SAUCE (PAGE 48)

SCALLOPS WITH SAUTÉED SWEET POTATO
RELISH (PAGE 52)

BLACK BEAN CAKES WITH BUTTERFLIED
SHRIMP AND CHILI BUERRE BLANC (PAGE 58)

LOBSTER PANCAKES WITH STINGYTIME SAUCE
(PAGE 64)

GARLIC-CRUSTED CRAYFISH TAILS (PAGE 66)

GRILLED SWORDFISH WITH SOY-GINGER BUERRE BLANC (PAGE 78)

SALMON TOURNEDOS WITH MANGO, BRIE CHEESE AND A ROASTED TOMATO VELOUTÉ (PAGE 82)

BARBECUED SWORDFISH AND CRISPY FRIED GULF SHRIMP
WITH ROCK LOBSTER AND SQUID INK RISOTTO, TROPICAL MANGO SALSA,
AND PINEAPPLE-CILANTRO DRESSING (PAGE 80)

Colombo of Black Mussels with Leeks

Benoit Pepin
Little Dix Bay Resort
Virgin Gorda, British Virgin Islands

SERVES 4

VEGETABLE NAGE

1	small leek, white and light green parts thinly sliced
1	stalk celery, thinly sliced
1	small carrot, thinly sliced
½	white onion, thinly sliced
½	fennel bulb, thinly sliced
2	tablespoons sliced fresh gingerroot
	Fresh herb sprigs (2 each): thyme, rosemary, basil, Italian parsley
2	bay leaves
2	whole star anise
2	whole cloves
2	teaspoons colombo or Madras curry powder (colombo is a Caribbean curry powder)
½	teaspoon fennel seed
½	teaspoon black peppercorns
½	teaspoon coriander seed

	Pinch salt
2	cups dry white wine or vermouth
2	cups water

MUSSELS

4	tablespoons unsalted butter
2	shallots, chopped
1	cup dry white wine or vermouth
36	large fresh black mussels
2	teaspoons colombo or Madras curry powder

GARNISH

20	slices leek, poached
8	large Swiss card leaves, steamed
1	tomato, diced
4	large garlic croutons
	Chervil sprigs

❋ | FOR THE VEGETABLE NAGE: In a 3-quart saucepan combine all ingredients. Bring to a simmer and cook for 25 minutes.

❋ | FOR THE MUSSELS: In a large sauté pan heat 1 tablespoon of the butter and sauté one of the shallots for 2 minutes. Add the wine and bring to a simmer. Add the mussels, cover, and simmer about 3 minutes until the mussels open. Pour the mussels into a colander, reserving the mussel juice. Cool. Remove the mussels from their shells and set aside.

❋ | In the same sauté pan melt 1 tablespoon of the butter. Sauté the remaining shallot for 1 minute. Add the curry powder; sauté 1 minute. Add the reserved mussel juice. Strain the vegetable nage, pressing on the solids to extract all juices. Discard the vegetables. Add the juices to the sauté pan. Simmer gently for 15 minutes. Stir in the remaining 2 tablespoons of butter and reserved mussels. Heat just until the butter melts and the mussels are hot.

❋ | TO SERVE: Arrange 5 slices of poached leek star fashion in the bottom of 4 shallow bowls. Arrange the chard in the center of the leeks. Spoon the mussels and sauce over the chard and leeks. Garnish with tomato, garlic croutons, and chervil sprigs.

CALABAZA RISOTTO

RAMESH PILLAI

El Conquistador
Fajardo, Puerto Rico

SERVES 6

Calabaza is a Caribbean pumpkin. Any pumpkin, or even hard winter squash, will work for the recipe. The stock should be made at least a day ahead so the flavors can blend; it may be prepared even earlier and frozen until ready to make the risotto. Check the amount of cayenne; if you prefer foods on the milder side, reduce the amount of cayenne used.

CALABAZA STOCK

2	tablespoons canola oil
2	medium onions, coarsely chopped
8	garlic cloves, crushed
2	carrots, peeled and coarsely chopped
3	celery ribs including leaves, cut into 1-inch pieces
1	small calabaza or pumpkin, peeled and cut into chunks
1	bay leaf
1	star anise
3	sprigs parsley
½	teaspoon nutmeg
2	quarts water
	Salt and freshly ground black pepper to taste

PLANTAIN BASKETS

8	plantains
	Canola oil for frying

CALABAZA RISOTTO

3	tablespoons unsalted butter
3	shallots, minced
3	garlic cloves, minced
½	teaspoon saffron
2	cups dry white wine
1	cup Arborio rice
2	cups calabaza stock (above)
	Salt and freshly ground black pepper
1	cup calabaza, cut into medium dice

¼	cup heavy (whipping) cream
¼	cup shaved parmesan cheese

INDIAN PORK PICKLE

1½	pounds lean pork, cut into 1-inch dice
1	tablespoon plus 1 teaspoon turmeric powder
2	teaspoons cayenne, to taste
1	teaspoon salt
1	tablespoon unsalted butter
6	shallots, sliced
2	cloves garlic, minced
2	tablespoons grated fresh ginger
3	teaspoons coriander powder
1	to 2 teaspoons cayenne to taste
2	tablespoons extra-virgin olive oil
1	teaspoon cardamom
¼	teaspoon cloves, powdered
¾	teaspoon cinnamon
¼	cup distilled white vinegar

MANGO RELISH

½	mango, diced
1	small red onion, diced
½	red bell pepper, seeded, deribbed, and diced
1	teaspoon cilantro, chopped
	Pinch salt
	Pinch cayenne

½	cup Balsamic Syrup (see page 238)
1	green onion

❀| To make the stock: In a large stock pan heat the oil and sauté the onions and garlic until soft. Add the carrots and celery and sauté for 1 minute. Add the remaining ingredients and bring to a boil over medium-high heat. Skim the foam from the top, reduce the heat to low, and simmer for 30 minutes. Remove, let cool, and refrigerate overnight. Bring the stock back to a simmer over medium heat, then strain through a fine-mesh sieve. Remove the calabaza and purée; strain back into the stock and stir to blend. Store in the refrigerator for 24 hours to allow the flavors to blend.

❀| To make the plantain baskets: Peel the plantains and cut into thin lengthwise slices, ⅛ inch thick. In a large skillet over medium-high heat, heat 2 inches of oil to 350°F, or until a breadcrumb immediately sizzles and comes to the top when dropped in. On a work surface, crisscross 2 plantain slices, pressing at the center. Criss-cross them with 4 more plantain slices to create a "star," pressing together at the center each time more slices are added. Using a large spatula, drop into the hot oil. Fry the plantain "star," turning once, about 3 to 4 minutes until lightly browned and crisp. Invert a cup or small bowl and lay a paper towel over the bottom. Remove the plantain "star" from the oil with a slotted spoon and lay over the inverted cup or bowl, pressing the sides down around the cup. Let stand until cooled, then remove and set aside on more paper towels. Repeat this process with the remaining plantains to complete 3 more cups.

❀| To make the risotto: In a large skillet melt 1 tablespoon of the butter over medium-high heat and sauté the shallots and garlic until softened. Stir in the saffron. Pour in ½ cup of the white wine, deglaze the pan by stirring up the browned bits, and add the remainder of the wine. Cook until reduced by half. Add the rice and half of the stock. Cook, stirring constantly, until the rice has absorbed the stock. Season with salt and pepper. Add half of the remaining stock and continue to stir the mixture as it cooks, until the stock is absorbed. Stir in the calabaza and cook 30 minutes longer, until the calabaza is tender. Add more stock as needed, stirring the mixture often. Add the remaining butter and the cream and stir until the butter has melted. Add the cheese and stir until melted. Set aside, covered, and keep warm.

❀| To make the pickled pork: Season the meat with 1 tablespoon of turmeric, 1 teaspoon of the cayenne, and salt, working the seasonings into the meat with your hands. Set aside. In a medium saucepan melt the butter over medium-high heat and sauté the shallots and garlic until soft. Stir in the remaining turmeric, ginger, coriander, and cayenne to taste, and cook 1 minute to bring up the aroma of the spices. Stir in the pork and toss to coat. Cook until the mixture is almost dry, then stir in the olive oil. Continue cooking for 10 more minutes. Mix the cardamom, cloves, and cinnamon powder and add to the pork mixture. Cook for 30 seconds, add the vinegar, and cook for 30 more seconds. Remove from heat and set aside.

❀| To make the relish: In a medium bowl toss all ingredients together.

❀| To serve: Place a 4-inch ring mold in the center of a serving plate and fill with risotto. Press down in the center of the risotto to form a concave top. Remove the ring mold and place a plantain basket in the top of the risotto. Fill the basket with pork. Put balsamic syrup in a squeeze bottle and draw 3 curved designs on the plate with the syrup. Place a dot of oil from the pork inside each curve of syrup. Place 4 small spoonfuls of relish around the edge of the plate. Cut the green tips from the inner portions of the onion and place them in the center of the pork for garnish.

PARMESAN BASKET WITH POLENTA AND ROASTED VEGETABLES

JANICE BARBER

The White House Inn
St. Kitts

SERVES 4

Baskets made of freshly grated Parmesan cheese melted together and formed into cups hold a piece of polenta and a selection of roasted vegetables. This is an easy recipe to work with; the only "trick" is that the cheese must be freshly grated. Any selection of vegetables can be used.

PARMESAN BASKETS

8	ounces Parmesan cheese, coarsely grated

TOMATO SAUCE

1	tablespoon olive oil
4	garlic cloves, minced
1	small onion, minced
2	tomatoes, peeled, seeded, and chopped

PESTO OIL

⅓	cup olive oil
10	to 12 basil leaves
2	ounces Parmesan cheese, finely grated

POLENTA

2	cups Vegetable Stock (see page 236)
½	cup cornmeal
1	tablespoon olive oil
	Salt and freshly ground black pepper

ROASTED VEGETABLES

1	pound mixed vegetables, cubed (eggplant, zucchini, tomatoes, shallots)
2	tablespoons olive oil
1	teaspoon chopped basil
	Salt and freshly ground black pepper
8	basil leaves, cut in chiffonade
4	sprigs fresh basil

❁ | TO MAKE THE BASKET: Preheat the oven to 400°F. Spread the Parmesan cheese into 4 circles on a Teflon baking sheet, making sure the pieces within each circle overlap and the thickness is even. You will need to use 2 baking sheets, or bake in two batches. Bake for 8 to 10 minutes or until the cheese has fused to itself; test by lifting one side with a plastic spatula. Remove and immediately place over an inverted glass, shaping the cheese into a basket. Allow to cool and harden. Remove from the glasses and store in an airtight container until used.

❋| To MAKE THE TOMATO SAUCE: In a small sauté pan heat the olive oil and sauté the garlic and onion over medium heat until translucent. Add the tomatoes, reduce the heat to low, and cook about 15 minutes until the tomatoes lose their shape and the mixture thickens slightly. Put in a squeeze bottle.

❋| To MAKE THE PESTO OIL: Process the ingredients in a food processor or blender until liquefied. Put in a squeeze bottle.

❋| To MAKE THE POLENTA: Grease a baking sheet. In a large saucepan bring the stock to a boil over medium-high heat. Gradually whisk in the cornmeal, olive oil, and seasonings. Lower the heat to medium and cook for 20 minutes, stirring continually. Spread onto the prepared baking sheet and allow to set. Cut into 2½-inch circles.

❋| To MAKE THE VEGETABLES: Preheat the oven to 400°F. Toss the vegetables with olive oil, basil, salt, and pepper. Spread on a baking sheet and roast for 30 minutes.

❋| To SERVE: Reheat the polenta in the oven, or sauté for 2 minutes a side in olive oil. Place a Parmesan basket on each serving plate. Press a polenta circle into the bottom of each basket. Fill with vegetables. Drizzle the plate with tomato and pesto oils. Garnish each plate with chiffonade of basil leaves and a fresh basil sprig.

BONITO TARTARE

DAYN SMITH
Stingray Cafe
El Conquistador, Puerto Rico

SERVES 4

CILANTRO PURÉE

1	cup packed cilantro leaves without stems
2	tablespoons vegetable oil

CILANTRO AIOLI

1	egg yolk*
1	tablespoon lemon juice
1	teaspoon Dijon mustard
3	cloves roasted garlic, mashed or 1½ teaspoons bottled minced roasted garlic
½	cup vegetable oil
	Cilantro purée
	Salt, cayenne and freshly ground white pepper

TARTARE

1	pound sushi-quality bonito or ahi tuna
1	tablespoon minced Bermuda (red) onion
½	teaspoon minced fresh ginger root
¼	teaspoon cayenne pepper
1	teaspoon fresh lemon or lime juice
1	teaspoon rice wine vinegar
	Salt and freshly ground black pepper

GARNISH

	Teriyaki glaze or thick sweet soy sauce
12	long deep fried yuca chips
	Mesclun or mixed baby salad greens
	White wine vinaigrette
	Onion sprouts

❀ | FOR THE CILANTRO PURÉE: Place the cilantro in a food processor or blender. Add the oil and process to make a thick purée, scraping down the sides of the container once.

❀ | FOR THE CILANTRO AIOLI: In a food processor or blender place the egg yolk, lemon juice, mustard, and garlic. With the motor running, add the oil in a stream and process until thick. (Alternately, the mixture may be whisked by hand.) Add the cilantro purée and process 10 seconds. Add salt, cayenne, and white pepper to taste. Add additional lemon juice, if desired. Process 10 seconds.

❀ | FOR THE TARTARE: Cut the tuna into ¼-inch dice and place in a large bowl. Add the onion, 3 tablespoons of the cilantro aioli, ginger, cayenne pepper, lemon juice, and vinegar and mix gently. Add salt and pepper to taste. Pack into four 3-inch high, 2-inch diameter plastic molds (have plastic PVC pipes cut to order), or pack into plastic wrap–lined small custard cups or ramekins. Cover and chill at least 30 minutes or up to 4 hours before serving.

❀ | TO SERVE: Place the remaining cilantro aioli in a squeeze bottle. Squeeze the sauce attractively over 4 serving plates. Place the teriyaki glaze in a squeeze bottle. Squeeze over aioli in the opposite direction. Unmold the tartare in the center of the plates. Garnish the tops of the tartare with yuca chips. Dress the salad greens lightly with vinaigrette. Place greens and onion sprouts over the tartare.

*The egg yolk in this recipe is not cooked; if you are concerned about possible salmonella contamination in the eggs you buy, heavy cream may be substituted.

Seared Yellowfin Tuna Tartare

Michael Madsen
**Divi Resort & Casino
St. Croix, U.S. Virgin Islands**

SERVES 4

TUNA TARTARE

6	ounces very fresh yellowfin (ahi) tuna, chopped
¼	cup finely chopped shallots or sweet onion
2	tablespoons chopped chives
2	tablespoons drained capers
1	egg yolk*
¼	teaspoon salt
¼	teaspoon freshly ground black pepper
4	slices very fresh yellowfin (ahi) tuna medallions, cut ½ inch thick
1	tablespoon olive or vegetable oil

SAGE-CREAM SAUCE

2	tablespoons unsalted butter
¼	cup chopped shallots or sweet onion
2	tablespoons sliced fresh sage leaves
½	cup dry white wine such as Chardonnay
½	cup heavy cream
	Salt and freshly ground black pepper to taste
4	cups small romaine lettuce leaves or mesclun salad greens

OPTIONAL GARNISHES

Freshly grated horseradish
Whole sage leaves, dredged in cornmeal and deep-fried until crisp

❈ | FOR THE TUNA: In a medium bowl combine the chopped tuna, shallots, chives, capers, egg yolk, salt, and pepper and mix well. Spread the mixture evenly over the tuna medallions. In a large non-stick skillet heat the oil over medium-high heat until hot. Add the medallions (in batches, if necessary) to the skillet and cook until the bottom of each medallion is seared, about 2 minutes (the chopped tuna mixture on top will be uncooked).

❈ | FOR THE SAGE-CREAM SAUCE: In a large skillet melt the butter over medium heat. Add the shallots and sauté for 3 minutes. Add the sage and sauté for 1 minute. Add the wine and simmer about 3 minutes until reduced by half. Add the cream and simmer about 2 minutes until slightly thickened. Season the sauce with salt and pepper.

❈ | TO SERVE: For each serving, wilt 1 cup of lettuce leaves briefly in the hot sauce, turning to coat lightly with the sauce. Transfer to a serving plate. Top with a tuna medallion. Garnish with horseradish and fried sage leaves, if desired.

*The egg yolk in this recipe is not cooked; if you are concerned about possible salmonella contamination in the eggs you buy, heavy cream may be substituted.

SALT FISH SPRING ROLLS

RICHARD BUTTAFUSO

The Sugar Mill Hotel
Tortola, British Virgin Islands

SERVES 4

The salty flavor of the fish complements the crisp fried crust of the spring rolls. While the mustard is a traditional flavor associated with spring rolls, the mango coulis is a piquant island touch.

SALT FISH

4	ounces salt cod
½	cup sugar
1	teaspoon honey

VEGETABLES

2	red peppers
12	large spinach leaves
1	onion, julienned
1	tablespoon butter
	Salt to taste

MANGO COULIS

2	mangoes, pitted and diced
2	tablespoons sugar
	Juice of 1 lemon

MUSTARD SAUCE

1	cup mayonnaise
¼	cup prepared Chinese hot mustard
1	teaspoon lemon juice
½	cup heavy (whipping) cream
1½	tablespoons soy sauce
	Salt and freshly ground white pepper to taste

SPRING ROLL ASSEMBLY

1	egg
¼	cup milk or water
4	large egg roll wrappers (5 to 6 inches)
1	plantain, quartered lengthwise
	Canola oil for frying

❀ | TO PREPARE THE SALT FISH: In a saucepan place the salt cod, ¼ cup of the sugar, and honey in cold water and bring to a boil over medium-high heat. Pour off the water, add fresh water and the remaining sugar, and bring to a boil again. Cook until the fish has softened. Drain, cool the fish, and remove and discard the bones and skin. Mix the salt cod with the honey and refrigerate.

❀ | TO PREPARE THE VEGETABLES: Roast the peppers over direct flame until charred. Rub with a cold moist towel to remove the skin. Cut the peppers in half, remove the seeds, and cut into long strips. Blanch the spinach leaves in boiling water for 5 seconds. Drain. Spread on a dry towel, roll up the towel, and squeeze to remove all the water. Chop the spinach. In a skillet sauté the onions in the butter over medium heat about 3 minutes until translucent and lightly browned. Keep the vegetables separate; season to taste.

❀ | TO MAKE THE COULIS: Toss all ingredients together in a bowl and set aside.

❀ | TO PREPARE THE MUSTARD SAUCE: In a medium bowl mix the mayonnaise with the Chinese mustard. Add the lemon juice. Stir in the heavy cream. Add the soy sauce. Season to taste.

❀ | To ASSEMBLE THE ROLLS: Mix the egg and milk or water to form an egg wash. Lay 4 wrappers on a work surface. Place the chopped spinach diagonally along the center of each. Lay some slices of pepper on the spinach. Sprinkle with onion. Arrange the salt cod on top of the peppers. Top each with a plantain quarter, cut into 2 pieces. Brush egg wash on the edges of the spring roll wrappers. Fold the bottom corner to the center of a roll. Fold the sides in to the center, then roll toward the top corner. Lightly press the edges to seal. Repeat with the remaining rolls.

❀ | In a deep-fat fryer or deep pot heat the oil to 350°F. Drop the rolls into the hot fat and fry for 2 to 3 minutes or until golden brown. Remove with a slotted spoon and drain on paper towels.

❀ | To SERVE: Slice each roll diagonally through the center. Stand 2 halves, points up, on each plate. Spoon mustard sauce around the rolls. Garnish the plates with spoonfuls of mango coulis.

CARIBBEAN LOBSTER SPRING ROLLS WITH CRISP LEEKS AND RED CURRY-HONEY DIPPING SAUCE

DAVID KENDRICK

Kendrick's
St. Croix, U.S. Virgin Islands

SERVES 4

Crisp lobster spring rolls stand at attention around a mound of fried leeks. The curry-based dipping sauce covers the plates. These wonderful rolls could also be made with shrimp.

FILLING

8	lobster tails
¼	cup olive oil
4	garlic cloves, minced
3	yellow bell peppers
8	leeks, white part only
2	large carrots
2	small zucchini, julienned
4	sprigs cilantro
4	sprigs thyme
	Salt and freshly ground black pepper to taste
12	spring roll wrappers
	Light vegetable oil for frying

DIPPING SAUCE

¼	cup red Thai curry paste
4	teaspoons sesame oil
2	cups honey
4	garlic cloves, minced
3	sprigs parsley, minced
½	cup (1 stick) unsalted butter
4	teaspoons rice wine vinegar

CRISPY LEEKS

12	leeks, white part only, cleaned and julienned
	Flour for dusting
	Vegetable oil for deep-fat frying
4	sprigs cilantro, stemmed and cut into chiffonade

❈ | To MAKE THE FILLING: Bring a pot of salted water to a rolling boil and drop in the lobster tails. Cook for 8 to 10 minutes, until opaque throughout. Remove, drain, and let cool. Remove the shells and cut into chunks. In a medium sauté pan heat the olive oil over medium-high heat and sauté the pepper for 30 seconds. Add the leeks, carrots, zucchini, cilantro, and thyme, and toss to coat. Sauté for 1 to 2 minutes until soft. Season with salt and pepper. Add the lobster meat and toss, then sauté for 30 seconds. Remove from the heat.

❈ | To MAKE THE SPRING ROLLS: Heat the oven to 350°F. Place the wrappers flat on the work surface. Put a heaping tablespoon of filling in the center of each wrapper, extending it in a line across the center. Fold in the left and right sides of a wrapper. Fold up the bottom and continue rolling, tucking in the filling, until the wrapper is completely sealed around the filling. Moisten the edge and press to seal. Repeat with the remaining wrappers and filling. In a deep fryer or large deep saucepan heat the oil to 350°F. Lightly fry the spring rolls until pale golden brown, turning 3 times to cook all sides. Drain on paper towels. Place on a baking sheet, and bake for 7 to 8 minutes to complete the cooking.

❈| To make the dipping sauce: In a dry sauté pan heat the curry paste over medium heat. Reduce the heat to medium-low. Whisk in the oil, honey, garlic, and parsley. When blended, remove from heat, stir in the butter, and return to the heat until thick and bubbly. Remove from the heat and cool. When cool, whisk in the rice wine vinegar.

❈| To make the crispy leeks: In a deep fryer or deep saucepan heat the oil to 350°F . Dust the leeks with flour, shaking off the excess. Fry a handful at a time for 30 seconds, until golden. Remove with a slotted spoon and drain on paper towels. Repeat until all the leeks have been fried.

❈| To serve: Cut a thin piece straight across the ends of the lobster rolls to square them, then cut through the center on the diagonal. Spoon the sauce into the plates in a thin layer. Place a cluster of leeks in the center. Stand 6 lobster roll sections around the leeks. Sprinkle with the cilantro chiffonade.

AHI TUNA TEMPURA, GRILLED RICE PAPER, AND MANGO-BLACK BEAN DRESSING

MARTIN FROST
Four Seasons Resort
Nevis

SERVES 4

Each colorful tuna roll shows off its filling when it is cut on the bias and stood up on the plate. An unusual garnish is the toasted rice paper, used vertically as a divider on the plates. The mango-black bean dressing could be used with other fish dishes. This dish depends on the quality of the tuna.

MANGO–BLACK BEAN DRESSING

½	cup cooked black beans
½	cup mango, peeled and diced
1	teaspoon cilantro, chopped
1	tablespoon sweet chili sauce
⅛	cup rice wine vinegar
⅛	cup sake
¼	cup soy sauce
	Freshly ground black pepper
1	tablespoon cilantro

4	3-ounce ahi tuna steaks
12	stems of pencil asparagus, blanched
¼	yellow bell pepper, seeded, deribbed, and cut into narrow strips

4	baby carrots, peeled and blanched
	Salt and freshly ground black pepper
2	sheets nori (dried seaweed)

TEMPURA

1	cup all-purpose flour
1	cup plus 2 tablespoons soda water
	Pinch salt
	Light vegetable oil for deep-frying
2	sheets rice paper dough
1	cup fresh mixed greens
8	whole chives

❀ | TO MAKE THE MANGO–BLACK BEAN DRESSING: In a small bowl combine all of the ingredients and set aside for at least 1 hour.

❀ | TO MAKE THE TUNA: With a sharp knife butterfly each tuna steak and open out flat. Split the asparagus and carrots in half lengthwise. Place the asparagus, pepper strips, and carrots in the center of each piece of tuna and roll the tuna around the vegetables into a cylinder. Keep the vegetables in the center of the tuna. Roll in plastic wrap, seal, and refrigerate for at least 1 hour, or up to 4 hours.

❀ | In a shallow bowl mix together the flour, 1 cup of the soda water, and salt. The batter should be loose, about the consistency of pancake batter; add more soda water, 1 tablespoon at a time, to thin the batter if necessary. In a deep fryer heat the oil to 325°F. Take the tuna rolls out of the refrigerator and unwrap. Cut each sheet of nori in half and wrap one half sheet around each tuna roll. Dip the chilled tuna rolls into the batter and deep-fry for 2 minutes. Remove with a slotted spoon and drain on paper towels. The object is to crisp the batter, not cook the tuna all the way through.

❀| TO MAKE THE RICE PAPER CRISPS: Heat the broiler as high as it will go. Cut the circles of rice paper in half. Lay the rice paper pieces on a baking sheet and broil until crispy, about 30 seconds. Watch as it cooks very quickly. When it just begins to brown, remove from the broiler. Curve the pieces while they are warm.

❀| TO SERVE: Stand a piece of grilled rice paper on each plate. Cut each tuna roll on the bias and stand 2 pieces cut side up on each side of the rice paper. Divide the greens among the plates. Divide the mango-black bean dressing among the plates. Garnish each plate with 2 chives.

MUSSELS WITH PARSLEY AND GARLIC

ERNESTO GARRIGOS

Virgilio's
St. Thomas, U.S.V.I.

SERVES 4

Olive oil, butter, white wine, and garlic create an Italian-style broth for fresh mussels. The mussels are served in shallow soup bowls to take full advantage of the flavorful broth.

¼	cup (½ stick) unsalted butter	1	bunch parsley, stemmed and minced
6	garlic cloves , minced	1½	cups dry white wine
24	to 32 fresh mussels	½	cup chicken stock
	Salt and freshly ground black pepper to taste	½	cup olive oil

❀| Place the butter, garlic, and mussels in a large skillet over medium-high heat, shaking the pan to distribute the mussels evenly. Cook for 30 seconds, then add three-fourths of the parsley and the wine. Avert your face, ignite the wine, and let the flames die down, shaking the pan constantly. Add the stock and olive oil. Shake the pan gently to blend the liquids, then cook until the mussels open, 4 to 5 minutes. Discard any mussels that do not open.

❀| TO SERVE: Divide the mussels among 4 shallow soup bowls. Ladle the broth into the bowls, and dust the bowls with the remaining minced parsley.

SCALLOPS WITH SAUTÉED SWEET POTATO RELISH

HUBERT LORENZ

Caneel Bay Resort
St. John, U.S. Virgin Islands

SERVES 4

Tamarind, also known as the Indian date, is grown locally on the Caribbean islands. Used to flavor Asian cuisines, it can be found in Asian markets in various forms. Tamarind paste is used in this recipe to add its very distinctive flavor to the sauce.

SWEET POTATO RELISH

1	tablespoon olive oil
1	cup peeled and diced sweet potato
2	slices red onion, diced
⅓	cup seeded, deribbed, and diced green bell pepper
⅓	cup seeded, deribbed, and diced red bell pepper
½	cup chicken stock
⅓	cup unpeeled, diced green zucchini
1	tablespoon unsalted butter

GUAVA-TAMARIND SAUCE

½	cup guava juice
1	tablespoon tamarind paste
12	sea scallops
	Salt and freshly ground black pepper to taste
4	tablespoons semolina
3	tablespoons olive oil

GARNISH

4	cilantro sprigs

❀ | TO MAKE THE SWEET POTATO RELISH: In a medium sauté pan or skillet heat the olive oil over medium-high heat. Add the sweet potato and red onion to the olive oil and sauté about 3 minutes until tender. Add the peppers and chicken stock and cook 2 more minutes. Add the zucchini and cook 1 minute. Remove from the heat and stir in the butter until melted. Set aside in a warm place.

❀ | TO MAKE THE SAUCE: In a small sauté pan heat the guava juice to simmering over medium heat and cook about 5 minutes until slightly reduced and thickened. Add the tamarind paste and cook 1 minute. Let the sauce cool and put it in a squeeze bottle.

❀ | TO PREPARE THE SCALLOPS: Season the scallops with salt and pepper. Dip each scallop into the semolina, one side only. In a medium sauté pan heat the olive oil over medium-high heat. Sear the scallops, semolina side first, 3 or 4 at a time, for 1 minute per side or until browned. Remove with a slotted spoon and drain on paper towels.

❀ | TO SERVE: Pipe the sauce over the plate in a swirled design. Arrange 3 small servings of sweet potato relish on the plate. Top each serving of relish with a scallop, semolina side up. Garnish the plate with a fresh cilantro sprig. Repeat with the remaining plates.

CRAYFISH MEDALLIONS WITH MANGO AND LEEK FONDUE AND OYSTER SABAYON

TROY SMITH
Necker Island, British Virgin Islands

SERVES 4

With advance preparation, this can be a quick and elegant meal. Caribbean crayfish, which are large like spiny lobsters, not small like mainland crayfish, are used; depending upon the size of the crayfish or lobster tails you find, you may want to increase the number of tails to allow 4 to 6 ounces of meat per serving.

MANGO AND LEEK FONDUE

2   tablespoons olive oil

      leeks, cleaned and chopped into ½-inch pieces

¼   yellow onion, finely diced

1   garlic clove, minced

½   cup white wine

2   cups (1 pint) heavy (whipping) cream

1   mango, pitted and diced

OYSTER SABAYON

2   egg yolks

1   egg

¼   cup white wine

⅛   cup white wine vinegar

6   oysters, chopped

1   tomato, peeled, seeded, and diced (see page 237)

      Salt and freshly ground black pepper to taste

      Juice of ½ lemon

10   to 12 chives, chopped

SAUTÉED CRAYFISH MEDALLIONS

2   to 4 crayfish (rock lobster) tails, shell removed

      Salt and freshly ground black pepper to taste

2   tablespoons olive oil

❀ | TO MAKE THE FONDUE: In a small skillet heat the olive oil and cook the leeks, onion, and garlic over medium heat until translucent, 1 to 2 minutes. Stir in the wine and cream, reduce the heat to medium-low, and cook about 6 minutes until the cream is reduced by half. Stir in the mango and cook for 2 more minutes. Set aside off the heat.

❀ | TO MAKE THE OYSTER SABAYON: In a bowl whisk together the egg yolks, egg, wine, and wine vinegar. Place the bowl in a larger bowl or pan of hot water and whisk until the mixture thickens. Remove from the heat and stir in the oysters and tomato. Season with salt, pepper, and lemon juice. Sprinkle with chives.

❀ | TO PREPARE THE CRAYFISH: Slice the crayfish tails into ½-inch medallions. Season with salt and pepper. Heat a sauté pan or skillet over medium-high heat and add the olive oil. When the oil is hot, sear the medallions for 1 to 2 minutes per side until browned. Remove from the heat and keep warm.

❀ | TO SERVE: Spoon fondue in the center of the plate. Arrange the medallions around the fondue. Spoon the sabayon sauce over the crayfish. Garnish with more chives and tomatoes.

RICE PAPER-WRAPPED GRILLED SHRIMP WITH AVOCADO AND ASIAN BROCCOLI SLAW

CHRIS FULCHER

Old Stone Farmhouse
St. Thomas, U.S.V.I.

SERVES 4

These beautiful shrimp spring rolls owe both inspiration and taste to Asian cuisine. The spring rolls are wrapped and chilled, then sliced into circles and arranged against a bed of Asian slaw. At last—a dish that uses broccoli stems, not florets!

THREE-FLAVOR INDONESIAN SAUCE

1	cup tomato juice
1	cup pineapple juice
1	tablespoon red chili peppers
2	tablespoons raisins
4	cloves garlic
2	tablespoons rice wine vinegar

ASIAN BROCCOLI SLAW

4	large broccoli stems
2	large carrots
4	green onions
1	sprig coriander (cilantro), minced
½	cup rice wine vinegar
1	tablespoon sugar
1	tablespoon pickled ginger
	Salt and freshly ground black pepper to taste

JASMINE RICE

1½	cups water
1	cup jasmine rice
¼	cup rice wine vinegar
1	teaspoon sugar
	Pinch salt

SPRING ROLLS

4	to 6 shrimp, shelled
	Olive oil
	Salt and pepper to taste
½	teaspoon sesame or olive oil
	Salt and freshly ground white pepper to taste
1	large carrot, pared
1	large cucumber
1	tablespoon wasabi
2	rice paper wrapper circles, approximately 15 inches in diameter
6	sprigs coriander (cilantro), stemmed and chopped
	Jasmine Rice (above)
1	tablespoon pickled ginger, chopped
1	avocado, julienned
1	red jalapeño pepper, seeded, deribbed, and julienned

GARNISH

¼	cup pickled ginger slices
4	green onions
4	sprigs coriander (cilantro)

❀ | TO MAKE THE THREE-FLAVOR INDONESIAN SAUCE: In a blender combine all of the ingredients and purée. Place in a squeeze bottle at room temperature.

❀ | TO MAKE THE ASIAN BROCCOLI SLAW: Pare the broccoli stems and carrots. Using a mandolin or V-slicer, cut the broccoli and carrots into very thin julienne. Cut the root end and the oldest part of the onion leaves away, leaving about 4 inches of green onion; cut lengthwise into narrow julienne. Put the vegetables in a nonaluminum bowl, add the coriander, and toss. Warm the rice wine vinegar in a small pan over medium heat and dissolve the sugar in the vinegar. Stir in the ginger. Pour the mixture into the rice, season with salt and pepper, and toss. Cover and refrigerate for at least 2 hours.

❀| To MAKE THE RICE: In a medium saucepan bring the water to a boil. Stir in the rice, cover, and turn the heat to medium-low. Simmer for 18 minutes, until all the water is absorbed. Remove from heat, uncover, fluff with a fork, and let cool. When the rice has cooled to room temperature, warm the rice wine vinegar in a small pan over medium heat and dissolve the sugar and salt in the vinegar. Pour the mixture into the rice and toss.

❀| To MAKE THE SPRING ROLLS: Toss the shrimp with the olive oil, salt, and pepper to coat. Heat the broiler to high and grill the shrimp, turning once, about 1 minute until opaque. Remove from the heat. Using a mandolin or V-slicer, cut the carrot and cucumber into very thin julienne. In a small bowl blend the wasabi with the oil to thin it. Moisten a rice paper circle in warm water and spread on a clean work surface. Sprinkle one-fourth of the chopped coriander across the center in a band. Mound half the rice across the coriander and pack it tightly together with your hands; the tighter the rice, the tighter the finished roll. Sprinkle with salt and pepper. Spoon a strip of wasabi sauce the length of the rice mound, then lay half of the ginger pieces on the wasabi. Place a line of avocado, carrot, cucumber, and jalapeño pieces along the top. Cut the shrimp in half through the center of the back, and lay half of the shrimp on the mound. Sprinkle with one-fourth of the chopped coriander. Lift one of the free sides of the rice paper circle and wrap it over the ingredients, pressing them into a tight log. Tuck the edge of the rice paper under the ingredients. Snug the roll again. Fold in the ends to keep the ingredients from spilling out, and roll up the spring roll completely. Shape it into a firm log with your hands again. Repeat with the second rice paper wrapper and remaining ingredients. Cover the rolls with plastic wrap, and chill for at least 2 hours.

❀| To PREPARE THE GARNISH: With a small sharp knife cut the roots from the onions, and cut off the long tops, leaving the onion about 5 inches long. Cut the top of the onions into narrow julienne, leaving them attached at the bulb. Place in ice water for at least 30 minutes.

❀| To SERVE: Place an open ring mold on each serving plate. Pack the slaw in the ring molds, then gently lift off the molds. Spoon a dab of wasabi beside the slaw. Overlap a few strips of pickled ginger, roll them up, and set the ginger roll beside the slaw. Unwrap the spring rolls and cut them crosswise in ¾-inch-thick slices, revealing the filling. Place 4 slices on each plate, overlapping them slightly. Drizzle the center of the plates with Three-Flavor Indonesian Sauce, and dot the edge of the plates with the sauce. Garnish each with a green onion and a coriander sprig.

STUFFED SHRIMP WITH SCALLOP MOUSSE IN A ROASTED RED BELL PEPPER-LIME SAUCE

PATRICK GAUDUCHEAU

Le Bistro
Saint John's, Antigua

SERVES 4

Red and yellow pepper sauces form the setting for shrimp filled with a light scallop mousse and poached in fish stock. Zucchini julienne garnish the dish. Chef Gauducheau poaches three shrimp in a pan, starting the cooking on top of the stove to quickly bring the stock to a boil, then finishing in the oven. In preparing a quantity for four, dividing the shrimp and stock between two pans would probably work best, and the stock quantity listed is enough for a divided preparation.

SCALLOP MOUSSE

1	pound fresh scallops
3	egg whites
	Salt and freshly ground white pepper to taste
1	cup heavy (whipping) cream

12	jumbo shrimp
1	shallot, crushed
3	ounces white wine
1½	quarts fish stock

PEPPER SAUCES

1	yellow bell pepper, roasted (see page 235), seeded, and deribbed

1	red bell pepper, roasted, seeded, and deribbed
2	tablespoons butter
2	shallots, minced
¼	cup dry white wine
½	cup heavy (whipping) cream
1	lime

GARNISH

2	tablespoons unsalted butter
1	zucchini, julienned
	Salt and freshly ground pepper to taste
4	black olives, sliced
4	tomato roses (optional)
4	sprigs fresh dill

❁ | TO PREPARE THE MOUSSE: Place the scallops, egg whites, salt, and pepper in the bowl of a food processor and begin to purée. With the machine running, slowly add the heavy cream. Continue processing for 2 to 3 minutes until the mixture has formed a soft, airy mousse. Cover and refrigerate for at least 20 minutes.

❁ | TO PREPARE THE SHRIMP: Preheat the oven to 450°F. Peel the shrimp, leaving the tails attached. With a sharp knife, cut through the curve of the back almost all the way through the shrimp. Open the shrimp out flat. Place the chilled mousse in a pastry bag fitted with a large plain tip and pipe the mousse into the butterflied shrimp. Place the shrimp in an ovenproof sauté pan or skillet, and add the shallot, wine, and fish stock. Cover, and bring to a boil over medium-high heat. As soon as the mixture boils, place the pan in the oven and bake for 5 to 6 minutes until the mousse is firm.

❁ | TO PREPARE THE PEPPER SAUCES: Cut the peppers into quarters. Remove the seeds and ribs. Julienne one segment each of the yellow and red peppers, and set aside. Purée the remaining yellow pepper and red pepper separately. In a small sauté pan over medium heat melt the butter and sauté the minced shallot until soft. Add the white wine and cook until reduced by half. Stir in the cream and cook until reduced by one-fourth. Divide the sauce base between 2 small bowls or pans. Stir the yellow pepper purée into one bowl, and red pepper purée into the other. Stir a squeeze of lime juice into each. Put the red pepper sauce into a squeeze bottle.

❀| To SERVE: In a medium sauté pan melt the butter over medium heat and sauté the zucchini about 2 minutes until soft. Season with salt and pepper and keep warm. Fill each serving plate with yellow pepper sauce. Lift the shrimp from the poaching broth with a slotted spoon and pat the bottoms dry with a towel. Place 3 shrimp in the center of each plate in a pinwheel design, tails to the center. Squeeze 3 large dots of red pepper sauce on the plates between the shrimp. Using the tip of a sharp knife or a toothpick, pull from the center of the red pepper sauce outward in a star design. Place an olive slice next to each red pepper sauce star. Mound zucchini over the tails. Garnish with a tomato rose, the reserved red and yellow pepper strips, and a sprig of fresh dill.

BLACK BEAN CAKES WITH BUTTERFLIED SHRIMP AND CHILI BEURRE BLANC

JANICE BARBER

The White House Inn
St. Kitts

SERVES 12

Creamy black bean cakes and grilled shrimp are treated to the extra bite of bright chilies in a smooth butter-based sauce. The same recipe could be used for a luncheon or light supper for four. Begin the night before to soak the beans overnight.

BLACK BEANS

1	pound black beans, soaked in water to cover overnight
4	to 5 cups Vegetable Stock (see page 236)
3	large bay leaves

BLACK BEAN CAKES

2	tablespoons peanut oil
1	onion, minced
1	garlic clove, crushed
1	red bell pepper, seeded, deribbed, and finely diced
1	green bell pepper, seeded, deribbed, and finely diced
1	jalapeño pepper, seeded, deribbed, and minced
1	to 2 tablespoons chili powder, depending on taste
1	pound cooked black beans (above)
½	teaspoon cumin seeds, ground
1	tablespoon cilantro, minced
	Squeeze of fresh lime juice
	Salt and freshly ground black pepper to taste

SALSA

1	garlic clove, minced
1	small onion, minced

1	green bell pepper, seeded, deribbed, and minced
1	jalapeño pepper, seeded, deribbed, and minced
	Juice of ½ lime
2	tablespoons olive oil
1	tablespoon tomato paste
½	tablespoon chopped fresh cilantro
	Salt, freshly ground black pepper, and cayenne to taste

BUTTERFLIED SHRIMP

60	21- to 25-count shrimp
	Olive oil
	Salt and freshly ground black pepper to taste

CHILI BEURRE BLANC

1	tablespoon shallots, diced
4	ounces white wine
1	tablespoon chili sauce
¼	cup heavy cream
1	cup unsalted butter, cubed and chilled
	Salt and freshly ground black pepper to taste

GARNISH

	Cilantro leaves
1	cup sour cream

❋ | TO COOK THE BEANS: Put the beans in a large stockpot and fill with vegetable stock to cover. Add bay leaves and bring to a boil. Boil for 10 minutes and skim the foam from the top. Reduce the heat, and simmer, covered, for 1 hour and 30 minutes, until the beans are soft. Drain and remove the bay leaves.

❀| TO PREPARE THE BEAN CAKES: Preheat the oven to 450°F. Grease a large baking sheet. In a large skillet heat the oil over medium-high heat and sauté the onion, garlic, and peppers until they begin to soften. Stir in the chili powder, reduce the heat to medium, and simmer 1 minute. Stir in the beans, cumin seeds, cilantro, lime juice, salt, and pepper. Remove two-thirds of the bean mixture and pass it through a potato masher, leaving a coarse texture. Return the "mashed" portion to the pan, and stir in the seasoning and lime juice. Remove from heat, spread out ¾ inch thick on a flat surface, and chill thoroughly in the refrigerator.

❀| Cut the cooled cake into 3-inch circles with a cookie cutter or steel ring. Place the cakes on the prepared baking sheet and bake for 5 minutes.

❀| TO PREPARE THE SALSA: In a medium bowl combine all of the ingredients and let stand for at least 1 hour to blend the flavors.

❀| TO PREPARE THE SHRIMP: Remove the shells from the shrimp, leaving the tails intact. With the tip of a sharp paring knife, remove the dark vein. Cut almost all the way through each shrimp following the curve of the back; open the shrimp out and press open. Mix together the olive oil and seasonings, and toss the shrimp in the mixture. Let marinate for 1 hour.

❀| When ready to serve, preheat the oven to 450°F. Place the shrimp on a flat baking sheet, cut sides up, and bake for 5 minutes. Or, preheat the grill and grill for 3 minutes until they just begin to color.

❀| TO PREPARE THE BEURRE BLANC: In a small pan place the shallots, wine, and chili sauce and bring to a boil over medium-high heat. Lower the heat to medium and cook until the volume is reduced to approximately 1 tablespoon. Add the cream and cook to reduce again to 1 tablespoon. Whisk in the butter 1 tablespoon at a time. Make sure each addition is fully incorporated before adding the next tablespoon. The sauce will resemble thick cream. Strain through a fine-mesh sieve and season with salt and pepper.

❀| TO SERVE: Place a bean cake in the center of each plate. Arrange 5 grilled shrimp in a spoke pattern around each bean cake. Place cilantro leaves between the shrimp. Drizzle beurre blanc around the bean cake and over the shrimp. Garnish the top of the bean cake with salsa and sour cream.

SHRIMP SAUTÉED IN TROPICAL FRUIT SALSA

MICHAEL MADSEN

Divi Resort & Casino
St. Croix, U.S. Virgin Islands

SERVES 4

This simple-to-prepare sauté of shrimp is colorful with bright tropical fruits. Served with just a salad and sweet potato chips, it is a light and easy luncheon or supper.

4	tablespoons clarified butter	1	red bell pepper, minced
16	large (16- to 20-count) shrimp	½	jalapeño, seeded, deribbed, and minced
1	pineapple, skinned, cored, and cut in chunks	1	cup dry white wine
2	star fruit, sliced		Salt and freshly ground black pepper
2	kiwi, skinned and sliced		
1	mango, skinned, pitted, and diced	12	chives
2	papaya, skinned, seeded, and diced		

In a large sauté pan heat half of the butter over medium-high heat. Add eight shrimp and sauté until they turn opaque, about 30 seconds per side. Set aside, heat the remaining butter in the same pan and sauté the remaining shrimp. Put the first shrimp back into the pan. Add the fruits and peppers and sauté for 1 to 1½ minutes, tossing or stirring gently. Add the wine and stir up the cooked bits from the bottom of the pan. Cook for 1 minute. Season with salt and pepper. Arrange on plates and crisscross the chives on the top.

CURRIED NUGGETS OF LOBSTER

NORMA SHIRLEY
Norma at the Wharfside
Montego Bay, Jamaica

SERVES 4

2	12-ounce fresh or thawed frozen lobster tails
1	tablespoon fresh lime juice
3	tablespoons unsalted butter
1	tablespoon minced fresh garlic or bottled garlic paste
¼	cup sliced scallion (green onion)
¼	cup chopped parsley
1	teaspoon sliced Scotch bonnet chili pepper or 1 tablespoon jalapeño chili pepper

1	tablespoon Madras curry powder
¾	cup water
	Salt
6	cups mesclun or gourmet salad greens or Bibb lettuce leaves
2	ripe papayas

Remove the lobster meat from the shell and cut into 1-inch chunks. Toss with lime juice and set aside. In a large skillet melt the butter over medium heat. Add the garlic and sauté for 1 minute. Add the green onion, parsley, and chili pepper, and sauté for 1 minute. Add the curry powder and sauté for 1 minute. Add the water and simmer for 1 minute. Transfer the mixture to a blender or food processor and purée. Add salt to taste.

Return the purée to the skillet and heat over medium-high heat until hot. Add the lobster mixture and simmer 4 to 5 minutes or until the lobster is cooked through, stirring frequently. Arrange the salad greens on 4 serving plates. Cut the papayas in half and discard the seeds. Place papaya halves, cut sides up, in the center of the plates. Using tongs, arrange the lobster nuggets in the papaya halves. Spoon the sauce over the lobster and greens.

CURRIED CONCH AND PLANTAIN RAVIOLI WITH MANGO AND PAPAYA COULIS

KEITH SCHEIBLE

St. James's Club
Antigua

SERVES 4

These lovely large ravioli are filled with curried conch with just a touch of hot pepper. They are served with mango and papaya coulis, and a warm wine sauce. Conch is hard to find outside of tropical areas; you may substitute chopped clams for conch if you can't get it in your seafood market. If you use the clams, omit the conch preparation steps.

RAVIOLI

1	pound 2 ounces (4½ cups) all-purpose flour
½	teaspoon salt
½	teaspoon olive oil
4	eggs
6	egg yolks
1	conch, removed from the shell
2	cups fish stock or clam juice
	Water to cover

CONCH CURRY FILLING

2	tablespoons olive oil
1	small red onion, diced
2	garlic cloves, chopped
	Pinch diced habañero or jalapeño pepper
½	inch fresh ginger, peeled and minced
1	plantain, diced
1	small tomato, peeled and diced
1	teaspoon freshly grated coconut

1	tablespoon curry powder
1	cup fresh pineapple juice

COULIS

2	mangoes, peeled and cut from pit
2	papayas, peeled and seeded
2	tablespoons sugar
1	egg
½	cup water

RED WINE GLAZE

½	cup red wine
1	tablespoon honey

GARNISH

	Crispy Fried Ginger (see page 238)
1	mango, quartered and cut from pit (leave skin attached)
	Red Wine Glaze (recipe above)

❀ | TO PREPARE THE RAVIOLI DOUGH: In a food processor or mixer with a paddle attachment combine the flour, salt, and olive oil and process for a few seconds to mix. Add the eggs and egg yolks and process until the dough starts to come together in a loose ball. Knead the pasta dough on a floured surface until smooth. Cut the dough into 8 equal pieces and roll them into balls. Wrap each ball in plastic wrap and refrigerate for 20 minutes. The dough may be frozen and thawed later for use.

❀ | TO PREPARE THE CONCH: Cut the hard dark skin off the conch meat. Bring the stock or clam broth to a boil. Add the conch, and enough water to cover, reduce the heat to low, and simmer for 3 to 4 hours, skimming any foam that forms. Remove the conch and let cool. Cut into large dice.

❀| TO PREPARE THE FILLING: In a skillet heat the olive oil and sauté the onion, garlic, pepper, and ginger about 1 minute until softened and translucent. Stir in the plantain and tomato and sauté for 30 seconds. Add the coconut and curry powder and sauté for 30 seconds. Stir in the conch. Add the pineapple juice and simmer for 20 minutes. Chill in the refrigerator.

❀| TO PREPARE THE COULIS: Place the mango and 1 tablespoon of sugar in a blender and purée, Press through a fine-mesh sieve and place in a squeeze bottle. Clean the blender and repeat with the papaya, putting the sieved purée in another squeeze bottle.

❀| TO COMPLETE THE RAVIOLI: Mix the egg and water together to form an egg wash. Remove the dough from the refrigerator and roll out one ball of dough. Cut out four 3-inch circles of dough. Brush the edges of 2 circles with egg wash. Put a spoonful of filling in the center of these 2 circles. Cover each with one of the remaining circles of dough and press around the edges to seal. Press again, using the tines of a fork. Repeat with the remaining dough.

❀| Bring a large pot of salted water to a boil and drop in the ravioli a few at a time; do not crowd them. When the ravioli float back to the top, cook 2½ minutes. Take one out with a slotted spoon or skimmer and check for doneness; when cooked through, remove and drain, then place on a warmed platter and keep warm in the oven while cooking the remaining ravioli.

❀| TO PREPARE THE RED WINE GLAZE: In a saucepan cook the wine and honey together over medium-low heat until reduced by one-fourth. Remove, cool, and place in a squeeze bottle.

❀| TO SERVE: Drizzle the mango and papaya coulis onto the plates. Place 2 cooked ravioli on the sauce, and cut one open to reveal the center. Garnish the center of the sliced ravioli with fried ginger. Keeping the skin attached, cut each mango quarter in a cross-hatch pattern. Place 1 mango piece on each plate. Drizzle the plates with red wine glaze.

Lobster Pancakes with Stingythyme Sauce

Vernon Hughes

The Cinnamon Reef Hotel
Anguilla

Sweet potato pancakes are lifted from the ordinary with pieces of lobster tail and a little nutmeg spice. Stingythyme, a variety of thyme indigenous to Anguilla, gives an intense flavor to the dish. Fresh thyme may be substituted; use a little more to simulate the stronger flavor of stingythyme.

SERVES 4

2	8- to 10-ounce lobster tails		1	tablespoon fresh lemon juice
			¼	cup tarragon vinegar
PANCAKES			4	shallots, minced
1	pound sweet potatoes		½	teaspoon peppercorns
2	tablespoons butter		2	sprigs parsley
	Salt and freshly ground black pepper to taste		1	pint heavy (whipping) cream
1	whole egg			
½	cup milk		**GARNISH**	
½	cup all-purpose flour		2	sweet potatoes, peeled
1	teaspoon baking powder		1½	cups peanut oil
½	teaspoon nutmeg, freshly grated		1	red onion, sliced
	Salt and freshly ground black pepper to taste		2	tablespoons unsalted butter
			2	tablespoons balsamic vinegar
SAUCE			¼	cup lobster roe
1	cup dry white wine		4	sprigs stingythyme, or 8 sprigs thyme
			2	tomatoes, skinned, seeded, and diced

❋ | To cook the lobster: Place a medium stockpot of lightly salted water over high heat and bring to a boil. Drop the lobster tails into the boiling water and cook 5 to 6 minutes. Using tongs, remove the tails and drop into a bowl of ice water to stop the cooking. When cooled, lightly crush each tail shell and carefully remove the meat in one piece. Slice each tail into very thin medallions and set aside.

❋ | To make the pancakes: Preheat the oven to 350°F. Wrap each sweet potato in foil with a dab of butter and a little salt and pepper. Roast about 1 hour until soft. Remove from the foil and let cool. Peel the sweet potatoes and mash in a small mixing bowl. In the bowl of a food processor combine the potatoes, egg, and milk and process until smooth, about 10 seconds. Add the flour, baking powder, and nutmeg and process again about 20 seconds until smooth. The mixture should be thick; it can be thinned with a little milk or thickened with more flour. Season to taste with salt and pepper. Heat a large sauté pan or skillet over medium-high heat until a drop of water immediately sizzles when sprinkled on it. Spritz with cooking oil, then pour three 3-inch circles of batter into the pan. When bubbles begin to appear on top of the pancake, place a lobster medallion on top and carefully turn the pancake. Cook the second side 1 to 2 minutes until golden. Remove to a warmed platter and place in the oven to keep warm. Repeat the process with the remaining batter and medallions to make 9 more pancakes.

❀ | To MAKE THE SAUCE: In a large heavy-bottomed saucepan combine all ingredients except the heavy cream. Bring to a simmer and let cook until it is reduced by two-thirds, about 12 to 15 minutes. Stir in the cream. Simmer 15 minutes and strain.

❀ | To PREPARE THE GARNISHES: Using a spiral slicer, mandolin, or V-slicer, slice or shred the peeled sweet potatoes into small strips. Pat dry. In a large saucepan heat the oil until it ripples. Plunge one-fourth of the potato strips into the hot oil; when they float to the surface, remove with a slotted spoon and drain on paper towels. Repeat with the remaining strips.

❀ | Cut the onion in half, then slice into rings. In a shallow skillet over medium-high heat, melt the butter and sauté the onions until they are browned. Remove from the heat and drain on paper towels, then place in a small bowl and toss with balsamic vinegar. Let stand.

❀ | To SERVE: Sprinkle lobster roe around the outer edges of the plates. Arrange stingythyme on the serving plates. Spoon the sauce onto the center of the plates over the stingythyme. Garnish the sauce with diced tomato. Place 3 pancakes in a circle, slightly overlapping each other. Garnish the pancakes with warm grilled onions, then top with fried sweet potato garnish. Add a stingythyme leaf to complete.

GARLIC-CRUSTED CRAYFISH TAILS

VERNON HUGHES

The Cinnamon Reef Hotel
Anguilla

SERVES 2

Caribbean crayfish are enormous by U.S. mainland standards, but there are many substitutions: Maine or Florida lobster tails, or even very large prawns. The dish works well with any of these, and makes a pretty presentation. The ragout itself would also be good as an accompaniment to fish.

6	whole Caribbean crayfish tails (spiny lobster tails, Maine lobster tails, or jumbo prawns may be substituted)	1	cup cooked white beans
		4	tablespoons chicken stock
	Salt and freshly ground black pepper to taste		
4	tablespoons extra-virgin olive oil		**CELERY ROOT SAUCE**
	Flour to dust	1½	tablespoons butter
4	tablespoons garlic, minced	½	celery root, diced
		1½	tablespoons all-purpose flour
		1	teaspoon celery seeds
POTATO–WHITE BEAN RAGOUT			Salt and freshly ground white pepper to taste
2	medium potatoes, cut into large dice		
1	teaspoon salt	1	cup milk
2	tablespoons olive oil		
4	shallots, diced	2	sprigs fresh parsley
⅛	teaspoon curry powder		

❀ | TO PREPARE THE CRAYFISH: Preheat the oven to 425°F. Lay the tails flat on a cutting board and split: Place a large sharp knife along the center of the tail, with the point of the knife just short of the tail fins, and strike the knife with a mallet or other heavy object. Lift the split shells off the tail meat, leaving the meat attached to the tail fins. Discard the shells, or save for use in stock for another dish. Season the tails with salt and pepper, drizzle with a little of the olive oil, and dust lightly with flour, shaking off the excess. In a large ovenproof sauté pan heat the remaining olive oil over medium-high heat and place the tails and garlic in the pan. Sear on one side, then turn and sear again, about 30 seconds per side. Place in the oven for about 3 minutes to finish cooking.

❀ | TO MAKE THE POTATO–WHITE BEAN RAGOUT: In a large pot place the potato cubes in cold salted water and bring to a boil. Remove from heat and drain immediately. In a medium sauté pan heat the olive oil and sauté the shallots over medium heat about 2 minutes until soft and translucent. Stir in the curry powder, white beans, and chicken stock. Gently stir in the potato cubes. Keep warm.

❀ | TO MAKE THE CELERY ROOT SAUCE: In a small saucepan over medium heat, melt the butter and sauté the celery root until softened. Whisk in the flour and cook, stirring constantly, for 30 seconds; do not allow it to brown. Whisk in the celery seeds and seasoning. Whisk in the milk, reduce the heat to medium-low, and cook, whisking slowly, until the mixture thickens and coats the back of a spoon, about 5 minutes. Pour the mixture over the vegetables and toss gently to coat.

※ | To SERVE: Place a ring mold on each serving plate and fill with ragout, pressing the ragout slightly to bind. Spoon sauce around the plate outside the ring mold. Remove the mold by lifting directly upward. Place 3 crayfish tails over each vegetable ragout and garnish with parsley.

ZUCCHINI-LOBSTER SOUFFLÉ

ROGER WILES

Half Moon Bay Club
Montego Bay, Jamaica

SERVES 4

SOUFFLÉ

2	large zucchini squash, about 1¼ pounds
¾	teaspoon salt, divided
¼	teaspoon freshly ground black pepper
4	ounces uncooked shelled lobster tail meat, cut into chunks
2	large eggs, separated
1	tablespoon brandy or cognac
¾	cup reduced Lobster Stock (see page 236), divided
2	tablespoons unsalted butter

SALT COD AND VEGETABLES

2	tablespoons unsalted butter
½	cup julienned yellow onion

4	ounces salt cod, soaked, poached, and flaked according to package directions
1	tablespoon lime juice
1	green bell pepper, roasted and peeled (see page 235), julienned
1	medium tomato, seeded and julienned
2	scallions (green onions), julienned or sliced
½	cup drained canned Jamaican ackee (optional)
2	tablespoons chopped garlic chives or chives
	Salt and freshly ground black pepper to taste

GARNISH

1	scallion (green onion), julienned

❁ | TO PREPARE THE SOUFFLÉ: Using the tip of a rotary vegetable peeler, score the zucchini lengthwise every ½ inch. Trim the ends and cut each zucchini crosswise into 4 equal pieces, about 2½ inches long. Using a melon baller or grapefruit knife, hollow out the zucchini, leaving a ¼-inch shell on the sides and bottom to form a cup. Sprinkle ¼ teaspoon of the salt and the pepper over the zucchini and let stand for 10 minutes. Invert onto a paper towel to drain.

❁ | Heat the oven to 375°F. In a blender or food processor finely chop the lobster meat. Add the remaining ½ teaspoon of salt, egg yolks, brandy, and ¼ cup of the stock; process 30 seconds. In a medium bowl beat the egg whites until soft peaks form. Gently fold in the lobster mixture. Spoon the mixture into the zucchini cups, mounding slightly. Place the filled cups in a shallow baking pan. Bake for 12 to 15 minutes or until puffed and set. In a skillet combine the remaining ¾ cup of lobster broth and butter. Cook over medium heat until the butter is melted and the sauce is slightly thickened. Keep warm.

❁ | TO PREPARE THE SALT COD AND VEGETABLES: In a large skillet melt the butter over medium heat. Add the yellow onion, and sauté for 4 minutes. Add the salt cod, and sprinkle with lime juice. Add the bell pepper and tomato, and sauté 4 minutes. Add the scallions, ackee, and chives, and sauté 3 minutes. Season with salt and pepper.

❀| To serve: Spoon lobster-butter sauce in the center of 4 warm serving plates. Top each with two zucchini-lobster soufflés. Spoon salt cod and vegetables around the edges of the plate; sprinkle with julienned scallion.

Foie Gras au Poireaux with Truffle Vinaigrette

Pierre Castagne
**Le Perroquet
St. Maarten**

This rich, elegant dish relies on the perfection of its ingredients. The foie gras contains enough fat to sear it without the addition of any oils. You can find truffle juice and truffles in fine food stores.

SERVES 2

Truffle Vinaigrette

1	teaspoon Dijon mustard
2	tablespoons vegetable oil
½	cup truffle juice
	Salt and freshly ground black pepper to taste

4	medium leeks, cleaned

1	foie gras, 1½ to 2 pounds
2	shallots, minced
2	truffle shavings
2	parsley sprigs

❀| To prepare the vinaigrette: In a nonaluminium bowl whisk together all of the ingredients and set aside.

❀| To prepare the leeks: In a medium sauté pan bring a small amount of water to a boil and cook the leeks for 4 to 5 minutes until soft. Remove from the heat, drain, plunge into cold water, drain again, and set aside.

❀| To prepare the foie gras: Soak the fresh foie gras in tepid water to cover for 1 hour. Pat dry and separate into the large and small lobes. Remove and discard the connecting tube and any blood vessels or nerve tissue that is visible. Slice them into ¼-inch-thick scallops. Preheat a dry nonstick sauté pan over high heat. Add the foie gras and sear for 15 seconds. Turn and cook another 15 seconds. Remove from the heat. Repeat until all pieces are seared.

❀| To serve: Divide the leeks between 2 serving plates. Top with foie gras slices. Sprinkle with minced shallots and truffle vinaigrette. Garnish with a piece of truffle and a sprig of parsley.

SUCKLING PIG PAUPIETTE WITH GUAVA SAUCE

PHILIPPE MONGEREAU

Casa de Campo
Dominican Republic

SERVES 8

Tender suckling pig chunks are mixed into a pork mousseline, and the whole is wrapped with glazed cabbage leaves—possibly the most elegant stuffed cabbage ever! Chef Mongereau uses a whole suckling pig, slow-roasting it until the meat is easily pulled apart. You may substitute large pork shoulders or butts, which are much easier to obtain and fit in a home oven.

ROAST SUCKLING PIG

1	suckling pig (5 pounds), or 2 large fresh pork shoulders or butts
½	cup olive oil
	Kosher salt
	Freshly ground black pepper

PORK MOUSSELINE

6	ounces pork tenderloin, diced
2	egg whites
1	cup heavy (whipping) cream
½	teaspoon salt
½	teaspoon freshly ground black pepper
¼	teaspoon cayenne pepper
1	tablespoon dry white wine
1	heaping tablespoon chopped chives

GLAZE

2	tablespoons honey

1	tablespoon soy sauce
	Juice of 1 lemon

CABBAGE PAUPIETTES

1	head green or Savoy cabbage (16 large leaves)
	Pork Mousseline (recipe above)

GUAVA SAUCE

8	guavas, or 3 ounces of guava paste
1	medium red onion, chopped
1	Anaheim pepper, seeded, deribbed, and chopped
2	tablespoons olive oil
2	tablespoons dry white wine
1	cup chicken stock
	Salt and freshly ground black pepper to taste
	Juice of 1 lemon

Fresh herbs for garnish

❀ | TO ROAST THE PIG: Preheat the oven to 350°F. Rub the pig or pork roasts with olive oil, salt, and coarsely ground black pepper. Roast to an internal temperature of 160°F, about 2 hours and 20 minutes. Halfway through the roasting, turn the pig over. Loosely cover with foil if the skin gets too brown. Remove from the oven and cool. Pull the meat from the bones. Trim the fat from the meat and cut the meat into bite-size pieces. Reserve the meat in the refrigerator until ready to use.

❀ | TO MAKE THE PORK MOUSSELINE: Place a food processor bowl and blade in the freezer to chill completely. Keep the pork tenderloin, egg whites, and cream cold; place in a bowl over a larger bowl of ice if necessary. In the food processor purée the pork tenderloin with the egg whites. Season with salt, pepper, and cayenne. Process again, slowly adding cream until the mixture is a creamy consistency. Spoon the mousseline into a large bowl, stir in the suckling pig chunks, white wine, and chives, and refrigerate.

爨 | To make the glaze: In a small bowl whisk together the honey, soy sauce, and lemon juice.

爨 | To make the paupiettes: Preheat the oven to 350°F. Spray a large baking pan with quick-release spray. Cut the heavy rib from the backs of the cabbage leaves so that they will be flexible. Bring a large pot of salted water to a boil. Plunge the leaves into the water and cook for 5 minutes until softened. Plunge into cold water to stop the cooking, then drain on paper towels and open out on a work surface. Place a large spoonful of mousseline in the center of each leaf. Roll up from the stem end to cover the filling and fold in the sides. Roll up toward the top of the leaves to seal. Place the cabbage rolls in the prepared baking pan and brush with glaze. Roast for 1 hour and 30 minutes. Remove from the oven and let rest for 5 minutes.

爨 | To make the guava sauce: Peel and seed the guavas and purée the pulp in a blender (or use guava paste). In a covered saucepan over medium heat, cook the onion and pepper in olive oil about 3 minutes until soft and translucent. Uncover, add the white wine and chicken stock, and cook over low heat about 5 minutes until reduced by half. Stir in the guava purée, salt, pepper, and lemon juice. Transfer to a food processor and purée. Strain into a sauté pan and cook over low heat for 2 to 3 minutes until sauce thickens. Keep warm until ready to use.

爨 | To serve: Spoon guava sauce on each serving plate. Cut each paupiette on the diagonal and arrange on the sauce. Garnish with fresh herbs.

GRILLED PORTOBELLOS

ERNESTO GARRIGOS

Virgilio's
St. Thomas U.S.V.I.

SERVES 4

Large portobello caps are grilled, then topped with a garlic-laced tomato ragout. Preparation is quick and simple, but allow time for the tomato ragout to marinate.

TOMATO RAGOUT

4	large tomatoes, roughly chopped
8	basil leaves, chopped
¾	cup olive oil
	Salt and freshly ground black pepper to taste
4	garlic cloves, minced

MUSHROOMS

1	cup balsamic vinegar
½	cup balsamic vinegar
½	cup olive oil
2	garlic cloves, minced
8	large portobello caps
1	bunch parsley, stemmed and minced

※ | TO PREPARE THE RAGOUT: Combine the ingredients in a large nonreactive bowl. Cover with plastic film and let stand for 3 hours.

※ | TO PREPARE THE MUSHROOMS: In a large bowl combine the balsamic vinegar, olive oil, and garlic. Toss the mushrooms in the mixture and let stand for 30 minutes. Heat a grill pan (one with grill ribs in the bottom) or a charcoal grill to medium-high heat. Place the caps, gills up, on the grill and sear for 30 seconds. With a spatula, turn the caps over and sear the gill side for 30 more seconds.

※ | TO SERVE: Place two portobello caps on each plate. Spoon the tomato ragout over them and dust the plates with minced parsley.

Fish and Seafood

SUGAR MILL ESCOVICHED FISH

HANS SCHENK

Sugar Mill Restaurant, Half Moon Bay
Montego Bay, Jamaica

SERVES 4

In this classic preparation of typical Jamaican fare, the grouper is served beneath a colorful array of julienned vegetables. Potatoes and pumpkin on the side add a perfect mix of textures.

FISH

4	6-ounce grouper fillets (mahimahi, snapper, or catfish may be substituted)
	Salt and freshly ground black pepper to taste
1	lemon, halved, seeds removed
½	cup all-purpose flour
½	cup olive oil for frying

SAUTÉED VEGETABLES IN VINAIGRETTE

1	medium green pepper, seeded, deribbed, and julienned
1	medium red pepper, seeded, deribbed, and julienned
1	medium onion, peeled and julienned
2	carrots, peeled and julienned

1	small habañero (Scotch bonnet) pepper, seeded and cut into very thin julienne
1	tomato, seeded and julienned
½	cup sherry vinegar or other flavored vinegar
	Salt and freshly ground black pepper to taste

GARNISH

1¼	pounds fresh pumpkin, calabaza, or winter squash, peeled and trimmed into 1-inch-by-2-inch ovals (tournéed)
6	small potatoes, peeled and trimmed into 1-inch-by-2-inch ovals (tournéed)
12	watermelon balls
4	Jamaican apple slices (optional)
4	stems fresh basil

❋ | TO PREPARE THE FISH: Season the fillets with salt and pepper, then squeeze lemon juice over each fillet. Dust the fish with flour on both sides, shaking off the excess. In a large sauté pan or skillet heat the olive oil over medium-high heat. Sauté the fillets, turning several times, for 2 to 3 minutes on each side until golden brown. Remove the fish from the pan, placing it in another skillet, and set aside to keep warm.

❋ | TO PREPARE THE VEGETABLES: Discard the oil from the skillet and put the green and red peppers, onion, carrot, habañero, and tomato in the skillet. Add the sherry vinegar and cook until softened, about 3 minutes. Season with salt and pepper. Return the fish to the stove and turn the heat to low. Mound the sautéed vegetables on the fish. Pour the liquid from the vegetables over all, allowing the flavors to blend a few minutes before serving.

❋ | TO PREPARE THE GARNISH: Place the pumpkin and the potato in separate sauté pans and cook in a small amount of water until fork-tender.

🏵| To serve: Divide the fish fillets among the serving plates and spoon the vegetables over them. Alternate pumpkin and potato ovals on each plate. Garnish with watermelon balls, apple slices (optional), and fresh basil.

Swordfish Piccata

David Kendrick
Kendrick's
St. Croix, U.S. Virgin Islands

SERVES 4

Star fruit gives a tropical touch to this traditional piccata preparation. The Parmesan cheese adds a bright flavor note to the batter as well. This preparation would also work with other firm-flesh fish.

BATTER

3	tablespoons all-purpose flour
1	cup freshly grated Parmesan cheese
3	eggs
¼	cup milk
4	1-inch-thick swordfish steaks
¼	cup clarified butter
¼	cup extra-virgin olive oil
	Flour for dusting

2	garlic cloves, minced

PICCATA SAUCE

	Juice of 1 lemon
¼	cup dry white wine
¼	cup capers, chopped
1	bunch parsley, chopped
	Salt and freshly ground black pepper to taste
4	tablespoons unsalted butter
1	star fruit, sliced thin

🏵| To prepare the batter: In a food processor combine the cheese, flour, eggs, and milk. The batter should be the consistency of heavy cream; add more cheese to thicken, or milk to thin.

🏵| To prepare the fish: Preheat the oven to 400°F. Cut each steak horizontally into 2 thin pieces. In a large ovenproof frying pan heat the clarified butter and oil over medium-high heat. Dust the fish with the flour and dip into the batter to coat. Place the fish and garlic in the pan and sear about 1 minute until the coating is golden brown, turning once. Place the pan in the oven and cook 7 to 8 minutes until just opaque. Transfer the fish to a warm plate.

🏵| To prepare the piccata sauce: Pour off any excess oil, leaving several tablespoons in the pan, and wipe the outside of the pan. Return the pan to the heat. Squeeze the lemon juice into the pan, add the wine, and stir to bring up any browned bits from the bottom. Stir in the capers and one half of the parsley. Add salt and pepper to taste. Stir in the butter.

🏵| To serve: Place 2 slices of fish on each plate. Pour the piccata sauce from the pan over the fish. Dip the edges of the star fruit in the remaining parsley, and place slices of star fruit on the fish.

PEPPER-CRUSTED YELLOWFIN TUNA FILET MIGNON WITH SWEET POTATO CAKE, RED PEPPER PURÉE, AND SUN-DRIED FRUIT AND TOMATO COMPOTE

KEITH GRIFFIN
Lantana's
Grand Cayman

SERVES 4

This fine tuna steak is treated like beef filet mignon: rolled in crushed peppercorns, and seared. It is started on top of the stove, and finished in the oven. When ready, it is stacked with greens, the sweet potato cakes, and a fruity compote for a tall presentation.

SWEET POTATO CAKES

1	pound sweet potatoes, peeled and sliced 1 inch thick
¾	cup water
¼	cup sugar
	Salt and freshly ground black pepper to taste
2	tablespoons butter
¼	cup seeded, deribbed, and diced red bell pepper
¼	cup seeded, deribbed, and diced green bell pepper
¼	cup chopped scallion
	Salt and freshly ground black pepper to taste
	Yellow cornmeal for dusting

SUN-DRIED FRUIT AND TOMATO COMPOTE

½	cup roughly chopped sun-dried mixed fruit
¼	cup skinned, seeded, and roughly chopped sun-dried tomatoes
1	cup water
1	tablespoon orange marmalade

RED PEPPER PURÉE

2	large red bell peppers
	Oil for brushing
	Salt and freshly ground black pepper to taste

TUNA

4	ounces crushed mixed peppercorns
	Pinch of salt
4	5-ounce tuna steaks
¼	cup extra-virgin olive oil
1	tablespoon clarified butter

GARNISH

1	tablespoon red wine vinegar
3	tablespoons extra-virgin olive oil
	Salt and freshly ground black pepper to taste
2	cups mixed baby greens
4	chives, cut into 2-inch pieces

❀ | TO MAKE THE POTATO CAKES: Place the sweet potatoes in a deep saucepan with the water and sugar and cover. Bring to a boil, reduce the heat to simmer, and cook for 12 minutes. Drain off the water and mash, seasoning with salt and pepper to taste. In a small frying pan heat the butter and sauté the peppers and scallion until soft. Add to the potatoes and mix together. Allow the mixture to cool, then shape into 4 patties. Dust with cornmeal and set aside.

❀ | TO MAKE THE COMPOTE: Soak the dried fruit and tomatoes separately in the water for 1 hour. In separate small pans simmer each until the liquid has evaporated. Cool. Mix with the marmalade.

❀ | To MAKE THE PEPPER PURÉE: Brush the peppers with oil and roast over hot coals or a gas flame until the skin is charred and blistered. Place in a bowl, cover with plastic wrap, and let sit for 10 minutes. Break open the pepper and wash off the skin and seeds under running water. In a food processor purée the pepper and season to taste. Place in a plastic squeeze bottle.

❀ | To PREPARE THE TUNA: Preheat the oven to 375°F. Combine the crushed peppercorns with the salt and press onto the outside edges of the tuna (do not cover the top and bottom of the fillets). Heat 1 tablespoon of the olive oil in a medium ovenproof skillet over medium-high heat and sear a tuna filet on all sides, 20 seconds per side. Set aside and repeat for the remaining tuna fillets. Place the tuna in the oven for 4 minutes (for medium).

❀ | In another medium ovenproof skillet heat the clarified butter over medium-high heat and fry the potato cakes until golden on both sides, and place them in the oven for 4 minutes.

❀ | To SERVE: Whisk together the vinegar and olive oil, and season with salt and pepper. Toss the greens in the mixture and divide among 4 serving plates. Place a potato cake on the greens, then place a tuna fillet on each potato cake. Place a rounded spoonful of compote on top of the tuna, and drizzle the plate with red pepper purée. Sprinkle chives on top of the compote.

GRILLED SWORDFISH WITH SOY-GINGER BEURRE BLANC

SCOTT WILLIAMS
Necker Island, B.V.I.

SERVES 8

Guests on luxurious, privately owned Necker Island don't need to lift a finger: Chef Scott Williams is ready to prepare dishes that are at once flavorful and quick to appear. This swordfish with soy-ginger sauce begins with quenelles of crushed—not mashed—potatoes. The grilled swordfish steaks lean against the potatoes, and are accented with the Asian-influenced sauce. Tuna, shark, or other fish steaks could be substituted, and the potatoes are good with almost any main dish.

SOY-GINGER SAUCE

1	cup dark soy sauce
1	medium gingerroot, peeled and chopped (1 cup chopped ginger)
10	medium shallots, chopped
1	tablespoon Clarified Butter (see page 234) or canola oil
1	sprig thyme
3	cloves garlic, chopped
½	cup white wine vinegar
¼	bottle dry white wine
1	cup heavy (whipping) cream
2	cups (4 sticks) chilled unsalted butter, diced

CRUSHED POTATOES

1	pound 4 ounces Yukon Gold or similar potatoes, peeled and rinsed
2	tablespoons kosher salt

½	cup extra-virgin olive oil
6	green onions, chopped
½	cup flat leaf parsley, stemmed and chopped

VEGETABLES

12	baby carrots, or 4 carrots, cut into ½-inch dice
1	butternut squash, peeled and cut into ½-inch dice
½	cup (1 stick) unsalted butter or canola oil
2	zucchini, cut into ½-inch dice
	Salt and freshly ground black pepper to taste

SWORDFISH

8	6-ounce swordfish steaks
	Salt and freshly ground black pepper to taste
½	cup extra-virgin olive oil

❉ | TO PREPARE THE SOY-GINGER SAUCE: Place the soy sauce and gingerroot in a small bowl and marinate for 1 hour (this can also be done overnight for a more pronounced ginger flavor). In a 3-quart saucepan cook the shallots in the butter or oil over medium heat about 1 minute until shiny and white. Add the garlic and thyme and cook an additional 2 minutes. Add the white wine vinegar, reduce the heat to medium-low, and cook about 4 minutes until reduced and nearly dry. Add the white wine and cook until reduced by half, about 5 more minutes. Gently whisk in the cream and cook about 4 minutes until reduced by half. Whisking continuously, blend in the butter 1 piece at a time, incorporating each piece completely before adding the next. When all of the butter has been added, remove the pan from the heat and stir in 2 tablespoons of the ginger-soy mixture (more can be added, according to taste; remaining marinade can be refrigerated for up to 1 week). Set aside.

❉ | TO MAKE THE POTATOES: Put the potatoes in a pot, cover with salted water, and boil over medium heat for about 10 to 15 minutes until just fork-tender. Drain and set aside the potatoes, keeping them warm. In the same pot heat the olive oil and cook the onions over medium heat about 1 minute until the onions soften. Put the potatoes back in the pot and reduce the heat to low. With the back of a spoon, crush the potatoes into large chunks. Stir in the parsley. Set aside and keep warm.

❀ | To MAKE THE VEGETABLES: Blanch the baby carrots in boiling salted water for 30 seconds. Remove with a slotted spoon and dip into ice water, drain, and set aside. Blanch the butternut squash in the same water for 2 to 3 minutes, dip into ice water, drain, and set aside. In a sauté pan over medium heat melt the butter and sauté the zucchini and squash about 2 minutes until tender. Season with salt and pepper. Add the carrots and toss. Set aside.

❀ | To MAKE THE SWORDFISH: Preheat the grill to the highest setting. Season 1 side of the steaks with salt and pepper. Rub with olive oil, turn over, and season and oil the other side. Grill for 2 to 3 minutes per side, turning once, to an internal temperature of 135°F for medium-rare.

❀ | To SERVE: Using 2 large spoons, scoop potatoes and form into quenelles, placing them in the centers of warmed serving plates. Lay a swordfish steak against the potatoes. Arrange an assortment of the vegetables to one side of the fish. Spoon the sauce at the base of the fish.

BARBECUED SWORDFISH AND CRISPY FRIED GULF SHRIMP WITH ROCK LOBSTER AND SQUID INK RISOTTO, TROPICAL MANGO SALSA, AND PINEAPPLE-CILANTRO DRESSING

KEITH GRIFFIN

Lantana's
Grand Cayman

SERVES 4

This is a simple, perfectly grilled fish surrounded by layers of flavor from barbecue sauce, mango salsa, a pineapple dressing, and a risotto that could be a dish in itself. The squid ink used in the risotto may be found in Asian markets.

BARBECUE SAUCE

1	tablespoon butter
1	red onion, roughly chopped
1	garlic clove, crushed
3	tomatoes, skinned, seeded, and roughly chopped
1	tablespoon ketchup
1	tablespoon whole grain mustard
1	tablespoon white vinegar
1	tablespoon honey
1	tablespoon paprika
¼	teaspoon hot pepper sauce
	Salt and freshly ground black pepper to taste

MANGO SALSA

2	tablespoons diced mango
2	tablespoons diced red bell pepper
1	tablespoon chopped cilantro
1	scallion, green part only, chopped
	Juice of 1 lime
1	tablespoon extra-virgin olive oil

PINEAPPLE-CILANTRO DRESSING

1	tablespoon extra-virgin olive oil
2	garlic cloves, crushed
1	cup diced fresh pineapple
¼	cup dark rum
½	cup pineapple juice
½	cup minced cilantro leaves

ROCK LOBSTER AND SQUID INK RISOTTO

1	pint fish or clam stock
4	tablespoons unsalted butter
1	onion, chopped
1	cup Arborio rice
1	teaspoon squid ink (1 packet)
4	ounces rock lobster meat, cut into chunks
1	cup calaloo (spinach may be substituted)
	Salt and freshly ground black pepper to taste
2	fennel bulbs, cut in half
½	cup olive oil

SWORDFISH AND SHRIMP

4	5-ounce swordfish steaks
	Salt and freshly ground black pepper to taste
4	jumbo Gulf shrimp, heads on
1	cup ice water
	Seasoned all-purpose flour for dredging

GARNISH

2	green plantains
8	whole chives

❀ | TO MAKE THE BARBECUE SAUCE: In a deep nonaluminum pan over medium-high heat melt the butter and sauté the onion and garlic until soft. Add the remaining ingredients and simmer 20 minutes. Purée and set aside. The sauce will last 3 to 4 days.

❀ | TO MAKE THE MANGO SALSA: In a nonreactive bowl combine all ingredients and toss together. Set aside.

❀ | TO MAKE THE PINEAPPLE-CILANTRO DRESSING: In a deep non-aluminum pan heat the oil over medium-high heat and sauté the garlic about 2 minutes until soft. Stir in the pineapple, rum, and pineapple juice, reduce the heat to medium, and simmer until reduced by half. Add the cilantro. In a blender or food processor, pulse several times to break up the large pieces; it should retain some texture. Set aside at room temperature.

❀ | TO MAKE THE RISOTTO: Heat the stock to a simmer over medium heat. In a deep pan over medium-high heat, melt 2 tablespoons of the butter and sauté the onion until soft. Add the rice, toss, and sauté for 1 minute, stirring frequently. Stir in the ink and ¾ cup of the hot stock, keeping the rice over medium heat and stirring constantly. When the rice has absorbed the stock, stir in another ¼ cup. Keep adding in this manner until the rice is tender, about 20 minutes (not all the stock may be needed). In a small frying pan over medium-high heat melt the remaining 2 tablespoons of butter and sauté the lobster and calaloo. When the lobster is cooked through and the callaloo has wilted, stir them into the risotto. Season to taste. Cover and keep warm.

❀ | TO PREPARE THE FENNEL: Cut away the wedge of tough fibrous core from the bottom of each half. In a saucepan place the fennel pieces, olive oil, and water to cover and bring to a boil. Reduce heat and simmer for 20 to 30 minutes until tender.

❀ | TO PREPARE THE FISH: Heat the broiler to high or prepare a charcoal fire. Sprinkle the swordfish with salt and pepper. Grill about 2 minutes per side; when almost finished, brush with a little barbecue sauce. At the same time, heat the oil to 350°F in a deep fryer. Season the flour with salt and pepper. Dip the shrimp into the ice water, then dredge in the seasoned flour. Deep-fry about 2 minutes until golden. Drain on paper towels.

❀ | TO SERVE: Place a spoonful of risotto in the center of each warmed dinner plate. Arrange the fish on top and place a spoonful of salsa on the fish. Place the shrimp against the fish. Place one-half fennel bulb on each plate. Drizzle the pineapple dressing around each plate, and garnish each plate with 2 chives.

SALMON TOURNEDOS WITH MANGO, BRIE CHEESE AND A ROASTED TOMATO VELOUTÉ

CHRIS FULCHER

Old Stone House Farm House
St. Thomas, U.S. Virgin Islands

SERVES 4

ROASTED TOMATO VELOUTE

2	cloves garlic, peeled
1	shallot, peeled
2	inner stems lemongrass, cut into ½-inch pieces
1	to 2 red or green jalapeño chili peppers, stemmed and seeded
½	cup fresh basil leaves
½	cup fresh cilantro leaves
2	tablespoons vegetable oil, divided
½	cup canned coconut milk
1	plum tomato, split in half and roasted until tender
2	tablespoons grated Romano or Parmesan cheese
	Salt and freshly ground black pepper

SALMON TOURNEDOS

8	skinless, boneless, center-cut salmon fillets, cut 1 inch thick (about 2 pounds)
	Salt and freshly ground black pepper

2	tablespoons olive oil
12	thin strips peeled ripe mango
8	(¼ inch thick by 2 inches long) strips Brie cheese
2	cups hot cooked mashed potatoes, seasoned with grated Parmesan cheese and freshly ground black pepper

ASIAN VEGETABLES

2	tablespoons vegetable oil
4	cups diced napa cabbage
½	cup julienned carrots
½	cup julienned yellow onion
½	cup julienned green onions
2	tablespoons bottled stir-fry sauce or teriyaki sauce

OPTIONAL GARNISHES

Blanched grilled broccoli stalks
Deep-fried julienned sweet potatoes
Hibiscus flowers

❀ | TO MAKE THE ROASTED TOMATO VELOUTÉ: In a food processor combine the garlic cloves, shallot, lemongrass, and chili peppers. Process until finely chopped. Add the basil and cilantro leaves, and process until finely chopped. Add 1 tablespoon of the oil and process until a paste forms. In a large skillet heat the remaining 1 tablespoon of oil over medium heat. Add half of the paste and sauté for 2 minutes. (Reserve the remaining paste for the Asian vegetables.) Add the coconut milk to the skillet and simmer for 1 to 2 minutes or until thickened. Add the tomato halves and heat through. Add the cheese, transfer to a food processor, and purée. Strain the sauce, if desired. Season to taste with salt and pepper and keep warm.

❀ | FOR THE TOURNEDOS: Preheat the oven to 375°F. Wrap 2 pieces of salmon together, forming a circle or tournado and tie with cotton string. Repeat with the remaining salmon. Sprinkle lightly with salt and pepper. In a large skillet heat the oil over medium-high heat. Add the tournedos (in batches if necessary) and sear for 1 minute per side. Transfer the salmon to a shallow roasting pan and roast in the oven for 5 to 7 minutes or until opaque in the center. Top the salmon with the mango strips and Brie; return to oven and roast for 2 to 3 minutes or until the Brie begins to melt.

For the vegetables: In a large skillet heat the oil over medium-high heat. Add the vegetables and stir-fry for 3 minutes or until the vegetables are crisp-tender. Add the reserved paste and stir-fry for 1 minute. Add the stir-fry sauce and stir-fry for 1 minute.

To serve: For each serving, spoon ½ cup of mashed potatoes into a 3-inch ring mold. Unmold onto the center of a warmed dinner plate (or spoon the potatoes into a 3-inch mound). Spoon velouté sauce around the potatoes. Spoon Asian vegetables in mounds around the potatoes. Top the potatoes with salmon. If desired, garnish each plate with broccoli, sweet potatoes, and a hibiscus flower.

YAUTIA-WRAPPED DORADO

DAYN SMITH

Stingray Cafe, El Conquistador Resort
Fajardo, Puerto Rico

SERVES 4

Strands of spiral-sliced yautia—or sweet potato, if yautia is not available in your market—are wrapped around fish fillets, protecting them as they fry and adding their own flavor and texture. The fish is served with braised vegetables and a salsa of tomatillos and tomatoes.

OVEN-DRIED TOMATILLO AND TOMATO SALSA

2	tomatoes
2	tomatillos
	Salt and freshly ground black pepper to taste
2	tablespoons olive oil
1	small onion, chopped
2	aji dulce (sweet peppers), seeded, deribbed, and minced
2	teaspoons ricao or cilantro, chopped
½	cup white wine vinegar
½	cup lime juice
½	teaspoon sugar

YUCA PURÉE

2	cups peeled, cored, and chopped yuca
3	cups milk
1	teaspoon kosher salt

VEGETABLES

1	fennel bulb

1	tablespoon butter
4	to 6 shallots, halved lengthwise
2	cups chicken stock
1	head romaine lettuce

CILANTRO OIL

1	bunch cilantro, stemmed
8	ounces grapeseed oil

DORADO

24	ounces dorado (mahimahi), filleted
	Kosher salt and freshly ground black pepper to taste
1	purple yautia, peeled (alternatively, 3 large sweet potatoes)
8	ounces vegetable oil
1	large red pepper, cut into very narrow julienne

❀ | TO MAKE THE SALSA: Preheat the oven to 200°F. Place a wire rack in a baking sheet. Quarter and seed the tomatoes and tomatillos. Place them on the wire rack, sprinkle with salt and pepper, and bake for 2 hours to 2 hours and 30 minutes, until nearly dried. Let cool and dice. In a medium skillet heat the oil over medium heat. Toss the dried tomatoes, tomatillos, onion, and peppers to coat, then cook about 1 minute until the onion and pepper are softened. Add the remaining ingredients, toss to coat, and remove from the heat. Set aside at room temperature for at least 1 hour to blend the flavors.

❀ | TO PREPARE THE YUCA PURÉE: In a saucepan bring the yuca, 2¾ cups milk, and salt to a simmer over medium heat. Cook for 20 minutes or until tender. Add ¼ cup of milk and purée in a food processor. Cover and set aside.

❈ | To PREPARE THE VEGETABLES: Preheat the oven to 350°F. Cut the fennel bulb vertically in ¼-inch-thick slices. In a sauté pan or skillet melt the butter over medium heat and sauté the fennel with the shallots about 2 minutes until the fennel is golden on both sides. Cover three-fourths of the way with stock, put in the oven, and braise for 10 minutes. Bring a pot of water to a boil over high heat and drop the lettuce into the water for 15 seconds. Remove with a slotted spoon or tongs and plunge into ice water to stop the cooking. Place the lettuce on a towel spread on a work surface, thick ends toward you, and pat dry with another towel. Cut off the heavy bases. Cut the lettuce lengthwise from base to tip into 2-inch-wide strips, then separate the strips. Using the towel to assist, fold the lettuce up one-third from the bottom and press with the towel, then lift the top end and fold over, forming a packet. Press with the towel. Lift the lettuce packets with a spatula, place in a skillet large enough to hold them in one layer, and add the remaining chicken stock. Place in the oven for 5 minutes.

❈ | To MAKE THE CILANTRO OIL: Bring a pan of water to a boil and plunge the cilantro into the water for 5 seconds. Remove with a slotted spoon and plunge into ice water. Remove and drain on a towel or paper towels. Place the cilantro and oil in a blender and purée. Strain through a fine-mesh sieve and put in a squeeze bottle.

❈ | To MAKE THE DORADO: Cut the dorado lengthwise into 6-ounce portions. Season with salt and pepper. Turn the yautia or sweet potato on a spiral slicer, making long spiral strands. Carefully wrap each fillet in the strands, making sure the strands are applied in a single layer all around the fish. Do not double the strands. In a sauté pan or skillet heat the oil over medium-high heat and pan-fry the fish until the crust is golden brown and the fish is cooked all the way through, about 5 minutes. Remove the fish and drain on paper towels. With a slotted spoon, place the red pepper julienne in the hot oil and let cook for 30 seconds, then remove and drain.

❈ | To SERVE: Cut a piece of fish diagonally into thirds and stand the 3 pieces in the center of a serving plate. Place a scoop of yuca purée beside the fish. Repeat with the other 3 serving plates. Divide the fennel and lettuce among the plates and place beside the yuca purée. Place small clusters of salsa around the other side of the plates and drizzle each with cilantro oil. Place a cluster of red pepper strips in the center of each plate.

FISH FILLET CAPRICE

OTTMAR WEBER

**Ottmar's at The Grand Pavilion Hotel
Grand Cayman**

SERVES 4

A simple sauce of mango and banana flavors fish that has been coated and sautéed until golden. The lovely cucumber garnish takes a bit of fiddling, but is unusual and attractive. Once you've mastered it you can use it to garnish many other dishes.

1	egg	2	mangoes, julienned
½	cup milk	2	bananas, sliced
	Flour for dredging	½	cup banana liqueur
	Salt and freshly ground black pepper to taste	½	cup water
6	12-ounce red snapper fillets, skinned		Salt and freshly ground black pepper to taste
¼	cup (½ stick) butter		
1	tablespoon light vegetable oil	1	cucumber
	Juice of 3 lemons	4	tomato roses
		4	sprigs rosemary

SAUCE

¼   cup (½ stick) butter

❊ | TO PREPARE THE FISH: In a large shallow bowl beat the egg with the milk. In a separate shallow bowl season the flour with salt and pepper. Cut each fish fillet in half cross-wise. In a large heavy skillet over medium heat melt the butter and stir in the vegetable oil. Dip the fish fillets in lemon juice, then in the egg mixture. Dredge in the seasoned flour. Fry for 5 minutes on each side until golden. Remove, drain on paper towels, and keep warm.

❊ | TO MAKE THE SAUCE: In the same skillet used for the fish melt the butter and add the mango and banana. Sauté for 3 minutes. Stir in the liqueur and water and bring to a boil. Cook until reduced by one-fourth in volume. Remove from the heat and taste for seasoning; add salt and pepper to taste.

❊ | TO MAKE THE CUCUMBER GARNISH: Cut the ends off each cucumber, and cut each cucumber in half. Slice each piece in half lengthwise. Cut each resulting piece almost all the way through in very thin slices, keeping them attached by a strip of skin. Fan a cucumber section, tucking every other slice of the cucumber back on itself. Repeat with the remaining sections.

❊ | TO SERVE: Place 3 pieces of fish on each plate. Put a tomato rose in the center. Spoon the warm sauce over the fish, placing banana slices on the fish. Garnish each plate with a cucumber section. Top the plates with sprigs of rosemary.

Fillet of Vivaneau with Endive and Confit Tomatoes

Thierry Alix
La Samanna Resort
St. Martin

SERVES 2

Vivaneau, or red mullet, resembles trout. You can substitute trout or other firm-fleshed fillets if you can't get mullet. The fish is seared to brown it, then served on endive and tomato with a black olive sauce. A simple basil sauce is drizzled on the plate for garnish.

Endive

4	tablespoons olive oil
2	whole endive, cleaned and separated
6	to 8 oven-dried tomatoes
1	tablespoon ground sea salt
	Freshly ground black pepper to taste

Basil Sauce

6	tablespoons olive oil
10	basil leaves
2	large garlic cloves, peeled and minced
	Sea salt to taste

Black Olive Sauce

1	tablespoon unsalted butter
1	shallot, minced
¾	cup veal stock
¼	cup red wine
4	large black olives, pitted and julienned

2	whole red mullet (about 12 ounces each)
2	tablespoons unsalted butter
1	tablespoon olive oil
2	sprigs basil
2	sprigs thyme
2	cherry tomatoes

❁ | To prepare the vegetables: In a sauté pan heat the olive oil over medium heat and cook the endive leaves, covered, about 5 minutes until wilted. Stir in the tomatoes. Adjust the seasoning to taste with salt and pepper, re-cover, and set aside off the heat.

❁ | To make the basil sauce: In a blender or food processor purée the ingredients together. Place in a squeeze bottle, and set aside.

❁ | To make the black olive sauce: In a sauté pan melt the butter over medium-high heat and sauté the shallots about 1 minute until soft. Add ½ cup of the veal stock and the wine, lower the heat to medium, and cook for 6 to 8 minutes until reduced by half. The veal stock may be made to this point, chilled, and rewarmed just before serving. To continue the preparation, stir the remaining ¼ cup of veal stock into the warmed reduction sauce. Simmer over low heat while cooking the fish.

❁ | To prepare the fish: With a sharp boning knife, make an incision just below the head, cutting all the way to the bone. Cut off the fins. Cut along the backbone from head to tail and lift off the fillet. Repeat on the other side. Gently tweeze out any remaining bones from the flesh of the fillets. Season on each side with salt and pepper. Score the skin to keep the fish from curling. In a sauté pan heat the butter and olive oil over medium-high heat and sear the fish on the skin side until browned. Take the pan off the heat, turn the fish over, and set aside to finish using just the heat of the pan.

❁ | TO SERVE: Add the olives to the veal stock sauce. Place a mound of endive in the center of the plate. Place 2 pieces of fish on the endive and pour the olive sauce around it. Drizzle the basil sauce around the fish and endive. Garnish with basil and thyme sprigs and a cherry tomato.

FILLET OF SEA BASS WITH A DOMINICAN CREOLE SAUCE AND TROPICAL PURÉE

PHILIPPE MONGEREAU

Casa de Campo
Dominican Republic

SERVES 4

TROPICAL PURÉE

2	pounds sweet potatoes, peeled and cubed
1	small white onion, peeled
1	small orange
1	bay leaf
1	cinnamon stick
	Salt and fresh finely ground white pepper to taste
¼	cup butter
¼	cup sugar
1	apple, peeled and cubed
1	small banana, peeled and cut into cubes
½	pineapple, peeled, cored, and cubed
¾	cup heavy (whipping) cream

CREOLE SAUCE

1	pound tomatoes, skinned, seeded, and cut into large pieces
3	tablespoons olive oil
6	Cuban (Anaheim) peppers, seeded, deribbed, and minced
1	small white onion, minced

1	bunch celery, deribbed and finely diced
2	cloves garlic, minced
¼	bunch of cilantro, stemmed
¼	cup dry white wine
1	bay leaf
	Juice of 1 lemon
	Salt and freshly ground black pepper to taste

BREADCRUMB TOPPING

1	cup breadcrumbs
½	cup cilantro, minced
2	garlic cloves, minced
	Salt and freshly ground black pepper to taste

2	tablespoons Dijon mustard
4	fillets of sea bass (about 2 pounds)
	Salt and freshly ground black pepper
4	tablespoons butter
4	garlic cloves, minced
1	cup white wine
½	cup water

❁ | TO MAKE THE TROPICAL PURÉE: Place the sweet potatoes and onion in a large pan and cover with water. Squeeze the orange and reserve the juice. Remove the rind from the orange, cut a piece about one-fourth of the whole rind, and add to the potatoes; the remaining rind pieces may be refrigerated, or added to granulated sugar to create flavored sugar. Add half the cinnamon stick and the bay leaf to the sweet potato mixture. Season with salt and pepper. Bring to a boil and simmer for 20 to 30 minutes until soft.

❀| While the potatoes are cooking, in a small sauté pan melt the butter and sugar together over medium heat and let cook until it forms a light caramel, slightly thickened and golden in color. Add the apple, banana, pineapple, remaining cinnamon stick piece, reserved orange juice, and heavy cream. Simmer for 5 to 8 minutes, until the fruit softens.

❀| Drain the potatoes and discard the orange peel, cinnamon, bay leaf, and onion. Remove the cinnamon from the caramelized fruit. In a food processor combine the potatoes and fruit and purée until smooth. Keep hot.

❀| TO MAKE THE SAUCE: Dice 1 of the tomatoes. In a sauté pan heat 2 tablespoons of the olive oil. Add the peppers, onion, celery, and garlic and sauté for 1 minute. Add the cilantro and sauté 1 more minute, or until the vegetables are translucent and soft. Stir in the diced tomato and set the vegetables aside. Place the remaining tomatoes in a saucepan with the white wine and bay leaf and bring to a boil over low heat. Cook for 3 to 4 minutes. Remove from the heat and press through a fine-mesh sieve. Add 1 tablespoon of olive oil and lemon juice and purée the mixture in a blender. Place the warm tomato juice in a bowl and season with salt and pepper. Stir in the vegetables.

❀| TO PREPARE THE BREADCRUMB TOPPING: Combine all ingredients on a large dish.

❀| TO PREPARE THE FISH: Preheat the oven to 300°F. Season the fillets with salt and pepper and paint with a thin layer of mustard. Place the fillets in the breadcrumb mixture, top down. Place the butter and garlic in 4 positions on a large ovenproof sauté pan and cover with the fish. Sear over medium-high heat for 1 minute. Add the wine and water and bake 3 to 4 minutes, until the fish are opaque throughout.

❀| TO SERVE: Spoon the sauce into 4 large plates, covering the bottom of each plate. Using 2 large spoons, scoop the tropical purée into oval quenelle shapes and place 2 on each plate. Top with a fish fillet.

SEARED RED SNAPPER WITH SWEET POTATOES AND CHRISTOPHENE, WITH CREOLE SAUCE

BENOIT PEPIN

Little Dix Bay
Virgin Gorda, BVI

SERVES 4

Red snapper fillets are seared and cooked from the skin side only. Three kinds of potatoes are served with this dish, including white potatoes that are carved into mushroom shapes.

CREOLE SAUCE

4	green onions, green part only, julienned
4	red bell peppers, peeled, seeded, deribbed, and minced
	Juice of 4 limes
1	Scotch bonnet pepper (habañero)
2	cups extra-virgin olive oil
	Salt and freshly ground black pepper to taste

VEGETABLES

4	white potatoes, skinned and carved into mushroom shapes
8	tablespoons (1 stick) unsalted butter

4	yellow Caribbean sweet potatoes, peeled and cut into large chunks
4	yams, tournéed (see page 239)
4	christophenes, cut into matchstick julienne
½	cup Curry Oil (see page 20)

4	7-ounce red snapper fillets, skin on
	Juice of 1 lemon
	Freshly ground black pepper to taste
	Sea salt to taste

4	sprigs chervil

❀ | TO MAKE THE CREOLE SAUCE: In a nonaluminum bowl combine the onion, bell pepper, lime juice, Scotch bonnet, olive oil, salt, and pepper and marinate for at least 1 hour. Remove and discard the Scotch bonnet.

❀ | TO PREPARE THE VEGETABLES: Place the white potatoes in a saucepan, cover with water, and bring to a boil over medium-high heat. Reduce the heat to medium, cover the pan, and cook until just soft when pierced with the point of a knife, 6 to 8 minutes. Remove from the heat and drain. Add 2 tablespoons of butter and cover. Set aside.

❀ | Place the sweet potatoes in a saucepan, cover with water, and bring to a boil over medium-high heat. Reduce the heat to medium, cover the pan, and cook until just soft, about 10 minutes. Remove from the heat and drain. Add 3 tablespoons of butter and cover. Set aside.

❀ | Place the tournéed yams in a sauté pan, cover with water, and bring to a boil over medium-high heat. Cook 5 minutes and drain. Add 3 tablespoons of butter and sauté over medium-low heat for 5 minutes.

✻ | Place the christophene in a sauté pan, cover with water, and bring to a boil over medium-high heat. Cook 3 minutes and drain. Add 2 tablespoons of curry oil, toss, and sauté over medium-low heat for 3 minutes.

✻ | TO PREPARE THE FISH: Cut each fish fillet in 3 pieces. Heat a nonstick sauté pan over medium-high heat and place the fish in the pan, skin side down. Cook for 3 to 4 minutes until opaque, using a spatula to keep the fish loose on the pan. Do not turn over. Season the top with lemon juice, pepper, and sea salt.

✻ | TO SERVE: Mash the sweet potatoes and butter. Place a 4-inch ring mold in the center of each plate and fill with sweet potato. Strew the plates with creole sauce. Lift off the mold. Place 3 pieces of snapper over each potato mold. Arrange the yams and christophene around the plates. Drizzle with curry oil and garnish with chervil.

GROUPER FILLET WITH CORN, TOMATO, AND PLANTAIN

HUBERT LORENZ
Caneel Bay Resort
St. John, U.S. Virgin Islands

SERVES 4

8	stalks lemongrass, cleaned		1	cup coconut milk
4	8-ounce grouper fillets, cleaned		1	pound French green beans (haricots)
	Juice of 2 limes			Salt and freshly ground black pepper to taste
			3	large tomatoes, peeled, seeded, and diced

VEGETABLE STEW

¼	cup olive oil		1	large plantain
¼	cup diced red onion		2	tablespoons olive oil
1	cup corn kernels			
1	green bell pepper, seeded, deribbed, and diced		12	tarragon flowers, or 4 sprigs tarragon

❀ | TO MARINATE THE FISH: Cut the lemongrass stalks in thin circles and spread half of them over the grouper fillets in a shallow dish. Squeeze the lime juice over the fish. Turn the fish and repeat on the other side. Marinate the grouper for 10 minutes.

❀ | TO MAKE THE VEGETABLE STEW: In a medium sauté pan heat the olive oil over medium heat. Add the onion and sauté for 1 minute. Add the corn kernels and cook for 30 seconds, tossing or stirring gently. Add the bell pepper and 2 tablespoons of the coconut milk and cook for 30 seconds. Add the green beans and remaining coconut milk and cook for 1 minute. Season with salt and pepper to taste. Stir in the tomatoes and remove from the heat; set aside.

❀ | TO COOK THE PLANTAINS: Peel the plantain and cut into thin slices on the bias. In a small sauté pan heat 1 tablespoon of olive oil over medium-high heat and sauté the plantain slices until golden on both sides, about 1 minute total. Season with salt.

❀ | TO COOK THE FISH: Preheat the oven to 450°F. In another large ovenproof sauté pan heat the remaining olive oil over medium-high heat and sear the fish fillet for 30 seconds on each side. Place in the oven and cook for 5 minutes, or until the center is opaque.

❀ | TO SERVE: Arrange the vegetable stew in the center of each plate. Place a fish fillet on top of the vegetables. Garnish with plantain and tarragon flowers or sprigs.

Pan-fried Red Snapper with Baby Arugula and Papaya Salad

Alfredo N. Ayala
Chayote Restaurant
San Juan, Puerto Rico

SERVES 4

Sour Sop and Nutmeg Dressing

¼	cup olive oil
¼	cup puréed sour sop or cherimoya*
3	tablespoons fresh lime juice
1	tablespoon cider vinegar
1	teaspoon freshly grated nutmeg
	Salt and freshly ground black pepper

Snapper and Salad

4	6- to 8-ounce red snapper fillets with skin
¾	teaspoon salt
¼	teaspoon freshly ground black pepper
¼	cup olive oil
4	ounces (3 cups packed) arugula leaves
1	cup diced ripe papaya

❋ | For the dressing: In a jar with a tight-fitting lid combine the oil, sour sop purée, lime juice, vinegar, and nutmeg. Cover jar; shake well. Season to taste with salt and pepper. Chill until serving time.

❋ | For the snapper and salad: Score the skinned side of each fillet to prevent curling while cooking. Sprinkle the meaty side of fillets with salt and pepper. In a large skillet heat the oil over medium-high heat until hot. Add the fillets, skin side down. Cook for 4 minutes or until deep golden brown. Turn; continue cooking 30 seconds to 1 minute or just until the fish is opaque in center. Drain on paper towels.

❋ | To serve: Toss the arugula and papaya with ¼ cup of the dressing; arrange in the center of 4 serving plates. Top with snapper fillets. Drizzle the remaining dressing around the edges of the plates.

* Note: Choose a ripe fruit, discard the peel and seeds, and purée the flesh in a blender or food processor. If these fruits are not available, substitute ¼ cup of mashed ripe banana.

GRILLED RED SNAPPER WITH CONCH AND CORN PANCAKE AND TAMARIND-PINEAPPLE VINAIGRETTE

MARTIN FROST

Four Seasons Resort
Nevis

SERVES 4

Grilled fish tops a conch and corn pancake, which in turn sits atop a vegetable melange. Tamarind, the spice that dominates the vinaigrette drizzled around this dish, is a predominant spice in Worcestershire sauce, and adds an acerbic bite to the flavors. Conch is hard to find in most locations; you can substitute chopped clams, or even use shrimp or crab, and still have a delicious dish even if it is not an exact duplicate.

VINAIGRETTE

½	cup diced pineapple
2	tablespoons tamarind juice
¼	cup olive oil
1	tablespoon honey

PANCAKES

½	cup cornmeal
½	cup boiling water
1	tablespoon honey
	Pinch of salt
¼	cup sifted all-purpose flour
1	tablespoon baking power
1	egg
½	cup milk
1	tablespoon melted butter
1	scallion, finely chopped
¼	cup fresh corn
1	cup conch, ground or chopped very fine

VEGETABLE CURLS

1	sweet potato, peeled

	Flour for dusting
	Vegetable oil for frying
4	large basil leaves, cut into chiffonade
½	bunch chervil, minced
½	bunch cilantro, minced
½	bunch parsley, minced
2	tablespoons extra-virgin olive oil
4	6- to 8-ounce red snapper fillets, skin on
¼	cup mixed herbs
2	teaspoons dry jerk seasoning

VEGETABLE SALAD

8	spears fresh pencil asparagus, blanched
2	tomatoes, peeled and cut into wedges
6	yellow currant tomatoes
2	leaves fresh basil, cut into chiffonade
1	tablespoon olive oil
1	tablespoon red wine vinegar
	Salt and freshly ground black pepper to taste

❀ | TO MAKE THE VINAIGRETTE: Whisk all ingredients together and put in a squeeze bottle.

❀ | TO MAKE THE PANCAKES: In a large bowl combine the cornmeal, boiling water, honey, and salt. Let cool. Sift together the flour and baking powder. Add the egg, milk, melted butter, and flour mixture, stirring just until mixed. Stir in the scallion, corn, and conch. Lightly spray a nonstick griddle or frying pan with vegetable oil spray. Make 3-inch pancakes: For each pancake, pour 2 large tablespoonfuls of batter on the hot pan, letting it spread without touching another pancake. Cook until bubbles form on the surface, about 1 minute. Flip with a plastic spatula and cook on the other side for 30 more seconds, or until it is golden and cooked through. Remove and keep warm. Extra pancakes may be frozen.

✿ | To MAKE THE VEGETABLE GARNISH: Using a spiral slicer or similar slicer, pare the potato in long very thin strips. Soak in ice water for 10 minutes. Pat with paper towels to dry thoroughly, then dust lightly with flour. In a deep-fat fryer or deep pan heat the oil to 350°F. With a slotted spoon, plunge the potato strips, a few at a time, into the hot oil. Fry for 20 to 30 seconds until crisp. Remove and set aside on paper towels to drain. Lightly dust the basil with the flour, shake off excess, and plunge the basil into the hot oil for 10 to 15 seconds until crisp. Remove with a slotted spoon and drain on paper towels.

✿ | To PREPARE THE FISH: In a small bowl toss the minced herbs together and stir in the olive oil. Preheat the grill to its highest setting, or prepare a charcoal fire. Brush the snapper with the herb oil and sprinkle with mixed herbs and jerk seasoning. Grill skin side down for 30 seconds, lift and rotate the fish 45 degrees, and grill again for 1 minute, leaving grill marks. Turn and grill on the other side for 2 minutes or until the fish is opaque throughout.

✿ | To SERVE: Toss the vegetable salad ingredients together and divide among the plates. Place a pancake on top of the greens on each plate, and top with a piece of fish. Garnish the top with vegetable curls. Drizzle the plate with the vinaigrette.

FILLET OF RED SNAPPER WITH SHRIMP

NORMA SHIRLEY

Norma at the Wharfside
Montego Bay, Jamaica

SERVES 2

Scotch bonnet adds a touch of Caribbean heat to the broth used to poach the fish. This easy-to-prepare fish gathers flavors from the broth as it cooks. The accompanying vegetables are simply blanched. If you are serving this to a Jamaican, Chef Shirley recommends keeping the Scotch bonnet and serving it on the side!

1	whole red snapper (approx. 1½ to 2 pounds), filleted
	Juice of 1 lime
2	cups fish, chicken, or vegetable stock
1	sprig fresh thyme
1	scotch bonnet pepper
2	scallions
1	small tomato

Salt and freshly ground black pepper to taste
6 to 8 large shrimp

VEGETABLES

1	carrot, cut into julienne
1	head of broccoli, stem removed, divided into pieces
1	chayote, cut into julienne

❈ | Wash the snapper with the lime juice. Cut the fish into large serving pieces. In a skillet or pan large enough to hold the fish in a single layer combine the stock, thyme, pepper, scallions, and tomato, and bring to a simmer over medium heat. Reduce the heat to medium-low until the liquid is barely simmering, and gently place the fish skin side up in the liquid. Poach until cooked through and tender; about 15 minutes (time varies with the thickness of the fish). Ladle the hot liquid over the fish as it cooks. Test for doneness by pushing a toothpick into the thickest part of the fish; it should encounter a little resistance in the center. Very gently remove the fish with a slotted spatula and place it on a warmed serving platter. Cover with foil. Increase the heat under the liquid to medium-high and boil until the volume is reduced by half. Remove the Scotch bonnet pepper. Season to taste. Remove the heads, legs, and shells from the shrimp, leaving the meat attached at the tail. Remove the back strip. Put the shrimp in the stock and cook until just pink and firm, about 1 minute. Remove the shrimp and thyme.

❈ | TO PREPARE THE VEGETABLES: Place the carrots and broccoli in boiling water and cook for 1 minute, stirring once. Add the chayote and cook 1 more minute. Remove from the heat, drain, and plunge into cold water.

❈ | TO SERVE: Place the fish on serving plates and pour some of the reduced stock and shrimp over it. Place a strip of scallion over the fish. Serve with the blanched vegetables.

Sea Scallops with Polenta

Stephane Bois

**Le Patio, Village St. Jean
St. Barts**

SERVES 4

32	medium or 12 large sea scallops (about 1¾ pounds)	2	tablespoons cognac or brandy
	Salt and freshly ground black pepper	¼	cup dry French bread crumbs
2	tablespoons unsalted butter	2	cups Fish Stock (see page 236), bottled clam juice, or chicken stock
3	tablespoons extra-virgin olive oil, divided	½	cup dry white wine or dry vermouth
3	cloves garlic, minced	¾	cup yellow cornmeal or quick-cooking polenta
6	tablespoons chopped parsley, divided		
1	cup diced tomato, divided		

❀ | Rinse the scallops and pat dry; sprinkle lightly with salt and pepper. Heat the butter and 1 tablespoon of the olive oil in a large skillet over medium-high heat until hot. Add half of the scallops in one layer and sear 2 minutes per side. Transfer to a plate and sear the remaining scallops. Return all scallops to the pan. Add the garlic, 3 tablespoons of the parsley, and ½ cup of the tomato. Add the cognac; carefully ignite with a long match or barbecue starter. Shake the skillet until the flames subside. Sprinkle breadcrumbs over the scallops and simmer over low heat 3 minutes or until the scallops are opaque in the center, turning once.

❀ | In a large saucepan bring the fish stock and wine to a boil. Slowly stir in the cornmeal. Reduce the heat to low and whisk constantly until the polenta is very thick, about 5 minutes. Season with salt and freshly ground pepper to taste.

❀ | To serve: Spoon the polenta in the center of 4 serving plates. Spoon the scallops with pan juices over the polenta. Drizzle the remaining 2 tablespoons of olive oil around the edges of the plates. Sprinkle the remaining 3 tablespoons of parsley and ½ cup of chopped tomato over the oil.

CARIBBEAN STUFFED LOBSTER

OTTMAR WEBER

Ottmar's at the Grand Pavilion Hotel
Grand Cayman

SERVES 2

There's a reason fine chefs tournée vegetables: They cook evenly and quickly. This elegant dish uses the lobster tail shells to hold seafood stuffing, topped with lobster medallions cooked in garlic butter. The mango and avocado in the stuffing add Caribbean flavor.

VEGETABLES

6	baby carrots, peeled
6	baby potatoes, peeled
6	baby zucchini
1	cup dry white wine
1	cup red wine
1	small red onion, diced
	Freshly ground black pepper
2	1½- to 2-pound whole Maine or Caribbean lobsters

STUFFING

4	tablespoons butter
½	small red onion, minced
2	tablespoons all-purpose flour
1½	cups light cream

½	cup dry white wine
¼	teaspoon salt
½	small red onion, minced
4	tablespoons butter
4	ounces scallops, cut into large chunks
4	ounces crab meat, cut into large chunks
6	large shrimp, shelled, deveined, and cut into large pieces
4	ounces avocado, cubed
4	ounces mango, cubed
2	ounces mushrooms, cut into large pieces
1	tablespoon butter
2	tablespoons Garlic Butter (see page 239)
2	teaspoons salt
2	teaspoons freshly ground black pepper
8	tablespoons breadcrumbs

❀ | TO MAKE THE VEGETABLES: Peel and tournée the vegetables: Cut them into uniform 2-inch oblongs. In 2 small sauté pans bring water to a boil. Place the carrots in one and the potatoes in the other and cook for 5 to 7 minutes until just tender. Remove from the heat, drain, and plunge into cold water. Drain again, and set aside. Repeat with the zucchini, cooking only 2 to 3 minutes.

❀ | TO PREPARE THE LOBSTER: Bring a large pot of salted water to a rolling boil and add the wines, onion, and pepper. Hold the lobster right side up on a work surface. Quickly insert the point of a sharp knife into the lobster's shell in the center of the cross mark behind the head to kill the lobster. Place in the boiling water and cook for 7 to 8 minutes. Remove with tongs and drain. Repeat with the second lobster. With a sharp knife, split the lobster in half lengthwise. Remove the meat from the claws and set aside. Remove the meat from the tails, remove the black vein, and cut the tails into medallions. Clean the shell halves.

❀ | To MAKE THE STUFFING: In a small saucepan over medium heat, melt the butter and sauté the diced half of the onion until softened and translucent. Whisk in the flour, reduce the heat to low, and cook, whisking constantly, for 2 minutes. Do not allow it to brown. Whisk in the cream, white wine, and salt, and decrease the heat to medium-low. Cook for 7 to 10 minutes, stirring occasionally, until it thickens and coats the back of a spoon. Adjust the seasoning with salt and pepper.

❀ | In a large skillet over medium-high heat, sauté the remaining minced onion in butter until softened and translucent. Stir in the scallops, crabmeat, and shrimp, and sauté for 2 minutes. Add the avocado, mango, and mushrooms, and stir. Pour the sauce through a fine-mesh sieve into the seafood, and toss gently to coat.

❀ | To FINISH: In a small sauté pan over medium heat melt 1 tablespoon of butter and add the tournéed vegetables, tossing to coat. Sauté for 2 minutes to warm through. Preheat the broiler. Stuff the seafood filling into the lobster shells. Melt the garlic butter in a medium skillet over medium-high heat and sauté the lobster medallions for 1 minute until lightly browned. Season with salt and pepper. Place on top of the seafood stuffing. Sprinkle with breadcrumbs, drizzle with the melted garlic butter, and broil about 1 minute until golden brown.

❀ | To SERVE: Place 2 lobster halves on each serving plate. Garnish the plates with the tournéed vegetables.

CREOLE BLAFF OF CARIBBEAN LOBSTER AND MEXICAN FOIE GRAS

MARK EHRLER

The Ritz-Carlton Cancún
Cancún, Mexico

SERVES 4

This dish is prepared with simplicity and respect for the French Creole tradition. The name "blaff" comes from the sound the broth makes as it simmers. While lobster and foie gras add elegance, the basic dish could also be made with simpler ingredients like snapper or chicken.

3	tablespoons olive oil	1	tablespoon whole black peppercorns
1	habañero pepper	1	cup dry white wine
1	small red onion, thinly sliced	6	cups water
8	small scallions, cleaned and ends trimmed		Salt and freshly ground pepper to taste
6	sprigs Italian parsley		
2	sprigs thyme	12	to 14 ounces fresh foie gras
1	clove garlic, minced	2	8-ounce lobster tails
1	bay leaf	2	tablespoons lime juice, freshly squeezed

In a large stock pot heat the olive oil over medium-high heat to nearly smoking. Using a long toothpick, poke a small hole in the side of the habañero. Add the red onion, scallions, habañero, parsley, thyme, garlic, bay leaf, and peppercorns to the olive oil. Toss the vegetables in the oil and cook until slightly softened, 3 to 4 minutes. Add the white wine, and simmer for 1 minute, then add the water. Add salt and pepper to taste. Bring the broth and vegetables to a boil and cook for 5 to 6 minutes. Place the foie gras and lobster tails in the broth. Cover the pot with a lid, remove from the heat, and set aside. After 12 to 14 minutes, remove the foie gras from the broth, setting on a rack to drain. After 4 minutes longer, remove the lobster tails to a rack to drain. Bring the broth and vegetables back to a boil. Remove the pot from the heat and add the lime juice, stirring to blend. Take out the habañero pepper and discard. Slice the foie gras diagonally into 4 slices. Remove the lobster tails from their shells and cut each tail in half lengthwise.

To SERVE: Place a small amount of broth and vegetables in the bottom of each serving bowl. Lay a lobster piece in the broth, garnishing it with a scallion from the broth pot. Top with a foie gras slice. Garnish the side of the bowl with herbs from the broth pot. Pour a small amount of broth over the top and serve.

Caribbean Lobster Tail Orquijdee

Philippe Mongereau
Casa de Campo, Dominican Republic

SERVES 4

Lobster and vegetables

4	12-ounce lobster tails, preferably Caribbean, thawed if frozen
½	teaspoon salt
2	tablespoons olive oil
1	tablespoon unsalted butter
1	chayote squash, peeled, seeded, and julienned
2	large carrots, julienned
1	medium red onion, julienned
	Salt and freshly ground black pepper to taste

Sauce

2	whole vanilla beans, cut crosswise in half
2	tablespoons apple cider vinegar
½	cup dry white wine
2	tablespoons water
4	tablespoons unsalted butter
2	teaspoons fresh lime or lemon juice

Garnish

Basil or other herb sprigs

❀ | For the lobster and vegetables: Split the lobster tails in half lengthwise; discard the vein. Sprinkle the cut sides of the tails lightly with the salt. In a large skillet heat the oil over medium heat until hot. In batches add the tails cut side down and cook 3 to 4 minutes until browned. Transfer the tails as they are browned to a roasting pan and roast at 350°F for about 10 minutes until opaque. (Do not wash the skillet.)

❀ | Meanwhile, in another skillet melt the butter and sauté the julienned vegetables over medium heat until tender, 4 to 6 minutes. Season to taste with salt and freshly ground black pepper and keep warm while preparing the sauce.

❀ | For the sauce: Add the vanilla beans to the skillet used to cook the lobster tails and deglaze the pan with the vinegar. Add the wine and water and boil gently until the liquid is reduced by half. Whisk in the butter until melted and add the lime juice. Remove the lobster tails from their shells; add to the skillet to heat through.

❀ | To serve: Arrange the sautéed vegetables in 4 shallow bowls. Place the lobster tails over the vegetables and drizzle with the sauce. Garnish each serving with 1 of the halved vanilla beans and a basil sprig.

Sweet Potato-wrapped Spiny Lobster Tail with Avocado and Green Papaya Roti Taco and Beetroot Syrup

Martin Frost

Four Seasons Resort
Nevis

MAKES 4

This recipe makes good use of the Asian spiral slicers that are turning out long spiral garnishes at restaurants everywhere. While a spiral slicer will make a pretty wrap, you can create long thin slices on a regular slicer or grater and get the same flavor for this dish. The pretty potato-wrapped lobster medallions stud a salad of avocado and green papaya held in attractive cups. If you can't find triangular molds, take a trip to the hardware store for some lengths of right-angle aluminum, then wrap it in aluminum foil to make a mold.

Beet Syrup

½   cup beet juice
1   tablespoon honey

Sweet Potato-wrapped Lobster Tails

1   sprig parsley
1   sprig chervil
1   sprig cilantro
4   6-ounce spiny lobster tails
      Salt and freshly ground black pepper
2   sweet potatoes, peeled
      Vegetable oil for deep-frying

1   plantain, peeled

Avocado and Green Papaya Salad

1   avocado, peeled and sliced
1   medium jicama, peeled and julienned
½   medium green papaya, peeled, seeded, and
         julienned
2   tablespoons rice wine vinegar
      Juice of 2 limes
2   tablespoons sweet chili sauce
1   teaspoon chopped fresh ginger

4   roti shells (flour tortillas)

❀ | To make the syrup: Cook the beet juice and honey together in a saucepan over medium-low heat until reduced by one-fourth, to the consistency of maple syrup. Remove, cool, and place in a squeeze bottle.

❀ | To make the lobster: Pull the leaves from the herbs and mince them together. Peel the shells from the lobster tails, leaving the tail fins attached: Cut the shells down both sides of the tail, peel back, and cut off at the tail fins. Roll the lobster in the herbs and season with salt and pepper. Place 2 skewers through each tail to hold it straight during cooking. On a spiral vegetable slicer, make strings of the sweet potato and wrap these around the lobster tails. Wrap the prepared tails in plastic wrap and refrigerate for at least 30 minutes.

❀ | In a deep fryer or skillet heat the oil to 275°F. Remove the plastic and fry the tails for 8 to 9

FILLET OF VIVANEAU WITH ENDIVE AND CONFIT TOMATOES (PAGE 87)

FILLET OF SEA BASS WITH A DOMINICAN CREOLE SAUCE AND TROPICAL PURÉE
(PAGE 88)

SEARED RED SNAPPER WITH SWEET POTATOES AND CRISTOPHENE,
WITH CREOLE SAUCE (PAGE 90)

GROUPER FILLET WITH CORN, TOMATO, AND PLANTAIN (PAGE 92)

CARIBBEAN STUFFED LOBSTER (PAGE 98)

PAN-FRIED RED SNAPPER WITH BABY ARUGULA AND PAPAYA SALAD (PAGE 93)

CREOLE BLAFF OF CARIBBEAN
LOBSTER AND MEXICAN
FOIE GRAS (PAGE 100)

SWEET POTATO-WRAPPED SPINY
LOBSTER TAIL WITH AVOCADO
AND GREEN PAPAYA ROTI TACO
AND BEETROOT SYRUP
(PAGE 102)

BASIL-SCENTED CARIBBEAN LOBSTER (PAGE 120)

CHICKEN TRINIDAD WITH ORANGE-RUM SAUCE (PAGE 124)

SUGAR MILL PLANTATION PORK (PAGE 130)

GRILLED DUCK BREAST WITH A PINK PEPPERCORN-PASSION FRUIT SAUCE
AND WILD MUSHROOMS (PAGE 126)

112

VEAL OSCAR (PAGE 134)

LAMB CHOP WITH MOFONGO AND CILANTRO PESTO (PAGE 136)

BROILED BABY LAMB CHOPS (PAGE 138)

COFFEE-COCOA-SPICED RACK OF LAMB (PAGE 139)

RACK OF LAMB CRUSTED WITH HAZELNUTS AND DIJON MUSTARD ON FRAMBOISE
DEMI-GLACE (PAGE 140)

GUAVA MOUSSE IN A TROPICAL FRUIT
SOUP WITH MASCARPONE ICE CREAM
(PAGE 144)

MANGO-LIME MOUSSE TART WITH
COCONUT ICE CREAM (PAGE 146)

PASSION FRUIT MOUSSE IN A TUILE CONE
WITH STRAWBERRY AND MANGO COULIS (PAGE 148)

minutes. Remove and drain on paper towels. Slice the plantain into very thin chips and deep-fry in the same oil until golden brown, about 30 seconds. Remove and drain on paper towels.

❧ | To MAKE THE SALAD: Toss all ingredients together until the vegetables are coated.

❧ | To MAKE THE ROTI (TACO) SHELLS: Preheat the oven to 350°F. Place triangular molds on a baking sheet. Lay the tortillas over triangular molds and bake for 5 minutes, until crisp. Remove and let cool.

❧ | To SERVE: Place one shell on each plate and fill with the salad. Remove the skewers and slice the lobster tails into medallions. Place over the salad greens. Garnish with plantain chips and drizzle the plate with beet syrup.

BASIL-SCENTED CARIBBEAN LOBSTER

ROY KHOO

The Ritz-Carlton St. Thomas
St. Thomas U.S. Virgin Islands

SERVES 4

Chef Roy Khoo brings his Malaysian heritage and fresh Caribbean ingredients together. A spicy sambal—a thick pastelike sauce similar to American chili sauce—is made first, then used to flavor the lobster-basil-spinach mixture that is poured over the rice. Jasmine rice is a particular type of rice that has a flowery bouquet; plain rice may be substituted. The pigeon peas are used for garnish and may be eliminated. They must soak overnight before preparation.

½   cup pigeon peas

SPICY LEMONGRASS-GINGER SAMBAL

4   ounces tamarind
1½   cups warm water
1   pound shallots, peeled
4   garlic cloves, peeled
1½   inches fresh gingerroot, peeled
2   medium tomatoes, quartered
1   tablespoon ground chili paste
1½   tablespoons ground turmeric
1   tablespoon ground coriander
5   ounces Macadamia nuts
3   lemongrass stalks
2   tablespoons extra-virgin olive oil
¼   cup sugar
1   tablespoon salt

COCONUT-JASMINE RICE

1   tablespoon olive oil
2   shallots, sliced thin

Salt and freshly ground white pepper to
         taste
1½   cups coconut milk
2   cups Jasmine rice
1½   cups water

LOBSTER

1   tablespoon extra-virgin olive oil
1   garlic clove, diced
1   shallot, diced
2   cups diced Caribbean lobster meat
4   basil leaves, cut into julienne
3   tablespoons Spicy Lemongrass-Ginger
         Sambal (above)
1   cup coconut milk
1   cup blanched spinach
2   Kaffir lime leaves, cut into julienne

GARNISH

         Sweet Potato Spirals

❀ | TO PREPARE THE PIGEON PEAS: Place the peas in a small deep saucepan and cover them with warm water. Let soak overnight. Drain the water, add new water to cover, and boil until soft, about 1 hour. Drain and reserve.

❀ | TO MAKE THE SAMBAL: In a small mixing bowl crush the tamarind slightly, adding the warm water. Let soak for 15 minutes, then strain through a fine-mesh sieve. In a food processor or food mill grind the shallots, garlic, ginger, tomatoes, chili paste, turmeric, coriander, Macadamia nuts, and lemongrass into a paste. In a sauté pan heat the olive oil over medium heat and add the paste mixture, sugar, and salt. Sauté, stirring continuously, until slightly browned, about 30 to 40 minutes. Add the reserved tamarind juice to the paste mixture. Cook until a loose paste forms, 5 to 7 minutes.

❋ | To MAKE THE RICE: In a medium saucepan heat the olive oil over medium-high heat and sauté the shallots until soft. Add salt and pepper and toss together. Stir in the coconut milk, rice, and water. Bring to a boil. Lower the heat to simmer, cover, and cook about 20 minutes until the rice is soft.

❋ | To MAKE THE LOBSTER: In a medium skillet heat the olive oil and sauté the garlic and shallots over medium-high heat until soft. Add the lobster meat and basil and stir. Add the sambal and coconut milk and cook until bubbling and slightly thickened, about 3 minutes. Stir in the spinach and Kaffir lime leaf pieces and cook 30 seconds longer.

❋ | To SERVE: Place the coconut rice in the center of each serving plate. Top with the lobster mixture. Place fried sweet potato garnish on top and sprinkle each plate with pigeon peas.

THAI-BARBECUED LACQUERED WAHOO OVER A LEMONGRASS-GINGER BROTH ON UDON NOODLES

PHILIP FITZPATRICK
Villa Madeleine
St. Croix, U.S.V.I.

SERVES 4

Eastern ingredients flavor a popular West Indies fish: the wahoo is a firm-fleshed fish eaten throughout the Caribbean islands. Salmon is a good mainland substitute. Thai barbecue sauce glazes the fish, which is served over firm udon noodles in a fresh broth scented with lemongrass and ginger.

LEMONGRASS-GINGER BROTH

4	cups (1 quart) water
1	teaspoon Hon Dashi or other bonito-type soup stock
6	lemongrass stalks
1	gingerroot

THAI BARBECUE SAUCE

1	cup Thai chili sauce
2	Thai peppers
¼	cup ketchup
1	sprig mint, stemmed and finely chopped
1	teaspoon togarashi
2	Thai basil leaves

Salt and freshly ground black pepper

2	tablespoons safflower oil
1½	pounds wahoo or salmon, cut into four 2-inch-thick blocks
	Kosher salt for sprinkling
¼	cup (½ stick) unsalted butter
1	sprig parsley, stemmed and minced
2	basil leaves, minced
½	cup dry white wine
¼	cup water
8	ounces udon noodles

1	red bell pepper, seeded, deribbed, and cut into very thin lengthwise slivers	1	cup shiitake caps, cut into very thin slivers
1	yellow bell pepper, seeded, deribbed, and cut into very thin lengthwise slivers	2	scallions, cut on the bias
1	medium carrot, pared and shaved into very thin slivers	3	whole chives

❀| To MAKE THE BROTH: In a large pot over medium-high heat, bring the water to a boil. Add the hon dashi and reduce heat to medium-low. Smash the lemongrass and gingerroot with a mallet or other heavy flat object. Add to the hon dashi mixture and simmer for 15 to 20 minutes.

❀| To MAKE THE THAI BARBECUE SAUCE: Strain the chili sauce into a non-reactive bowl through a fine-mesh sieve to remove the seeds. Seed the pepper and purée; strain the juice through a fine-mesh sieve into the chili sauce. Stir in the ketchup, mint, togarashi, basil, and salt and pepper.

❀| To PREPARE THE FISH: Preheat the oven to 425°F. Heat the oil in a large skillet over medium-high heat. Sprinkle the fish with salt and pepper and sear on each side for 30 seconds to seal. Pour off the grease and add the butter and herbs to the pan. Deglaze with white wine, return the pan to the heat, and add the water. Stir gently and let the mixture bubble up. Remove from heat, paint the fish with Thai Barbecue Sauce, and put in the oven for 4 minutes. Remove from oven, paint with another layer of barbecue sauce, and put back in the oven for 2 to 4 minutes, until just cooked through. Heat the broiler to highest setting. Remove from oven and paint with barbecue sauce. Place under the broiler for 30 seconds, until glazed but not blackened.

❀| To MAKE THE NOODLES: Bring a large pot of salted water to a boil. Drop the noodles into the water and boil for 4 to 5 minutes, until al dente. Drain in a colander.

❀| To SERVE: Arrange pieces of bell pepper, carrot, shiitake, and scallions in the bottom of a shallow soup bowl. With tongs, lift about ½ cup of noodles and place them in the center of the bowl, twisting with the tongs before releasing the noodles to mound them. Place a piece of fish on the noodles. Repeat with remaining bowls. Ladle the broth over the fish and vegetables, dividing it between the bowls; do not stir up the bits from the bottom of the broth pot, so that you are using clear broth. Garnish each bowl with 3 whole chives.

Meats and Poultry

❀

CHICKEN TRINIDAD WITH ORANGE-RUM SAUCE

OTTMAR WEBER
Ottmar's at The Grand Pavilion Hotel
Grand Cayman

SERVES 4

A stuffing of nuts, grapes, and apples, a coconut crust, and orange-rum sauce give an island taste to chicken rolls. The stuffed chicken breasts are browned on top of the stove, then finished in the oven so that they cook completely while retaining a tender crust.

4	6- to 8-ounce chicken breasts
¼	cup Angostura Bitters
	Salt and freshly ground black pepper to taste
2	apples, peeled and diced
8	ounces blue seedless grapes, cut into halves
6	ounces blanched sliced almonds
1	pint peanut oil
1	cup all-purpose flour
3	eggs, beaten
2	cups grated coconut

ORANGE-RUM SAUCE

6	ounces concentrated orange juice
2	ounces rum
¾	cup cold unsalted butter, cut into 8 pieces
3	to 4 tablespoons heavy (whipping) cream

GARNISH

8	small whole green onions
¼	cup tomato ketchup
½	cup blanched sliced almonds

❋ | Remove the bones from the chicken breasts. Place the breasts between sheets of plastic film wrap and pound with a mallet or other blunt heavy object until very flat. Remove the top layer of plastic wrap and sprinkle the breasts with bitters, salt, and pepper to taste. Divide the apples, grapes, and almonds among the breasts, and roll up each breast around the filling, pressing the ends to seal.

❋ | Preheat the oven to 350°F. In a deep pot or deep fryer heat the peanut oil until rippling, about 360° to 380°F. Dip each breast in flour, shake to remove excess, then dip in the beaten egg. Roll the breasts in the coconut flakes. Using tongs, lower into the hot oil and fry until golden brown, about 20 to 30 seconds. With tongs, lift the breasts from the oil, drain on paper towels, and place on a baking sheet. Place in the oven and bake for 20 minutes or until the juices run clear. Remove from the oven and set aside.

❋ | TO MAKE THE ORANGE-RUM SAUCE: In a deep saucepan combine the orange juice and rum and boil over medium heat for 5 minutes. Remove from the heat and beat in the butter, 1 piece at a time, with an electric mixer set on medium. Stir in the heavy cream.

❋ | TO MAKE THE GARNISH: Cut the tops and roots from the onions, leaving a little of the green part attached to the bulb. Lay the onions on their sides and slice the green portion vertically into fringe. Place in ice water for 30 minutes.

❀ | To SERVE: Pour the sauce on the serving plates. Slice the breasts diagonally and reassemble the slices on the sauce, revealing the stuffed centers. Put the ketchup in a squeeze bottle and dot the sauce with ketchup in 5 places on each place. Pull through the ketchup with the tip of a sharp knife to create stars. Garnish with onion frills and a sprinkling of sliced almonds.

GRILLED DUCK BREAST WITH A PINK PEPPERCORN-PASSION FRUIT SAUCE AND WILD MUSHROOMS

PATRICK GAUDUCHEAU

Le Bistro
St. John's, Antigua

SERVES 4

PHYLLO BASKETS

1	sheet phyllo dough (need 24 3- to 4-inch squares)
2	tablespoons butter, melted and cooled

MUSHROOM POTATOES

32	new potatoes (waxy type, like red-skinned, yellow Finn, or white rose)
½	cup olive oil

VEGETABLES

1	butternut squash, pared and diced
1	large carrot
16	pencil-size asparagus stalks, blanched
16	chunky green beans, blanched
½	small red cabbage, separated and blanched
4	8-ounce duck breasts
	Salt and freshly ground black pepper to taste
¼	cup olive oil

PINK PEPPERCORN–PASSION FRUIT SAUCE

2	tablespoons unsalted butter
3	shallots, minced
1	ounce pink peppercorns
1	scallion, chopped
¼	cup cognac
1	cup dry white wine
1	cup chicken stock
24	passion fruit, peeled, diced and puréed, or 1 cup passion fruit purée
6	cups heavy (whipping) cream
3	sprigs parsley, stemmed and chopped
	Salt and freshly ground black pepper
8	ounces (2 sticks) unsalted butter, cut into 3 pieces

SAUTÉED MUSHROOMS

4	tablespoons (½ stick) unsalted butter
3	cups mixed wild mushrooms, cleaned and sliced
3	sprigs parsley, stemmed and chopped
4	garlic cloves, minced
3	tablespoons olive oil

GARNISH

4	sprigs rosemary
4	tomato roses
8	whole chives

❀ | TO MAKE THE PHYLLO BASKETS: Preheat the oven to 400°F. Cut the phyllo into 3- to 4-inch squares and separate into thin layers. Working quickly, place one square on a work surface, dip your finger in the butter and dot the center of the phyllo, and cover with a second square of phyllo, set slightly off angle to the first. Repeat, making 6 layers of phyllo tacked together with butter at the center. Lift, pressing at the center, and press into a small muffin tin cup. Repeat with the remaining squares. Bake for 2 minutes, until crisp. Remove and keep in a dry place until ready to use.

❀ | To make the mushroom potatoes: Preheat the oven to 325°F. Pare the potatoes and carve them into mushroom shapes. Pat dry with paper towels. Heat the olive oil in a large sauté pan over medium-high heat and sauté the potatoes until lightly browned. Place in the oven for 20 to 25 minutes to finish cooking.

❀ | To make the vegetables: Place the squash in a medium saucepan, cover with water, and bring to a boil. Cook for 10 minutes or until the pieces are soft when pierced with a fork. Drain, cover, and set aside. Cut the carrot with a large scalloped cutter, and cut the center out with a smaller cutter, creating a ring. Slip asparagus stalks into the rings.

❀ | To prepare the duck breasts: Heat the broiler to high or prepare a charcoal fire. Brush the duck breasts with oil and season with salt and pepper, pressing it onto the meat. Sear for 30 seconds, then turn one fourth of the way around and sear again on the same side to create grill marks. Grill for 2½ minutes, turn over, and grill for 2½ minutes on the other side (for rare). Remove and keep warm.

❀ | To make the pink peppercorn-passion fruit sauce: In a sauté pan melt the butter over medium-high heat and sauté the shallots for 30 seconds. Add the pink peppercorns and scallion and sauté for 2 minutes. Add the brandy, avert your face, and flame. When the flame dies down, add the white wine and stir up the browned bits from the bottom. Add the chicken stock and passion fruit purée and simmer to reduce for 1 minute. Whisk in the cream and parsley, and season with salt and pepper to taste. Whisk in the butter in three additions, blending well between each addition.

❀ | To prepare the mushrooms: In a sauté pan heat the butter over medium-high heat and sauté the mushrooms, parsley, and garlic until the vegetables are softened and begin to color. Set aside and keep warm.

❀ | To serve: Drain the squash again. In a large pan heat the olive oil and warm the vegetables. Slice the duck breast very thinly. Pool the sauce on the plate. Fan duck slices across the sauce. Place a spoonful of sautéed mushrooms to the side of the plate. Garnish with a sprig of basil or rosemary. Place 7 to 8 mushroom potatoes on the other side of the plate. Fill a phyllo cup with squash and place on the plate. Slip asparagus spears through a carrot ring and place on the plate. Complete the plate with green beans, a small mound of cabbage, 1 tomato rose, and a rosemary sprig. Cross 2 chives over the dish.

JERK-SEASONED PORK WITH SWEET POTATO, CALLALOO, AND GOAT CHEESE GNOCCHI

ROGER WILES

Half Moon Bay Club
Montego Bay, Jamaica

SERVES 4

GNOCCHI

1	large (12-ounce) sweet potato, peeled, boiled, and cut into chunks
4	ounces goat cheese, softened, divided
1	egg yolk
2	tablespoons unsalted butter
1	10-ounce package frozen chopped spinach, thawed and squeezed dry
½	teaspoon salt
¼	teaspoon freshly ground black pepper
⅛	teaspoon nutmeg
¼	to ½ cup all-purpose flour
1	cup heavy cream

PORK

4	well-trimmed boneless pork loin chops, cut 1½ inches thick
4	ounces boneless pork, cut into cubes
⅓	cup pumpkin purée (fresh or canned)

1	large egg
¼	teaspoon salt
¼	teaspoon freshly ground black pepper
¼	cup chopped scallion (green onion)
2	tablespoons Caribbean jerk seasoning mix (available in the spice section of the supermarket)
3	tablespoons unsalted butter, divided
2	tablespoons fresh lime juice
1	cup chicken stock or broth
¼	cup Veal Demi-Glace (see page 237) or reduced beef or veal stock
2	tablespoons rum (optional)

OPTIONAL GARNISHES

2	large tomatoes, halved and hollowed
	Blanched baby eggplant, chayote squash, and green beans

❧ | TO MAKE THE GNOCCHI: While still warm, mash the sweet potato with 2 ounces of the goat cheese in a food mill or food processor. Stir in the egg yolk. In a large skillet melt the butter over medium heat. Add half of the spinach, salt, pepper and nutmeg; sauté 4 minutes. Add the spinach mixture to the sweet potato mixture. Stir in the flour, 1 tablespoon at a time until dough is no longer sticky. Divide the dough in half and roll each half on lightly floured surface into a ½-inch thick rope. Cut the rope into 1-inch-long pieces. If desired, roll each piece of dough on a butter paddle to create a scored appearance. Let the gnocchi dry slightly for 20 minutes at room temperature.

❧ | Bring a large pot of salted water to a boil. Add one-fourth of the gnocchi and cook 3 to 4 minutes or until the gnocchi rise to the surface of the water and are firm. Using a strainer, transfer the cooked gnocchi to a plate. Set aside. Repeat with the remaining gnocchi.

❧ | In a large skillet cook the cream over medium-high heat until reduced to ¾ cup. Stir in the remaining 2 ounces of goat cheese until melted. Stir in the remaining spinach and heat through.

Season the sauce to taste with salt, pepper, and nutmeg. Add the gnocchi and cook for 2 minutes, stirring to coat the gnocchi with sauce.

❀| To MAKE THE PORK: Using a sharp, thin boning knife, cut a pocket in the center of each pork chop leaving the smallest opening possible. In a food processor finely chop the pork cubes. Add the pumpkin and egg yolk and process until fairly smooth. Stir in the salt, pepper, and scallion. Place in a pastry bag and pipe the mixture into the pockets in pork chops. Rub seasoning mix over both sides of the pork chops. Let stand at room temperature for 10 to 20 minutes.

❀| Preheat the oven to 400°F. In a skillet melt 1 tablespoon of the butter over medium-high heat. Add the chops to the skillet; sear for 2 minutes per side or until browned. Transfer to a shallow roasting pan. Repeat with the remaining 2 chops. Sprinkle the chops with lime juice and transfer to the oven. Bake for 20 to 25 minutes or until the pork is no longer pink inside.

❀| While the chops are cooking, add the chicken stock to the skillet and cook over medium-high heat until reduced to ½ cup. Add the demi-glace and, if desired, rum. Reduce the mixture to ½ cup. Remove from the heat and stir in the remaining 2 tablespoons of butter until melted and the sauce thickens.

❀| To SERVE: Carve the pork crosswise into ½-inch-thick slices; fan out onto serving plates and nap with the sauce. Fill the tomato shells with gnocchi. Garnish each plate with eggplant, squash, and green beans, if desired.

SUGAR MILL PLANTATION PORK

RICHARD BUTTAFUSO
The Sugar Mill Hotel
Tortola, British Virgin Islands

SERVES 4 TO 6

PORK AND STUFFING

2	large well-trimmed pork tenderloins, about 1 pound each
	Salt and freshly ground black pepper to taste
4	sour oranges, juiced or ½ cup orange juice plus 3 tablespoons lime juice
½	cup pineapple juice
2	tablespoons soy sauce
2	cloves garlic, minced
1	ripe plantain, skinned and coarsely chopped (if plantain is not available, substitute 1 large firm banana)
1	egg white
½	cup diced ham
¼	cup sliced green onions
½	cup seasoned dry Italian bread crumbs
2	tablespoons butter, melted

MANGO SALSA

1	ripe mango, peeled, seeded, and diced
¼	cup diced red bell pepper
¼	cup sliced green onions
2	tablespoons seasoned rice vinegar

BLACK BEAN SAUCE

½	cup diced smoked bacon
1	medium onion, chopped
2	cloves garlic, minced
1	red bell pepper, cored, seeded, diced
1	yellow bell pepper, cored, seeded, diced
1	teaspoon Cajun seasoning mix
½	teaspoon ground coriander
½	teaspoon ground cumin
¼	teaspoon ground ginger
¼	teaspoon ground cloves
2	cups rinsed and drained cooked black beans
½	cup chicken stock or water
1	teaspoon sugar
	Hot sauce

GARNISH

½	cup sour cream
1	tablespoon water
	Deep-fried julienned potato and sautéed julienned vegetables (optional)

❧ | FOR THE PORK AND STUFFING: Cut each tenderloin lengthwise three-fourths of the way through. Open like a book and pound to ½-inch thickness, forming a rectangular shape. Sprinkle lightly with salt and freshly ground black pepper. Place each tenderloin in a resealable plastic food storage bag or on a shallow plate. Combine the orange juice, pineapple juice, soy sauce, and garlic. Pour evenly over the tenderloins, turning to coat. Cover and marinate in the refrigerator for 1 to 2 hours.

❧ | Meanwhile, in a food processor combine the plantain and egg white and process until the plantain is puréed. Transfer to a medium bowl. Stir in the ham, green onions, and breadcrumbs. Cover and refrigerate.

❀ | FOR THE MANGO SALSA: Combine all ingredients and toss well. Cover and chill until serving time.

❀ | FOR THE BLACK BEAN SAUCE: In a large sauté pan cook the bacon until most of the fat is rendered. If desired, spoon off and discard half of the fat. Add the onion and garlic and sauté for 5 minutes. Add the bell peppers and sauté for 2 minutes. Add the Cajun seasoning, coriander, cumin, ginger, and cloves, and cook for 1 minute. Stir in beans, broth, and sugar and simmer 10 minutes, stirring and partially mashing the beans occasionally. Add hot sauce to taste. The sauce may be made up to 2 hours ahead and reheated before serving.

❀ | Heat the oven to 375°F. Drain the tenderloins and transfer to a work surface. Spread the stuffing over the tenderloins, leaving a ½-inch border. Roll up lengthwise and enclose the filling. Tie with cotton string at 2-inch intervals. Brush the tenderloins with melted butter and place in shallow roasting pan. Roast in the oven for about 40 minutes until the internal temperature of the pork is 155 degrees, turning after 20 minutes of roasting. Transfer to a carving board and tent with foil. Let stand for 5 to 10 minutes before slicing.

❀ | TO SERVE: Combine the sour cream and water, mixing well. Transfer to a squeeze bottle. Slice the tenderloins crosswise into ½-inch-thick slices. Spoon black bean sauce onto 6 serving plates and drizzle sour cream garnish attractively over the sauce. Arrange the tenderloin slices in a row to one side of the sauce and top with mango salsa. Garnish the plate with fried potatoes and sautéed vegetables, if desired.

VEAL ROULADE WITH SAGE SAUCE

STEPHANE BOIS
Le Patio
Village St. Jean, St. Barts

SERVES 4

VEAL ROULADE

4	large slices veal leg, cut ¼-inch thickness (about 1½ pounds)
8	thin slices deli mortadella (about 4 ounces)
4	ounces fresh mozzarella cheese, drained and sliced
2	tablespoons sliced sage leaves
	Salt and freshly ground black pepper
2	tablespoons olive oil, divided

SAGE SAUCE

2	tablespoons cognac or brandy
1	cup reduced veal stock (see page 00)
3	garlic cloves, minced
¼	cup diced tomato
2	tablespoons sliced sage leaves
2	tablespoons chopped parsley
1	tablespoon unsalted butter
	Salt and freshly ground black pepper

GARNISH

10	ounces fresh spinach leaves, blanched
¼	cup chopped tomato
2	tablespoons chopped parsley

❀ | FOR THE VEAL ROULADE: Heat the oven to 200°F. Between sheets of plastic wrap, pound each slice of veal to ⅛-inch thickness. Place on a work surface. Layer the mortadella and mozzarella cheese over the center of the veal and sprinkle with sage. Sprinkle very lightly with salt and pepper. Starting at the long end, roll up the veal and secure with wooden picks.

❀ | In a large skillet heat 1 tablespoon of the oil over medium-high heat. Add 2 roulades to the hot oil and brown on all sides, about 4 minutes. Transfer the browned roulades to a roasting pan and keep warm in the oven. Repeat with the remaining 1 tablespoon of oil and remaining 2 roulades.

❀ | FOR THE SAGE SAUCE: Add cognac to the same skillet and carefully ignite with a long-handled match. Shake the skillet until the flames subside. Add the veal stock and garlic and simmer for 2 minutes. Add the tomato, sage, and parsley, and simmer 2 minutes. Stir in the butter just until melted and the sauce thickens. Season with salt and pepper to taste.

❀ | TO SERVE: Remove the wooden picks from the roulades. Transfer to 4 warm serving plates. Spoon sage sauce over the roulades. Arrange the blanched spinach alongside the roulades. Top with tomato. Sprinkle parsley around the edges of the plates.

Veal Chop with Potatoes à la Provençale

Patrick Gateau
The Carl Gustaf Hotel
St.-Barthélemy

SERVES 4

2	cups veal stock or 1 can (about 14 ounces) low-salt chicken broth	2	thick slices smoked bacon, diced
4	veal rib or loin chops, cut 1 inch thick	1	large onion, thinly sliced, separated into rings
1½	teaspoons salt, divided	2	pounds small yukon gold or red potatoes, peeled, steamed, or boiled until almost tender
¾	teaspoon freshly ground black pepper, divided		
1	tablespoon olive oil	¼	cup chopped parsley
5	tablespoons unsalted butter, divided		

❀ | In a medium saucepan bring the veal stock to a boil over high heat. Reduce the heat and boil gently until the mixture is reduced to ¼ cup, about 15 minutes.

❀ | Meanwhile, preheat the oven to 400°F. Sprinkle both sides of the veal chops with 1 teaspoon of the salt and ½ teaspoon of the pepper. In a large skillet or sauté pan combine the oil and 1 table-spoon of the butter and place over medium-high heat. When the butter sizzles, add the veal chops (in two batches, if necessary) and cook until browned, about 3 minutes per side. Transfer to a shallow baking pan. Roast in the oven for 15 minutes for medium-rare or until the desired doneness.

❀ | Pour off fat from the skillet. Add the bacon and cook for 2 minutes over medium heat. Add the onion rings; cover and cook for 10 minutes or until the onions are golden brown and tender, stirring occasionally. Add the potatoes; sprinkle with the remaining ½ teaspoon of salt and ¼ teaspoon of pepper. Cover and cook for 8 minutes or until heated through, stirring occasionally.

❀ | After the stock has reduced to ¼ cup, add the remaining 4 tablespoons of butter, 1 tablespoon at a time, whisking over low heat until the butter is melted and the sauce thickens. Whisk in any juices from the veal baking pan.

❀ | To serve: Arrange the veal chops on 4 serving plates. Spoon the potato and onion mixture around the chops and sprinkle with parsley. Spoon the sauce over the veal and potatoes.

VEAL OSCAR

BENT RASMUSSEN
Top Hat
St. Croix, U.S. Virgin Islands

SERVES 2

GARNISH

2	tablespoons unsalted butter
2	green papayas, peeled, seeded, cut into ½-inch cubes
½	cup water
	Salt, freshly ground black pepper, and lime juice to taste
½	cup vegetable oil
½	cup thinly sliced yuca

SAUCE BEARNAISE

¾	cup unsalted butter
3	tablespoons white wine
2	tablespoons white wine vinegar
2	small shallots, minced
1	tablespoon dried tarragon
½	teaspoon cracked black peppercorns
3	egg yolks
1	tablespoon water
1	tablespoon fresh lemon juice
	Salt to taste

ASPARAGUS, VEAL, AND LOBSTER

½	pound asparagus
3	tablespoons butter, divided
2	6-ounce boneless veal cutlets
½	teaspoon salt
½	teaspoon freshly ground black pepper
2	tablespoons all-purpose flour
½	cup Veal Demi-Glace (see page 237)
1	small lobster tail, cooked, cooled, and sliced into medallions
½	black truffle, thinly sliced (optional)

❈ | TO MAKE THE GARNISH: In a small sauté pan melt the butter over medium-high heat and sauté the papaya for 1 minute. Add ½ cup of water and simmer uncovered until soft, about 1 minute. Season with salt, pepper, and lime, and set aside.

❈ | In a small heavy saucepan heat the oil to 350°F. Add several yuca slices at a time and fry until golden brown. Drain on paper towels; set aside.

❈ | TO MAKE THE SAUCE BEARNAISE: Clarify the butter: In a small saucepan melt the butter over low heat until it separates, and pour the oil portion into a cup. Discard the solids at the bottom. In another small pan combine the wine, vinegar, shallots, tarragon, and peppercorns, and cook over medium-high heat until the liquid evaporates. In a small heavy saucepan whisk together the egg yolks, water, and salt. Place over low heat and continue whisking constantly until the mixture is creamy and thick enough for the whisk to leave marks in the sauce. The mixture should not be allowed to become too hot; remove the pan from the heat periodically to control the temperature. When the mixture is thick enough, remove it from the heat and whisk vigorously for 30 seconds. Whisk in the butter drop by drop until the sauce has absorbed about 2 or 3 tablespoons of butter. Then begin pouring in the remaining butter in a thin stream, whisking constantly to incorporate it. Whisk in the lemon juice and the herb reduction. Adjust the flavor with salt to taste. The sauce is best served immediately; it must be kept warm and whisked frequently, or may be stored in a thermos until ready for serving.

🦋 | To MAKE THE ASPARAGUS, VEAL, AND LOBSTER: Cut the top 3 inches (tips) off the asparagus spears. Reserve the remaining stalks for future use. Bring a small amount of water to a boil and drop the tips in the water. Cook for 3 to 4 minutes until almost tender. Drain. Add 1 tablespoon of the butter, cover the pan, and set aside.

🦋 | Season the cutlets with salt and pepper and dredge in the flour. In a large sauté pan over medium-high heat melt the remaining 2 tablespoons of butter and sauté the veal for 2 minutes. Do not allow the cutlets to touch each other. Turn and sauté on the other side until lightly browned, about 2 minutes. Remove the cutlets and keep warm. Deglaze the pan with the demi-glace, lower the heat, and cook to reduce the sauce by one-fourth. Set aside.

🦋 | To SERVE: Place a cutlet on each warm serving plate and top with asparagus tips. Pour the reduced demi-glace over the asparagus and cutlets. Press warm lobster medallions on top of the asparagus. Pour Sauce Bearnaise over the medallions and garnish with truffle slices. Place yuca chips and green papaya beside the cutlets.

LAMB CHOP WITH MOFONGO AND CILANTRO PESTO

JEREMIE CRUZ
El Conquistador Resort
Fajardo, Puerto Rico

SERVES 4

Mofongo is a Caribbean plantain preparation used as a mild counterpoint to the seared lamb chops and spicy sauces. There is some last-minute preparation for this dish, cooking the lamb and vegetables, but none of this last-minute effort takes a lot of time. You could even prepare the vegetables early, then heat them for the table in the last-minute sauté.

CILANTRO PESTO

2	cups cilantro
¾	cup olive oil
½	cup grated Parmesan cheese
1	teaspoon cassava seasoning
2	tablespoons lemon juice
⅓	cup chopped walnuts or pine nuts
4	garlic cloves
	Pinch of salt and freshly ground black pepper

CHIMICHURRI SAUCE

2	garlic cloves
1	bay leaf
1	jalapeño chili, coarsely chopped with seeds
½	tablespoon salt
2	tablespoons Jamaican jerk seasoning
⅛	cup finely minced fresh parsley
⅛	cup finely minced flat-leaf parsley
⅛	cup finely minced fresh cilantro
⅛	cup distilled white vinegar
¼	cup extra-virgin olive oil
8	double lamb chops
	Salt and freshly ground black pepper to taste
⅛	cup Chimichurri Sauce (above)
1	tablespoon extra-virgin olive oil

MOFONGO

3	large green plantains
3	cups water with ½ tablespoon salt
½	slice bacon
3	cloves garlic, minced
½	cup virgin olive oil
	Salt and freshly ground black pepper to taste
¼	teaspoon cassava seasoning
¼	cup corn oil
¼	cup Chimichurri Sauce (above)

LATIN ROOT VEGETABLES

2	purple potatoes, diced (yellow potatoes may be substituted)
1	small calabaza, diced (pumpkin may be substituted)
2	chayote squash, diced
5	large ribs of celery, diced
2	cups malanga (optional)
1	teaspoon olive oil
1	teaspoon minced garlic
	Salt and freshly ground black pepper to taste
½	cup balsamic vinegar
6	large Plantain Chips (see page 239)

TO MAKE THE CILANTRO PESTO: In a food processor combine all of the ingredients and blend until almost smooth and pasty.

❀| To make the chimichurri sauce: Grind the garlic, bay leaf, jalapeño, and salt with a mortar and pestle until a smooth paste is formed. Or, purée with a small amount of vinegar in a food processor or blender. Transfer to a mixing bowl and add the jerk seasoning. Stir in the parsleys and cilantro. Whisk in the vinegar and olive oil until well mixed and set aside. Use half for the sauce, and half to marinate the lamb chops.

❀| To prepare the chops: Season the chops with salt and pepper and place them in a shallow baking dish. Pour half the chimichurri sauce over the chops, turn the chops, and cover the dish with plastic wrap. Marinate in the refrigerator for 2 to 4 hours. Preheat the oven to 425°F. In a large ovenproof pan heat the olive oil over medium-high heat and sear the lamb chops on both sides, about 30 seconds per side. Place the chops in the oven and roast until the internal temperature is 120°F for medium-rare.

❀| To make the mofongo: Peel the plantains and cut them into ½-inch slices. Place them in the salted water. In a small skillet fry the bacon over medium-high heat. Drain and discard the fat. Chop and set aside. In a small bowl, combine the garlic, olive oil, and seasonings. In a large skillet heat the corn oil over medium-high heat and fry the plantain slices until golden brown. Drain on paper towels.

❀| To prepare the Latin root vegetables: Bring a large pot of water to a boil over medium-high heat. Plunge the vegetables into the pot and return it to a boil. Boil 3 minutes, drain, and refill the pot with cold water. Drain again. In a large skillet heat the olive oil and garlic over medium-high heat and sauté until the garlic softens. Add the drained vegetables and toss to coat. Season and keep warm.

❀| To make the balsamic syrup: Warm the balsamic vinegar over low heat and simmer until it is reduced and syrupy, 15 to 20 minutes. Transfer to a squeeze bottle and keep warm.

❀| To serve: For each serving plate, put a few teaspoons of the garlic-oil mixture for the mofongo in a small bowl. Add one-sixth of the bacon pieces and 5 or 6 slices of plantain. Mash and press firmly into the mortar until the mixture forms a thick paste. Invert the mofongo in the center of each warmed plate and form into a pyramid. Drizzle the plate with balsamic syrup. Lean the lamb chops against the mofongo. Place scoops of sautéed vegetables decoratively around the plate. Place a dollop of cilantro pesto on the chops. Finish with a plantain chip standing against the "back" of the plate, and spoon cilantro pesto and chimichurri sauce on the plate.

BROILED BABY LAMB CHOPS

NORMA SHIRLEY

Norma at the Warfside
Montego Bay, Jamaica

SERVES 4

LAMB CHOPS

12	lamb chops cut from 2 racks, Frenched
½	teaspoon salt
½	teaspoon freshly ground black pepper
4	ounces feta cheese, crumbled
2	tablespoons minced scallion (green onion)
1	tablespoon chopped fresh thyme
¼	cup dry breadcrumbs
¼	cup chopped fresh parsley
3	tablespoons prepared vinaigrette salad dressing

VEGETABLE NEST

1	tablespoon unsalted butter
1	cup julienned yellow or sweet onion
1	large tomato, diced
1	teaspoon minced fresh Scotch bonnet chili pepper or 1 tablespoon minced jalapeño pepper
10	ounces fresh calaloo or spinach leaves, stems discarded
	Salt and freshly ground black pepper

GARNISH

12	whole shallots, roasted or sautéed until tender
3	tablespoons chopped fresh parsley

❀ | FOR THE LAMB CHOPS: Place the lamb chops on a broiler pan. Sprinkle with salt and pepper. Broil 4 to 5 inches from the heat source for 5 minutes. Remove from the broiler; turn the chops over.

❀ | Combine the cheese, scallion, and thyme, and mix well. Press the mixture evenly over the chops. Top with breadcrumbs and parsley, and drizzle with vinaigrette. Return to the broiler for 3 to 4 minutes or until the topping is brown and the lamb is pink in the center.

❀ | FOR THE VEGETABLE NEST: In a large skillet melt the butter over medium heat. Add the onion and sauté for 5 minutes. Add the tomato and chili pepper, and sauté for 3 minutes. Blanch the callaloo leaves in boiling water just until wilted. Drain and add to the skillet. Turn the mixture with tongs until well combined and hot. Season with salt and pepper to taste.

❀ | TO SERVE: Arrange the vegetable mixture in the center of 4 warmed dinner plates, forming a nest. Arrange 3 lamb chops around each nest with the bones forming a pyramid over the nest. Garnish each plate with 3 shallots and sprinkle the edges of the plates with chopped parsley.

COFFEE-COCOA-SPICED RACK OF LAMB

JEFFREY VIGILLA

The Ritz-Carlton Cancún
Cancún, Mexico

SERVES 4

Lamb racks are seasoned with a mixture of brown sugar and cinnamon, roasted, and then serve with a dark sauce of coffee, cocoa, and more cinnamon. The exotic flavors are unusual yet blend together perfectly with the lamb. They would also be wonderful with duck or pork. It is easier to carve the lamb racks into individual chops if you have the butcher cut through the backbone between the ribs.

SPICE MIXTURE

4	tablespoons firmly packed brown sugar
2	tablespoons ground cinnamon

SAUCE

2	tablespoons olive oil
3	shallots, sliced
1	cup brewed coffee

1	cup brewed espresso
1	cup balsamic vinegar
2	cinnamon sticks
1	tablespoon unsweetened cocoa powder
4	cups Lamb Demi-Glace (see page 237)

2	racks of lamb, French trimmed
	Salt and freshly ground black pepper to taste
1	tablespoon olive oil

❀ | TO MAKE THE SPICE MIXTURE: In a small bowl blend the brown sugar and cinnamon together.

❀ | TO MAKE THE SAUCE: In a heavy sauté pan heat the olive oil and sauté the shallots over medium heat until translucent, about 3 minutes. Add half of the spice mixture and cook, stirring constantly, for 1 minute. Pour the coffee, espresso, and balsamic vinegar into the mixture and cook until reduced by half. Add the cinnamon sticks, cocoa powder, and demi-glace. Reduce by half again, until a syrupy consistency. Reserve and keep warm.

❀ | TO COOK THE LAMB: Preheat the oven to 400°F. Season the racks with the remaining half of the spice mixture, salt, and pepper. In a large ovenproof sauté pan or skillet heat the olive oil over medium-high heat and sear the lamb racks on all sides. Place the lamb in the oven and roast 25 minutes for medium-rare (140° internal temperature). Remove from the oven, tent with foil, and let rest for 10 minutes. Carve into individual chops.

❀ | TO SERVE: Arrange the chops on the plates and pour the sauce over them. Suggested accompaniments are braised chayote squash, garlic mashed potatoes, and plantain chips.

RACK OF LAMB CRUSTED WITH HAZELNUTS AND DIJON MUSTARD ON FRAMBOISE DEMI-GLACE

MICHAEL MADSEN
Divi Resort & Casino
St. Croix, U.S. Virgin Islands

SERVES 4

Lamb racks are seared, coated with a crust of Dijon mustard and hazelnuts, and roasted to medium rare. The rich sauce combines demi-glace and raspberries; although fruit is frequently paired with lamb, it is seldom as luxurious as this. The chops are served with a simple sauté of vegetables that could accompany any main dish.

¼	cup olive oil
4	racks of lamb (4 chops each), French trimmed
½	cup Dijon mustard
2	shallots, minced
1	cup hazelnuts, chopped
	Salt and freshly ground black pepper

FRAMBOISE DEMI-GLACE

2	shallots, minced
½	cup Clarified Butter (see page 234)
1	cup raspberries

¼	cup Chambord or other raspberry-flavored liqueur
2	cups Demi-Glace (see page 237)
	Salt and freshly ground pepper to taste

VEGETABLES

1	tablespoon olive oil
2	shallots, minced
16	shiitake mushrooms, sliced
1	pound sugar snap peas, julienned
1	pound cherry tomatoes, cut into half
	Salt and freshly ground pepper to taste
¼	cup balsamic vinegar

❀ | TO PREPARE THE LAMB: Preheat the oven to 400°F. In a large skillet or sauté pan heat the olive oil over medium-high heat and brown the racks of lamb on both sides, about 1 minute per side. Remove each one as it is browned and place in a large roasting pan so that the bones are pointing downward. In a small bowl mix the mustard, shallots, hazelnuts, and salt and pepper together. Coat the tops of the racks with the mustard mixture. Bake 10 to 12 minutes for medium-rare.

❀ | TO PREPARE THE FRAMBOISE DEMI-GLACE: Sauté shallots in the clarified butter over medium-high heat until just translucent. Add the raspberries and sauté for 10 seconds. Add the Chambord and cook for 15 seconds. Stir in the demi-glace and season with salt and pepper. Heat for 15 more seconds, then remove from heat and set aside.

❀ | TO PREPARE THE VEGETABLES: In a medium sauté pan heat the olive oil over medium-high heat and sauté the shallots until translucent, about 30 seconds. Add the shiitakes, sugar snaps, and tomatoes, tossing to coat. Cook for 30 seconds, tossing or stirring to keep them from sticking. Season with salt and pepper, and add the balsamic vinegar. Toss and remove from the heat.

✿ | To serve: Cut each lamb rack into 3 pieces—2 separate chops, and 2 chops joined. Pool the sauce off-center on each serving plate. Crisscross two chops on each plate, then place a double chop over each. Divide the vegetables among the plates.

Osso Buco

ERNESTO GARRIGOS
Virgilio's
St. Thomas, U.S.V.I.

SERVES 4

Rich savory sauce flavored with garlic and herbs accompanies traditional osso buco. Pasta tossed with parsley and butter accompanies the dish. Start early enough to allow the tomatoes to marinate for 1 hour.

4	large tomatoes, roughly chopped	¼	cup olive oil
	Salt and freshly ground black pepper to taste	4	center-cut veal shanks, 2 inches thick
2	tablespoons dried oregano, crushed		Flour for dredging

VEGETABLE RAGOUT

¼	cup olive oil	2	tablespoons olive oil
6	large garlic cloves, minced		
	Salt to taste	**PASTA**	
4	carrots, cut into small dice	8	ounces fettuccine
4	large ribs of celery, cut into small dice	1	teaspoon olive oil
1	white onion, cut into small dice	¼	cup (½ stick) butter
2	cups red wine	1	bunch parsley, stemmed and minced

✿ | To prepare the tomatoes: In a medium non-reactive bowl, mix the tomatoes, salt, pepper, and oregano, pressing down on the tomatoes to break them up. Cover with plastic wrap and let marinate for 1 hour.

✿ | To make the vegetable ragout: In a large skillet heat the olive oil over medium-high heat. Add the garlic and salt and cook for 30 seconds, until slightly softened, shaking the pan to prevent sticking. Add the carrot, celery, and onion, toss to coat, and cook for 1 minute. Add the tomatoes, toss to blend, and turn the heat to medium-low. Let cook while the bones are prepared.

✿ | To cook the osso buco: Preheat the oven to 325°F. In a large skillet heat 1 tablespoon of the olive oil over medium-high heat. Dredge the bones in the flour, shaking off the excess. Sear the bones in the olive oil for 1 minute, turn, and sear the other side, 1 minute. Turn the heat to medium and let cook for 1 more minute. With tongs, lift the bones and place them in the pan with the vegetable mixture, spooning the vegetables over the meat. Drizzle the top of the bones and vegetables with the 2 tablespoons of the olive oil. Place the pan in the oven and bake for 3 hours hours, until the meat is cooked all the way through.

🐢 | TO PREPARE THE PASTA: Bring a large pot of salted water to a boil. Add the olive oil and pasta and cook, uncovered, until al dente, 3 to 5 minutes. Drain the pasta. In a large skillet over medium-low heat melt the butter and stir in the parsley. Toss the pasta in the butter mixture until coated.

🐢 | TO SERVE: Place 1 osso buco on each of 4 serving plates. Divide the vegetable mixture among the plates and pour it over the meat. Place a scoop of pasta beside the meat on each plate. Sprinkle the plates with the remaining minced parsley.

Desserts

✿

GUAVA MOUSSE IN A TROPICAL FRUIT SOUP WITH MASCARPONE ICE CREAM

KEVIN BOXX

The Ritz-Carlton St. Thomas
St. Thomas, U.S. Virgin Islands

SERVES 6

This dish is colorful, and the different textures and temperatures are delightful. The actual fruits chosen for the soup can vary according to season and availability.

MASCARPONE ICE CREAM

1	cup sugar
½	cup water at room temperature
3	vanilla beans, split
2	tablespoons lemon juice
1	tablespoon lemon zest
5	egg yolks
	Pinch of salt
1	pound mascarpone cheese
2	cups buttermilk

DOBOS BISCUIT

½	cup (1 stick) unsalted butter
¾	cup confectioners' sugar
2	eggs, separated
1	teaspoon lemon juice
½	teaspoon vanilla extract
⅓	cup all-purpose flour

GUAVA MOUSSE

1	packet (1 tablespoon) unflavored gelatin
¼	cup cold water
1	cup guava purée
⅓	cup sugar
	Juice of 2 key limes
1	cup heavy (whipping) cream, whipped

TROPICAL FRUIT SOUP

6	guavas
4	mangoes
4	passion fruit
1	pineapple
	Pinch of saffron
2	star anise
1	teaspoon ground cardamom
2	vanilla beans

MACADAMIA NUT TUILES

¼	cup (½ stick) unsalted butter
½	cup brown sugar, packed
¼	cup light corn syrup
½	cup all-purpose flour
	Pinch of salt
½	cup toasted macadamia nuts, finely ground

❦ | TO MAKE THE MASCARPONE ICE CREAM: In a heavy 2-quart saucepan combine ½ cup of the sugar, the water, vanilla beans, lemon juice, and zest. Bring to a boil. Beat together the egg yolks, the remaining ½ cup of sugar, and salt. When the sugar-water mixture comes to a boil, gradually add a little of the hot syrup to the eggs, beating continuously to keep from cooking the eggs. Add the tempered eggs back to the saucepan, stirring to blend, and cook the mixture until just thickened. Remove from the heat and stir in the mascarpone. Strain into a large bowl and mix in the buttermilk. Place in the container of an ice cream maker and freeze according to the manufacturer's instructions.

❀| TO MAKE THE DOBOS BISCUIT: Line a small sheet pan with parchment paper and spray with non-stick cooking spray. Preheat the oven to 375°F. In a medium mixing bowl cream the butter and half the confectioners' sugar until light and fluffy. Add the egg yolks, lemon juice, and vanilla and beat until smooth. Set aside. In a separate bowl whisk the egg whites with the remaining confectioners' sugar until stiff peaks form. Sift the flour over the beaten egg whites and gently fold together. Fold the egg white and flour mixture into the egg yolk mixture. Spread evenly onto the parchment-covered sheet pan. Bake for 8 minutes or until set and beginning to brown around the edges. Take out of the oven and allow to cool. Cut into twelve 2½-inch rounds with a cookie cutter. Set aside 6 of the rounds for use; the remaining 6 can be wrapped and frozen.

❀| TO MAKE THE GUAVA MOUSSE: Cover a baking sheet with parchment paper. Sprinkle the gelatin into the water and let soften. In a 2-quart saucepan combine ½ cup of the guava purée, the sugar, and lime juice. Heat over medium heat until the sugar is dissolved. Remove from the heat and stir in the gelatin mixture (do not add until the mixture has stopped boiling). Transfer to a large mixing bowl and add the remaining purée. Cover with plastic wrap and chill. While the mixture is chilling, place one dobos biscuit in the bottom of a 2½-inch ring mold and place on the baking sheet. Repeat with the remaining biscuits. Set aside. In a large mixing bowl using a whisk or an electric mixer with a whisk attachment, whip the cream to soft peaks. Remove the guava mixture from the refrigerator and quickly stir half of the whipped cream into the mousse. Gently fold in the remaining whipped cream. Transfer to a pastry bag fitted with a large plain tip and pipe into the molds, or spoon the mousse into the molds and smooth off the tops. Cover with plastic wrap and freeze at least 4 hours.

❀| TO MAKE THE TROPICAL FRUIT SOUP: Reserve 2 guavas and 1 mango for garnish. Peel and purée the remaining guavas and mangoes and the passion fruit separately, and press the purées through a fine-mesh sieve. Peel and core the pineapple and remove the eyes. Cut the pineapple into medium dice and reserve 1 cup for garnish. Purée the remaining pineapple and pass through a fine-mesh sieve. Ina a large saucepan combine the fruit purées with the spices and vanilla and bring to a simmer over medium-low heat. Remove from the heat and steep for 2 hours, then strain and cool. Refrigerate until serving time.

❀| TO MAKE THE MACADAMIA NUT TUILES: In the bowl of an electric mixer cream the butter with the sugar. Add the corn syrup and mix well. Combine the flour and salt and beat into the butter mixture. Stir in the nuts with a wooden spoon. Preheat the oven to 350°F. Line cookie sheets with parchment paper. Lightly draw 3-inch circles on the paper and spread the batter as thinly as possible within the area of each circle, smoothing with the back of a spoon. Bake for 3 to 5 minutes, or until golden. Remove from the oven and remove a tuile cookie with a spatula, pressing the cookie over the bottom of an inverted small bowl or custard cup. Repeat with the remaining tuiles; if they become brittle, place them back in the oven for a moment to rewarm them. Let cool. Set aside.

❀| TO SERVE: Cut the reserved fruit into ¼-inch dice. Remove the molded mousse from the freezer and allow to sit at room temperature for a few minutes. Unmold and place a mousse in the center of each chilled shallow soup bowl. Spoon chilled soup around the mousse and garnish with the diced fruit. Place the soup bowls on large serving plates and put a tuile cup on each plate beside the soup bowl. Fill each tuile cup with a scoop of mascarpone ice cream.

MANGO-LIME MOUSSE TART WITH COCONUT ICE CREAM

PEGGY HUGHES

**The Cinnamon Reef Hotel
Anguilla**

SERVES 8

Slices of lime tart are served with mango, mango coulis, and coconut creme anglaise. A phyllo cup of coconut ice cream accompanies the dish. The coconut ice cream can be made several days in advance. The pastry tart shells can be made and frozen in advance, and thawed before being filled with mousse. Doing these steps ahead of time saves time on the day you plan to serve the dessert.

COCONUT ICE CREAM

| | Ice Cream Base, less 1 cup heavy (whipping) cream (see page 240) |
| 1 | cup coconut milk |

SUGAR PASTRY

2	cups all-purpose flour
¾	cup confectioners' sugar
1½	teaspoons baking powder
2	cups (4 sticks) minus 2 tablespoons unsalted butter
¼	cup almonds, finely chopped
2	eggs, beaten

MANGO-LIME MOUSSE

3	eggs
3	egg yolks
¾	cup sugar
1	packet (1 tablespoon) unflavored gelatin

½	cup lime juice
4	14 x 18-inch sheets of phyllo dough
2	tablespoons butter, melted and cooled

COCONUT CRÈME ANGLAISE

1	cup coconut milk
1	cup whole milk
5	egg yolks
½	cup sugar

GARNISH

½	cup coconut, toasted (see page 240)
1	mango
2	tablespoons rum
1	cup Mango Coulis (see page 240)
½	cup heavy (whipping) cream, whipped to soft peaks
8	mint sprigs

❀ | To MAKE THE COCONUT ICE CREAM: Follow the directions for Ice Cream Base (page 240), substituting 1 cup of coconut milk for 1 cup of heavy cream in the basic recipe. Pour into the freezer container of an ice cream maker and freeze according to the manufacturer's directions. Store in the freezer.

❀ | To MAKE THE SUGAR PASTRY: In the bowl of an electric mixer fitted with a paddle attachment combine the flour, sugar, and baking powder. Mix on low speed, adding the butter in three parts, until the dough resembles coarse meal. Alternatively, blend the ingredients with a pastry blender until it resembles coarse meal. Add the almonds and eggs and mix 30 seconds to blend. Avoid overmixing. Form into a dough, wrap in plastic wrap, and chill for 30 minutes or overnight.

❀| Preheat the oven to 375°F. On a floured surface, roll out the dough to ¼-inch thickness. Cut two 11-inch circles and press into 2 fluted tart pans with removable bottoms. Prick the bottoms and sides of the pastry shells with a fork and fill the shells with dried beans to hold the pastry down while baking. Bake for 15 to 20 minutes, until golden. Cool. Freeze one shell for later use.

❀| To MAKE THE MANGO-LIME MOUSSE: Whisk the eggs and egg yolks with the sugar in the top of a double boiler over barely simmering water until they are as thick as cake batter. Remove from heat. In a small bowl combine the gelatin and ½ cup of the lime juice and let stand to dissolve the gelatin. Whisk the remaining lime juice into the egg mixture, then whisk in the gelatin. Place the bowl into a larger bowl filled with ice and beat the mixture with an electric mixer for 6 to 8 minutes, until the mousse thickens. Pour into the pastry shell and chill.

❀| To MAKE THE PHYLLO CUPS: Preheat the oven to 400°F. Grease a muffin tin. Stack 4 sheets of phyllo and use a heavy sharp knife to cut into 12 equal pieces about 4 inches square, cutting straight down through the layers. Lay plastic wrap over the squares and cover with a damp towel. Working quickly, place one square on a work surface, dip your finger in the butter and dot the center of the filo, and cover with a second square of phyllo, set at a 45° angle to the first. Repeat, making 4 layers of filo tacked together with butter at the center. Lift, pressing at the center, and press into a muffin cup. Repeat with the remaining squares. Bake for 2 minutes until crisp. Remove and keep in a dry place until ready to use. Extras may be frozen.

❀| To MAKE THE CREME ANGLAISE: In a saucepan over medium-low heat bring the coconut milk and whole milk to a simmer. Beat the egg yolks and sugar until light and fluffy. Add a little warm milk to the egg mixture, beating to blend, then add the egg mixture slowly to the milk, stirring constantly. Cook, stirring, until it is thick or until it registers 170° on an instant-read thermometer. Do not boil. Remove from the heat, place the pan in a large bowl filled with ice, and whisk to cool. Strain through a fine-mesh sieve and refrigerate.

❀| To PREPARE THE GARNISH: Preheat the oven to 350°F. Spread the coconut in a single layer on a baking sheet. Bake for 5 to 10 minutes or until lightly toasted.

❀| To SERVE: Pit and slice the mango, and arrange on top of the tart. Brush the slices with rum. Cut the tart into 8 servings. Put the mango coulis and the coconut crème anglaise in separate squeeze bottles and drizzle on cold serving plates. Arrange a slice of tart on each plate. Place a phyllo cup next to the tart slice and fill with a scoop of coconut ice cream. Garnish each with whipped cream, toasted coconut, and a sprig of mint.

PASSION FRUIT MOUSSE IN A TUILE CONE WITH STRAWBERRY AND MANGO COULIS

JANICE BARBER
The White House Inn
St. Kitts

SERVES 4

Light-as-a-feather passion fruit mousse is piped into tuile cones decorated with chocolate swirls and served on a colorful plate of strawberry and mango purées. The recipe draws on many techniques, simple to master, which create an eye-catching dessert.

PASSION FRUIT MOUSSE

8	passion fruits
1	tablespoon water
1	packet powdered gelatin
	Juice of 2 limes
4	eggs, separated
1	cup superfine sugar
½	cup plus 2 tablespoons heavy (whipping) cream

TUILE CONES

¾	cup all-purpose flour
¼	cup superfine sugar
3	egg whites
2	tablespoons (¼ stick) unsalted butter
	Rind of 1 lime, grated
1	tablespoon cocoa powder
8	large strawberries
½	cup heavy (whipping) cream
1	cup Mango Coulis (see page 234)
1	cup Strawberry Coulis (see page 234)
2	mangoes, peeled, pitted, and sliced
4	mint sprigs

❀ | TO MAKE THE MOUSSE: Cut the passion fruits in half and scoop out the pulp. Press through a sieve into the bowl of a food processor or blender and add the water. Purée. Dissolve the gelatin in the lime juice. In the top of a double boiler over boiling water, whisk the egg yolks and sugar until the sugar is completely dissolved, about 2 minutes. Remove from the heat. Stir in the gelatin until dissolved, about 1 minute, then fold in the passion fruit purée. Let cool to room temperature. In a deep bowl, beat the egg whites until stiff peaks form. Fold into the mousse mixture. In a deep bowl beat the cream until soft peaks form. Fold into the mousse mixture, cover with plastic film, and chill until set.

❀ | TO MAKE THE TUILE CONES: Preheat the oven to 350°F. Line a baking sheet with silicone (Teflon®) paper, or use a teflon-lined pan. Cut 6-inch circles from a sheet of thin cardboard or stiff plastic, making a stencil. Mix all ingredients together in a large bowl until smooth. Scoop out ½ cup of batter, add 1 tablespoon of cocoa powder, and mix. Place in a pastry bag fitted with a very small plain tip, or put in a small plastic bag. Place the stencil on the baking sheet and spread the cutout with a thin layer of batter, smoothing with a spatula or the back of a spoon. Lift the stencil, reposition, and repeat to make 8 circles. Draw a zigzag design across each circle with the chocolate batter; if using the plastic bag with the chocolate batter, snip a tiny hole in one corner and use it as a pastry bag. Bake for 10 minutes or until the edges just start to brown. Remove from the oven and immediately lift the circles with a spatula, one at a time, and roll into cones, holding momentarily until they cool enough to stiffen and hold shape. If the tuiles become too stiff to roll, return them momentarily to the oven to soften. Set the cones aside to cool completely.

❀ | TO SERVE: Cut the strawberries into thin slices from the tip almost to the green caps and fan out. Put the heavy cream in a squeeze bottle and draw a line across the center of each plate. Spoon mango coulis on one side of the line, filling that half of the plate; fill the other half of the plate with strawberry coulis. With a toothpick or the point of a sharp knife, pull through the cream in alternating directions to create a design across the plate. Put the mousse in a pastry bag fitted with a large fluted tip and pipe into the cones. Cross 2 filled cones in the center of each plate. Garnish the plates with slices of mango, strawberry fans, and mint sprigs.

Lemon-Lime Mousse with Chocolate Crunch

Chris Fulcher

Old Stone Farmhouse
St. Thomas, U.S. Virgin Islands

SERVES 8

The crisp, cool flavor of the mousse is a perfect foil for the crunchy chocolate-marshmallow-cereal disc under it. The simple granite adds a cooling bite of its own. The surprise is the "secret ingredient"—Frosted Flakes® cereal!

Chocolate Crunch

2	ounces chocolate chips
3	marshmallows
1	ounce unsalted butter
1	cup Frosted Flakes® cereal or similar sugared crunch cereal
1	cup toasted almonds

Passion Fruit Granite

2	cups water
¼	cup sugar
1	cup passion fruit purée
1¼	cups dry white wine

Lemon-Lime Mousse

¼	cup heavy (whipping) cream
1	14-ounce can sweetened condensed milk
	Zest of 2 limes
	Juice of 2 lemons
	Juice of 6 limes
2	egg whites

Garnish

1¼	cups Strawberry or Raspberry Coulis (see page 234)
1	cup Chocolate Sauce (see page 239)

❀ | To make the chocolate crunch: Line a large baking sheet with parchment paper, or butter the baking sheet. In a double boiler over boiling water, melt the chocolate chips, marshmallows, and butter. Mix well. In a large bowl combine the cereal and almonds. Pour the chocolate mixture over the cereal and mix gently to combine. Turn out onto baking sheet, flatten into a circle, and freeze until set.

❀ | To make the passion fruit granite: In a small saucepan heat the water and sugar together to make simple syrup. Transfer to a heatproof glass mixing bowl. Add the purée and wine. Pour into a shallow 2-quart pan and cover with foil. Freeze for 4 hours, stirring with a fork every 30 minutes. The crystals will be coarse.

❀ | To make the mousse: Beat the cream until soft peaks form. Place a large dollop of whipped cream in a large mixing bowl. Pour the condensed milk over the cream. Add the zest and juices to the bowl. Mix thoroughly. Whisk in the remaining whipped cream. Beat the egg whites until stiff peaks form. Fold the egg whites into the cream mixture. Refrigerate to keep cold while the molds are prepared. Line a baking sheet with parchment paper. Using a ring mold as a guide, cut 8 rounds out of the chocolate crunch. Place the molds on the prepared baking sheet. Press a chocolate crunch round

LEMON-LIME MOUSSE WITH CHOCOLATE CRUNCH (PAGE 150)

PASSION FRUIT AND RASPBERRY MOUSSE (PAGE 168)

FROZEN MANGO SOUFFLÉ (PAGE 170)

ICED BANANA SOUFFLÉ ON A CHOCOLATE TART
WITH SHAVED MANGOES (PAGE 172)

CLASSIC PLANTAIN TART (PAGE 176)

CRUZAN BANANAS (PAGE 177)

ROASTED PINEAPPLE WITH BLACK CURRANT, MARTINIQUE AGED RUM,
AND VANILLA BEANS (PAGE 180)

TROPICAL FRUIT PUDDING (PAGE 182)

159

CRÈME BRULÉE WITH SAUTÉED
EXOTIC FRUITS (PAGE 191)

FRUIT AND CEREAL SALAD WITH
LEMON CREAM IN A WHITE
CHOCOLATE CRUST (PAGE 194)

SPONGE CAKE WITH SAUTÉED BANANAS AND SPICED RUM BUTTER (PAGE 196)

ALMOND STICKS (KRANSEKAGE) (PAGE 201)

SWEET YUCA FRITTERS (PAGE 202)

THE UNNAMEABLE DESSERT (PAGE 203)

CARAMELIZED APPLE PIE WITH MANGO ICE CREAM
AND FRESH FRUIT (PAGE 205)

CRISPY FEUILLANTINES WITH FRESH STRAWBERRIES
AND CARAMEL ICE CREAM (PAGE 206)

BANANA-CHOCOLATE TART WITH HAZELNUT SAUCE (PAGE 210)

HAZELNUT NAPOLEON FILLED WITH CHOCOLATE-KAHLUA MOUSSE AND PASSION
FRUIT GRANITE (PAGE 212)

into the bottom of each. Pipe or spoon the mousse into the molds and even the top with the back of a knife. Cover with plastic wrap and freeze to set, at least 4 hours.

🌸 | TO SERVE: Spoon a small pool of strawberry or raspberry coulis on cold dessert plates. Unmold a mousse and place on the purée on each plate. Put a scoop of passion fruit granite on top of the mousse and garnish plates with chocolate sauce and more strawberry or raspberry sauce.

Passion Fruit and Raspberry Mousse

Philippa Esposito

Le Bistro
St. John's, Antigua

SERVES 8

This beautiful and delicious mousse is cradled in teardrops of chocolate and served with tuiles filled with whipped cream and fresh fruit. The blend of passion fruit and raspberry is exotic and perfumy, and a perfect foil for the bittersweet chocolate wrapping.

TUILES

¼	cup (1 stick) unsalted butter
1	cup confectioners' sugar
3	egg whites
1	cup all-purpose flour
2	ounces bittersweet chocolate, chopped

CHOCOLATE RIBBON

10	ounces bittersweet chocolate, chopped

MOUSSE

2	pounds passion fruit, peeled and seeded
1¼	cups sugar
2	cups water
1	packet gelatin
¼	cup water
1	pound fresh raspberries
1	tablespoon sugar
1	pint heavy (whipping) cream

GARNISH

1	cup heavy (whipping) cream
1	tablespoon sugar
1	cup blackberries
1	pint strawberries
2	mangoes, pitted and julienned
	Mint sprigs

❀ | To MAKE THE TUILES: Line a baking sheet with parchment. Cut a 6-inch circle in a piece of cardboard or stiff plastic to create a stencil. In the bowl of a food processor or electric mixer, cream the butter and sugar together until light and fluffy. Add the egg whites one at a time. Fold in the flour. Refrigerate for 30 minutes. Preheat the oven to 400°F. In the top of a double boiler over barely simmering water melt the 2 ounces of chocolate. Place the stencil on the prepared baking sheet and fill evenly with batter, spreading thin with the back of a spoon. Lift the stencil and repeat. Put the melted chocolate in a squeeze bottle or a plastic bag. Drizzle the tuiles with the melted chocolate and bake for 2 to 3 minutes; do not let them become brown. Remove and immediately shape into cones. Let cool. If the tuiles become too stiff to mold, place them in the warm oven for a moment to reheat them.

❀ | To MAKE THE CHOCOLATE RIBBON MOLDS: Line a baking sheet with plastic wrap or parchment paper. In the top of a double boiler over barely simmering water melt the chocolate. Lay 8 heavy flexible 2½ x 15-inch plastic strips on a work surface. Spread chocolate ⅛ inch thick on a plastic strip, let cool until the sheen disappears, then lift both ends of the strip and bring them together at one end, chocolate-to-chocolate, forming a teardrop shape. Hold the ends together with a paper clip. Repeat with the remaining strips. Stand on the prepared baking sheet and put in the refrigerator.

❀ | To MAKE THE MOUSSE: Put the passion fruit pulp, sugar, and water in a medium saucepan and bring to a boil. Reduce the heat to low and simmer for 20 minutes. Remove from the heat, strain through a fine-mesh sieve, and place in a bowl set in a larger bowl of ice. Dissolve the gelatin in the water. Reserve ½ cup of raspberries for garnish. Purée the remaining raspberries with the tablespoon of sugar and press the pulp through a fine-mesh sieve to remove the seeds. Set aside ½ cup of each purée in separate containers for use as garnish.

❀ | Add the raspberry purée to the passion fruit purée and gently whisk the dissolved gelatin into the purée mixture. In a deep heavy bowl beat the cream at high speed until firm peaks form. Gently fold the cream into the purée mixture. Fill the chocolate molds with the mousse and chill in the refrigerator for 2 hours.

❀ | To SERVE: Beat the whipping cream with the sugar until soft peaks form. Place it in a pastry bag fitted with a medium star tip. Place one chocolate-wrapped mousse off center on each dessert plate. Spoon one strip of mango purée, one strip of heavy cream, and one strip of raspberry purée side by side near the large end of the mousse. Pull across the sauces with the point of a sharp knife or toothpick, alternating directions, to create a design. Place a dot of raspberry purée at the thin end of the mousse and pull through it to form a star design. Pipe whipped cream into the tuile cones and place 1 on each plate. Garnish the plate with fresh berries and a sprig of mint.

FROZEN MANGO SOUFFLÉ

ANDREW COMEY
Caneel Bay Resort
St. John, U.S. Virgin Islands

SERVES 8

Mango soufflés are frozen into tall cylinders, and set in tuile cookies shaped to fit around them. Begin a day ahead so that the soufflés have time to freeze. If fresh mangoes are not available, look for frozen mango purée in your market's frozen foods section. Other fruits may be substituted for the mango; the flavor will be different, but the dessert is still delicious.

MANGO PURÉE

2	mangoes

SOUFFLÉ

5	egg yolks
3	whole eggs
1	cup sugar
¼	cup Mango Purée (see above)
1	pint heavy (whipping) cream, whipped to stiff peaks

TUILES

7	ounces egg whites
3	cups confectioners' sugar
2	cups bread flour or all-purpose flour
1	cup melted butter

GARNISH

¼	pint raspberries
16	4-inch chocolate straws or strips

❀ | To make the MANGO PURÉE: Peel the mango and cut the flesh from the pit. Place in a blender or food processor and purée. Press through a fine-mesh sieve. Set aside ½ cup for the soufflé; place the remaining purée in a squeeze bottle.

❀ | To make the SOUFFLÉ: Cut 8 strips of parchment, 8 inches by 4 inches. Curve the strips inside eight 2½-inch ring molds set on a baking sheet; if the top of the parchment sticks up very high above the molds, reinforce it with a strip of aluminum foil wrapped around the outside. In the deep bowl of an electric mixer beat the egg yolks, eggs, and sugar on high speed until they thicken and form a ribbon when dribbled on top of the mixture. Fold in the mango purée. In a separate bowl beat the cream until firm peaks form. Gently fold a heaping spoonful of whipped cream into the mango mixture, then gently fold the mango mixture into the remaining whipped cream. Pipe into prepared molds, filling three-fourths of the way, and freeze overnight.

❀ | To make the TUILES: Prepare a stencil for the cookies: Cut a right triangle, 4 inches tall by 10 inches long on the perpendicular edges, from a heavy piece of cardboard or stiff plastic. In the large bowl of an electric mixer beat the egg whites at high speed until soft peaks form. Slowly pour in the sugar, continuing to beat at high speed. Slow the speed to medium and beat in the flour in 3 additions. Pour in the butter in a slow stream and beat until incorporated. Cover the bowl with plastic wrap and chill the batter overnight.

❀ | When ready to bake, preheat the oven to 375°F. Line a baking sheet with parchment paper. Take the batter from the refrigerator and stir to soften slightly. Lay the stencil on the parchment paper and put a spoonful of batter into the stencil; smooth with the back of the spoon. Repeat to make 8 triangles (you will probably have to make them in 2 batches). Bake until golden, about 12 minutes. Remove and immediately curve around the outside of the same size ring molds used for the frozen soufflés, overlapping at the pointed end. Let cool, remove from the molds, and store in a cool dry place. If the cookies become brittle before shaping, return them to the oven briefly to warm them again.

❀ | To make the raspberry purée: Reserve 24 fresh raspberries. Place the remaining berries in a blender or food processor and purée; press through a fine-mesh sieve. Place the purée in a squeeze bottle.

❀ | To serve: Take the soufflés from the freezer. Unwrap the paper from the soufflés and place 1 on each chilled dessert plate, off center. Slip a molded tuile over each soufflé. Garnish the plate with fresh mango strips and raspberries, and dot with mango and raspberry purées. Put 2 chocolate strips in the top of each soufflé.

ICED BANANA SOUFFLÉ ON A CHOCOLATE TART WITH SHAVED MANGOES

JOSEF TEUSCHLER
Four Seasons Resort Nevis
Nevis

SERVES 4

This beautiful tart makes dessert a true adventure! A sweet surprise of iced banana soufflé is hidden beneath the beautiful petals made of mango slices.

ICED BANANA SOUFFLÉ

4	egg whites
½	cup sugar
2	bananas, cut into 1-inch chunks
	Juice of 1 lemon
½	cup heavy (whipping) cream

SWEET DOUGH TART SHELLS

3	cups unbleached all-purpose flour
½	cup sugar
2	egg yolks
	Pinch of salt
1	teaspoon vanilla extract
1	cup butter at room temperature

CHOCOLATE GLAZE

4	ounces semisweet chocolate, chopped

COCONUT TART FILLING

3	egg yolks
¼	cup sugar
¼	cup canned coconut milk
1	cup whipping cream
1	cup flaked coconut
6	ounces semi-sweet chocolate, roughly chopped

GARNISH

½	cup Caramel Sauce (see page 239)
½	cup Crème Anglaise (see page 234)
3	large mangoes, pitted and sliced into 20 very thin pieces
4	unhulled fresh strawberries, halved
1	banana, sliced
4	fresh mint sprigs
2	chocolate cigarettes (optional)

❁ | TO MAKE THE ICED BANANA SOUFFLÉ: In a double boiler over simmering water, whip the egg whites and sugar together. Cook until the sugar has dissolved, then remove from the heat. In the bowl of an electric mixer beat the mixture at high speed until stiff peaks form. In a blender or food processor purée the bananas with the lemon juice. Beat the cream until soft peaks form. Fold the banana purée into the egg white mixture, then fold in the whipped cream. Place 6 paper drinking cones in tall glasses. Fill a pastry bag fitted with a large plain tip with the soufflé mixture and pipe into the cones, filling them nearly to the top. Set in the freezer and freeze for at least 3 hours.

❁ | TO MAKE THE SWEET DOUGH TART SHELLS: In a large mixing bowl sift the flour and sugar together. Add the egg yolks, salt, vanilla, and butter. Work the mixture together with your hands until a dough forms (the mixture may be turned out on a work surface when working it together if preferred). Form the dough into a ball, wrap in plastic wrap, and chill in the refrigerator for at least 1 hour.

❀ | On a lightly floured surface, roll the dough out to ⅛-inch thickness and cut four 7-inch circles. Press the circles into 5-inch tart pans. Run the rolling pin across the top of each tart pan to remove excess dough. Set the tarts aside on a baking sheet to let the dough rest while preparing the coconut filling.

❀ | To MAKE THE CHOCOLATE GLAZE: In the top of a double boiler over barely simmering water, melt the chocolate. Let the chocolate cool slightly, then brush onto each tart just covering the sides. Let the chocolate harden slightly.

❀ | To MAKE THE COCONUT FILLING: Preheat the oven to 350°F. In a medium bowl beat the egg yolks, sugar, coconut milk, and cream. Sprinkle ¼ cup of coconut flakes in the bottom of each tart shell, then fill with the coconut filling. Bake the tarts for 20 minutes or until a knife inserted in the center comes out clean. Remove from the oven and let cool.

❀ | To SERVE: Place the crème anglaise and caramel sauce in separate squeeze bottles. On each serving plate squeeze a strip of crème anglaise around the edge of the plate to form a circle. Squeeze another circle of caramel sauce inside the crème anglaise. Using a toothpick or the point of a sharp knife, pull through the circles in a spiral motion, creating a swirled design all the way around. Place a tart in the center of each plate. Dip the banana soufflé cups into warm water to loosen them. Invert a frozen soufflé on top of each tart, and pull off the paper cups. Place mango slices around each cone like petals to form a flower. Garnish the edges of the tarts with a strawberry half, banana slices, and sprig of mint. If using chocolate cigarettes, crisscross 2 in front of each cone, resting them on the cones.

Banana Napoleon with Chocolate Sabayon

Patrick Lassaque

The Ritz-Carlton Cancun
Cancun, Mexico

SERVES 9

Towers of puff pastry cookies and flambéed bananas are paired with coconut sauce and a rich chocolate "sabayon." This "sabayon" is not a traditional sabayon at all, but chilled and firm enough to scoop. The sugary puff pastry cookies add a touch of snap to a very creamy dessert.

COCO SAUCE

8	ounces raisins
3	ounces rum
1	fresh coconut, cracked, meat extracted, and juice reserved (see page 240) or 1 cup unsweetened frozen coconut
	Juice of 1 lemon

PUFF COOKIE

1	sheet frozen puff pastry dough, thawed
½	cup sugar
	Flour for dusting

CHOCOLATE SABAYON

1	packet (1 tablespoon) unflavored gelatin
½	cup cold water
6	ounces dark chocolate
2	tablespoons water
5	tablespoons sugar
2	eggs
3	egg yolks
1	cup plus 2 tablespoons heavy (whipping) cream

SAUTÉED BANANAS

2½	cups firmly packed brown sugar
1	cup water
9	bananas, sliced in half lengthwise, then cut in half crosswise
1	cup passion fruit liqueur, or rum

❋ | To make the coco sauce: Place the raisins in a glass bowl and add the rum. Cover and refrigerate overnight. In the bowl of a blender or food processor, purée the coconut with reserved coconut liquid and lemon juice. Strain the mixture into a bowl. Strain the raisins and add them to the purée. Refrigerate until needed; the mixture can be refrigerated for several days.

❋ | To make the puff cookie: Sprinkle the puff pastry with the sugar, roll up like a jelly roll, cover tightly with plastic wrap, and refrigerate overnight so that the sugar will caramelize into the layers when the pastry is baked. Butter a baking sheet or line a baking sheet with parchment paper. Preheat the oven to 400°F. Remove the pastry from the refrigerator and place on a floured surface. Cut into ¼-inch-thick slices, putting the slices on the floured surface. Dust a rolling pin with flour and roll out the cookies into thin circles. Cut the circles into squares and discard the cut-off dough. Place the squares on the prepared cookie sheet and bake for 12 minutes, or until golden. Remove and set aside to cool. The cookies are best used the day they are prepared; however, they will keep for a few days in an airtight container, or may be frozen for up to 2 weeks.

❀| To make the chocolate sabayon: Dissolve the gelatin in the water in a small pan, and allow to soften. Melt the chocolate in the top of a double boiler over barely simmering water. Remove the chocolate from the heat. In a small saucepan add 2 tablespoons of water to the sugar and bring to a boil. In a large mixing bowl beat the eggs and egg yolks at high speed until thick and pale, about 5 minutes. Lower the speed to medium and gradually pour in the hot sugar syrup while continuing to beat the eggs. Beat until the mixture cools. Warm the gelatin mixture in the top of a double boiler over simmering water until it is thin and completely dissolved (do not allow it to boil). Add a large spoonful of sabayon to the gelatin and mix well. Pour the gelatin mixture into the sabayon and whisk. Fold the entire mixture into the warm chocolate. Whip the cream to soft peaks and fold into the chocolate mixture. Pour into a large bowl, cover with plastic wrap, and refrigerate for at least 4 hours (preferably overnight).

❀| To prepare the sautéed bananas: In a medium skillet over medium heat, melt the sugar in the water and heat until it begins to caramelize (brown). Add the banana slices and sauté briefly, turning to cook evenly. The bananas should be softened slightly. Remove from the heat and add the liqueur or rum. Avert your face and ignite the alcohol using a long match. Let the flames die down.

❀| To serve: Place a puff cookie on each chilled dessert plate. Place 2 slices of banana on top of each cookie. Top with another cookie and 2 more slices of banana. Add a final cookie to the top. Spoon coco sauce around the plate. Top with a scoop of the chocolate sabayon.

CLASSIC PLANTAIN TART

ROLSTON HECTOR

St. James's Club
Antigua

MAKES ONE 10-INCH TART

A large slice of plantain tart is served in a plate covered with rum sauce, a true taste of the Caribbean. This method makes one large tart; separate small tarts could be made instead.

TART SHELL

4½	cups all-purpose flour
2	tablespoons sugar
1	teaspoon salt
1	cup (2 sticks) unsalted butter
½	cup shortening
¾	cup ice water

FILLING

1	cup (2 sticks) unsalted butter
¾	cup rum
¾	cup banana liqueur

½	cup sugar
4	large plantains, peeled and cut into disks

RUM SAUCE

6	tablespoons cornstarch
1	cup water
1	quart heavy (whipping) cream
6	tablespoons sugar
1	cup dark rum
4	ounces bittersweet chocolate, cut into chunks

❈ | TO MAKE THE TART SHELL: In a large bowl stir the flour, sugar, and salt together. Cut in the butter and shortening with a pastry blender or fork until the mixture resembles cornmeal. Or, place the flour, sugar, salt, butter, and shortening in the bowl of a food processor and blend. Add half of the water and stir with a fork gently to bring the mixture together. Add the remaining water, a little at a time, until the dough forms a ball and pulls away from the sides of the bowl, about 1 minute. Wrap in plastic wrap and chill for 30 minutes.

❈ | Preheat the oven to 400°F. Roll out the pastry on a floured surface. Roll up the crust on your rolling pin; unroll it across a 10-inch pie tin and press into place. Put pie weights or dried beans in the bottom and bake for 8 minutes. Remove from the oven, take out the weights or beans, and let cool.

❈ | TO MAKE THE FILLING: In a large saucepan bring the butter, rum, liqueur, and sugar to a boil over medium-low heat, whisking to keep the mixture from boiling over. Cook until reduced by half in volume, about 10 minutes. When reduced and bubbling, stir in the plantains and cook for 1 minute. Remove the plantains from the heat. Preheat the oven to 350°F. Use a slotted spoon to lift the plantain disks from the liquid and put them in the cooled pie shell. Gently pour the liquid from the pan over the plantain pieces. Bake for 30 minutes or until set and golden. Remove from the oven and cool to room temperature. Cover with plastic wrap and refrigerate for 2 hours.

❀| To make the rum sauce: Dissolve the cornstarch in the water. In a saucepan bring the cream, sugar, and rum to a boil over medium heat. Remove from the heat and stir in the cornstarch. Let cool.

❀| To serve: In the top of a double boiler melt the chocolate over water that is barely simmering. Spoon rum sauce into the plates. Cut the tart into wedges and place 1 on each plate. Place the melted chocolate in a squeeze bottle or a plastic bag; cut a tiny snip in one corner if using a plastic bag. Drizzle melted chocolate into the rum sauce, swirling into a design.

Cruzan Bananas

Michael Madsen
Divi Resort & Casino
St. Croix, U.S. Virgin Islands

MAKES 4

Like New Orleans's famed "Bananas Foster," Cruzan Bananas are caramelized and served with vanilla ice cream. The spiced rum puts the Caribbean spin on this simple but delicious dish.

¼	cup Clarified Butter (see page 234)	½	cup heavy (whipping) cream
8	tablespoons dark brown sugar		
4	bananas, cut in half and split lengthwise	12	small scoops vanilla ice cream
1	cup Cruzan Clipper Spiced Rum or other spiced rum	½	cup chopped walnuts
		4	sprigs mint

❀| In a large sauté pan heat the butter over medium heat. Stir in the brown sugar and allow to melt in the butter. Add the bananas and cook until coated with the caramelized sugar. Stir in the rum, then stir in the cream. Cook for 30 seconds, stirring gently or tossing.

❀| To serve: Put 3 small scoops of ice cream in the center of each plate. Pour the bananas and syrup over the ice cream. Sprinkle with chopped walnuts and garnish with a mint sprig.

PINEAPPLE SURPRISE

ROLSTON HECTOR

St. James's Club
Antigua

SERVES 4

A meringue pineapple sporting pineapple leaves at its top reveals sponge cake and pineapple chunks
when sliced open.

SPONGE CAKE

4	eggs, separated
⅔	cup sugar
1½	teaspoons vanilla extract
½	teaspoon cream of tartar
	Pinch of salt
⅔	cup cake flour

2	pineapples
1¼	cups sugar, divided
4	cups water
½	tablespoon cornstarch
¼	cup cold water
7	egg whites
2	tablespoons sugar
¼	cup Chocolate Sauce (see page 239)

❋ | TO MAKE THE SPONGE CAKE: Preheat the oven to 350°F. Lightly grease a 10-inch round cake pan
and line with parchment paper. In a large bowl lightly beat the egg yolks, then add ¾ cup sugar. Beat
until the mixture is pale yellow in color and forms a ribbon on top of the mixture when dropped from
a spoon. Add the vanilla. In a deep mixing bowl beat the egg whites until foamy. Beat in the cream of
tartar, salt, and remaining sugar, and beat until stiff, glossy peaks form. Fold the flour into the egg
yolk mixture by thirds, then fold in one large spoonful of egg whites to lighten the mixture. Gently
fold the remaining egg whites into the batter. Pour into the prepared pan, smooth the top, and bake
until the top springs back when gently touched, about 15 minutes. Remove from the oven, cool, and
turn out onto a towel on a work surface.

❋ | Peel the pineapples and save some of the tender center leaves for garnish. Core out the eyes,
and chop the pineapple in small chunks. Place the pineapple chunks, 1¼ cups of sugar, and 4 cups of
water in a deep saucepan and bring to a boil. Boil 10 minutes, then set aside to cool. Strain and
squeeze all the juice out of the chunks into the saucepan and bring back to a boil. Dissolve the cornstarch in the cold water, and stir into the pineapple syrup to thicken. Purée one half of the cooked
pineapple and stir into the sauce. Let cool.

❋ | Cut the sponge cake in half horizontally and separate the layers. Cut out 8 disks. Place 1 piece
of cake, cut side up, on each of 4 heatproof plates. Divide the remaining pineapple chunks among the
cakes and cover with the remaining cake discs, cut side down.

❋ | In a deep bowl beat the egg whites until soft peaks form. Continue beating, adding the sugar,
until stiff peaks form. Preheat the broiler to the highest setting. Place the meringue in a pastry bag

fitted with a medium star tip and cover the sponge cake with meringue stars to look like a pineapple. Place under the broiler just long enough to singe the meringue, or, singe it with a small blowtorch. Fill the plates with the pineapple sauce. In a small heavy pan melt the chocolate over barely simmering water, place in a squeeze bottle, and dot the pineapple sauce with a row of chocolate dots around one-half of the plate. Pull the tip of a sharp knife through the chocolate dots in one direction, connecting the dots with a line of chocolate. Working with the tip of the knife, pull outward a short distance from each dot in a series of lines for a star-line effect. Garnish the other side of the dessert with a few pineapple leaves to make it resemble a pineapple.

ROASTED PINEAPPLE WITH BLACK CURRANT, MARTINIQUE AGED RUM, AND VANILLA BEANS

BENOIT PEPIN

Little Dix Bay Resort
Virgin Gorda, British Virgin Islands

MAKES 4

Crisp tuiles curve behind a slice of caramelized pineapple topped with whipped cream. Black currant jelly sauce creates a colorful contrast. As with any flambéed dish, be very aware of everything around the stove before you ignite the rum; there is a lot more room in a restaurant kitchen than in most home kitchens.

TUILES

5	tablespoons unsalted butter at room temperature
5	tablespoons confectioners' sugar
2	egg whites
3	tablespoons cake flour
¼	cup (½ stick) unsalted butter
¼	cup firmly packed light brown sugar

4	fresh pineapple slices
1½	cups aged rum
2	cups fresh pineapple juice
½	cup black currant jelly
2	vanilla beans, split
4	scoops vanilla ice cream
12	small pineapple leaves
4	mint sprigs

❀ | TO MAKE THE TUILES: Preheat the oven to 350°F. Lightly grease a baking sheet with butter, then dust it with flour. In a medium bowl beat the butter and confectioners' sugar until light and fluffy. Slowly add the egg whites and cake flour, mixing until fully incorporated. Spread the batter into 4 thin squares on the baking sheet, shaping with the back of the spoon. Use your fingers or the handle of a spoon to create small Swiss cheese-like holes in each square. Bake for 5 to 8 minutes until golden brown. Remove the cookies from the oven. Working quickly, lift a cookie with a spatula and drape it over a rolling pin, a glass placed on its side, or similar cylindrical object, letting a little of the cookie drape out flat on the counter. Let cool, slip off the mold, and set aside. If the cookies become too brittle to mold, return the pan to the oven briefly to warm them.

❀ | In a large saucepan melt the butter over medium heat and stir in the brown sugar until melted. Add the pineapple slices and sauté for 2 minutes, turning once. Add 1 cup of the pineapple juice and cook until the mixture is syrupy, about 3 minutes. Add the rum. Avert your face, ignite the rum with a long match, and shake the pan until the flames die down. Add the remaining pineapple juice and jelly. With the point of a sharp knife, scrape the vanilla seeds from the beans into the sauce. Cook for 2 minutes, turning the pineapple slices once.

❀ | TO SERVE: Place a pineapple slice on each plate. Spoon the sauce around the pineapple. Top the pineapple with a scoop of ice cream and stick 2 vanilla pieces in the ice cream. Drizzle the plate with the currant sauce. Position a tuile cookie on each plate, tucking the edge under the pineapple slice so that the tuile stands up. Garnish each plate with pineapple leaves and a mint sprig.

BANANA PUDDING

SCOTT WILLIAMS
Necker Island, British Virgin Islands

SERVES 8

These delicious puddings resemble moist muffins and are filled with pieces of banana. They are paired with butterscotch sauce and crème anglaise. The puddings and the crème anglaise may both be prepared ahead of time.

BANANA PUDDING

2	cups all-purpose flour
1	tablespoon baking soda
2	eggs, at room temperature
1	tablespoon vanilla extract
1½	cups sugar
	Pinch of salt
½	cup spiced rum
¼	cup (1 stick) softened unsalted butter
2	bananas, chopped

BUTTERSCOTCH SAUCE

½	cup (1 stick) unsalted butter
1¼	cups brown sugar

	Juice of ½ lemon
¼	cup spiced rum
¼	cup heavy (whipping) cream, warmed
4	tablespoons butter

CRÈME ANGLAISE

1½	cups milk
⅓	cup sugar
1	vanilla bean, split lengthwise
4	egg yolks

Sliced fresh fruit for garnish (optional)

❀ | TO MAKE THE PUDDING: Preheat the oven to 450°F. Grease and flour a muffin tin. Sift together the flour and baking soda. Set aside. In a food processor blend together the eggs, vanilla, sugar, salt, and rum. Add the butter and finish mixing. Remove to a large bowl. Fold in the flour mixture and mix until smooth. Add the chopped bananas. Spoon into the prepared muffin tin, filling the cups two-thirds of the way full. Bake for 10 to 12 minutes until a toothpick inserted in the centers comes out clean. Remove from pan when cool. The pudding will resemble moist muffins. Extra muffins can be wrapped and frozen for future use.

❀ | TO MAKE THE BUTTERSCOTCH SAUCE: In a 5-quart saucepan melt the butter and sugar until the sugar dissolves and begins to turn a dark brown color. Add the lemon juice. Remove from the heat and stir in the rum. Place it back on the heat and add the warmed cream. Simmer, whisking in the remaining butter until dissolved. Remove from the heat and set in a large bowl filled with ice. The sauce will thicken as it cools.

❀ | TO PREPARE THE CRÈME ANGLAISE: In a medium saucepan combine the milk and sugar. Scrape the seeds from the vanilla pods into the milk mixture, then put the whole pods into the milk. Bring to a simmer over medium heat. In a medium bowl whisk the egg yolks until pale in color. Slowly add the hot milk mixture to the egg yolks an ounce at a time, stirring constantly, until the eggs are warm to the touch. Then add the egg yolk mixture all at once back to the milk mixture in the saucepan. Stir constantly over medium-high heat until the custard begins to thicken. Do not let the mixture boil. When thickened, remove from the heat, place the pan in a large bowl of ice, and whisk to cool. Strain the custard through a fine-mesh sieve into a separate bowl. The custard may be made and kept refrigerated up to 2 days ahead.

🌸 | TO SERVE: On chilled plates spoon a pool of butterscotch sauce. Top with a banana pudding. Drizzle crème anglaise around the plate and over the pudding. Add the optional fresh fruit for garnish, if desired.

TROPICAL FRUIT PUDDING

GEORGE MCKIRDY
El San Juan Hotel & Casino
San Juan, Puerto Rico

SERVES 8

Layers of ladyfingers soaked with fruit juice alternate with coconut-ginger pastry cream and fresh fruit in this tropical version of English trifle. Chef George McKirdy uses strawberries and tropical fruits, but you could use a variety of berries, peaches, plums, or whatever local fruits are in season as well.

LADYFINGERS

5	egg yolks
¼	cup sugar
5	egg whites
½	cup sugar
3	drops white vinegar
1	teaspoon vanilla extract
¼	cup all-purpose flour
3	tablespoons (1 ounce) potato starch
	Pinch of salt

COCONUT-GINGER PASTRY CREAM

3	cups whole milk
1¼	cups sugar
½	vanilla bean, split
1½	tablespoons blanched ginger, finely grated
3½	cups cornstarch
1	cup coconut milk
16	egg yolks

FRUIT

1	quart water
1	cup sugar
2	tablespoons spiced rum
1	vanilla bean, split
1	ripe pineapple, cut into ¼-inch dice; reserve the leaves
2	ripe mangos, cut into ¼-inch dice
2	pints strawberries, stemmed and cut into small dice
2	cups sugar
¼	coconut
1	cup heavy (whipping) cream
4	ounces white chocolate, cut into curls
24	chocolate strips

❀| To MAKE THE LADYFINGERS: Preheat the oven to 400°F. Line 2 baking sheets with ungreased parchment paper. In the bowl of a mixer, beat the egg yolks and ¼ cup of sugar together until the mixture is light yellow in color and forms a ribbon when dribbled on the surface. In a deep bowl, beat the egg whites until foamy. Continue to beat, and slowly add the ½ cup sugar. Beat until stiff but not dry peaks form. Beat in the vinegar and vanilla. Fold one-fourth of the yolks into the whites, then alternately fold the dry ingredients and whites into the yolks, beginning and ending with the whites. Put the mixture in a pastry bag fitted with a ½-inch plain round tip and pipe onto the prepared sheets, leaving at least 1½ inches between each "line." Dust with confectioners' sugar. Bake for 8 to 10 minutes, or until slightly golden and baked through. Remove and let cool.

❀| To MAKE THE COCONUT-GINGER PASTRY CREAM: In a heavy saucepan heat the milk with one half of the sugar and the vanilla bean over medium heat. Bring to a boil, add the ginger, and remove from the heat. Allow to steep 4 to 5 minutes.

❀| Place the starch and remaining sugar in a bowl and mix together with the coconut milk. In a separate bowl beat the egg yolks until foamy. Add the yolks to the coconut milk mixture and stir to blend. Pour a small amount of the warm milk into the egg-coconut mixture, stirring constantly, then slowly pour in the remaining warm milk while stirring. Strain through a fine-mesh sieve or chinois into a stainless steel pot. Cook, stirring continuously. When the custard begins to thicken, stir more vigorously and cook for 3 more minutes, stirring vigorously to keep the bottom from scorching. After the first sign of boiling, remove the pan from the heat and pour into a glass or stainless steel bowl. Cover the surface with plastic wrap to keep it from forming a skin.

❀| To PREPARE THE FRUIT: Bring the water, sugar, rum, and vanilla bean to a rolling boil over medium-high heat. Reduce the heat to medium and add the pineapple. Cook 3 minutes (the riper the fruit, the less the time), remove from the heat, and stir in the mango. Let stand 1 minute, then stir in the strawberries. Allow to cool.

❀| To TOAST THE COCONUT: Heat the broiler to high. Cut the coconut into chunks and coarsely grate on a box-type grater. Spread the coconut in a single layer on a baking sheet and broil for 2 to 3 minutes, until lightly browned.

❀| To ASSEMBLE: Beat the pastry cream until smooth. In a deep bowl beat the whipping cream until stiff peaks form. Reserve 1 cup and fold the remainder into the pastry cream. Split the ladyfingers in half crosswise. Line the bottom of a large bowl with ladyfingers and brush them with the juice from the fruit. Spread an even layer of all three fruits across the ladyfingers. Top with one half of the coconut-ginger pastry cream. Repeat, pressing the ladyfingers down lightly. Top with a final layer of ladyfingers that have been dipped in the combined fruit juices, pressing them lightly into the cream. Chill at least 3 hours.

❀| To SERVE: Scoop the fruit pudding into large martini-style glasses. Top each with a dollop of the reserved whipped cream. Sprinkle with toasted coconut and white chocolate curls. Pull the tenderest leaves from the center of the reserved pineapple crown and stand them upright in the top of the dessert. Stand 3 chocolate strips in each dessert.

TROPICAL PARFAIT

IVOR PETERS
The Sugar Mill Hotel
Tortola, British Virgin Islands

SERVES 6

PARFAIT

3	large eggs, separated
¾	cup sugar
1	cup heavy cream
1	tablespoon lemon juice
1	tablespoon Grand Marnier liqueur
¼	cup passion fruit purée
¼	cup Mango Purée
¼	cup Guava Purée (see page 234 for preparing fruit purées)

PASTRY TULIPS

¾	cup bread flour or all-purpose flour

1	cup confectioners' sugar
1	tube or can (8 ounces) almond paste
½	cup milk
3	large egg whites
1	teaspoon vanilla

GARNISH

Mango or passion fruit purée
Guava purée
Diced mixed fresh fruit (optional)
Toasted coconut (optional)
Chocolate hummingbird (optional)

❁ | TO MAKE THE PARFAIT: In the bowl of an electric mixer combine the egg yolks and sugar. Beat with the wire whip attachment until thick and lemon colored, about 2 minutes. Place the bowl into a larger saucepan filled halfway with simmering water; whisk constantly until the temperature of the mixture is 160°F, about 3 minutes. Let stand at room temperature until cooled. Beat the egg whites until soft peaks form. In another deep bowl beat the cream until soft peaks form. Fold the egg yolk mixture and egg whites together, then fold them into the cream. Stir in the lemon juice and Grand Marnier. Divide the mixture into 3 bowls. Gently fold each purée separately into each bowl of the cream mixture. Fill 6 small tube-shaped molds or 6-ounce custard cups with 3 layers of the cream; cover and freeze for 4 to 6 hours or until firm.

❁ | TO MAKE THE PASTRY TULIPS: Line a baking sheet with baking parchment. Preheat the oven to 400°F. Cut a 9-inch circle from heavyweight plastic (about the weight of the cover of a margarine tub) and cut a stencil in the shape of a flower with 5 large petals.* In the bowl of an electric mixer combine the flour, sugar, and almond paste, blending until it is a coarse consistency. Slowly add the milk, scraping the bowl often. Slowly add the egg whites and vanilla, scraping the bowl. Place the stencil on the parchment-covered baking sheet and spread the batter inside with a spatula. Carefully lift off the stencil. Bake for 4 to 6 minutes or until the edges are slightly golden. (Do not overbake or the flower will crack.) Remove the baking sheet from the oven. Immediately transfer the cookie using a wide spatula and place it over an inverted custard cup to mold into a flower shape. Repeat with the remaining batter to form 5 more pastry flowers. Let the flowers cool completely; unmold them from the glasses and store in a cool, dry place.

❀ | To serve: Garnish each serving plate around the rim with small spoonfuls of mango purée; top with dots of guava purée. Run a knife through the centers of the purées attractively. Place an upturned pastry flower in the center of plate. Unmold the parfaits by dipping the mold quickly in warm water. Place the parfaits in the pastry flowers. Garnish with fruit and coconut, if desired. Place a chocolate hummingbird in each parfait, if desired.

*Alternately, cut a stencil of one 3-inch petal from plastic. Prepare 36 petals on a parchment-lined baking sheet and bake all at once. Arrange 6 cookie petals on each serving plate; unmold the parfait over the petals, and garnish plate as directed above.

CHOCOLATE-LAYERED LIME PARFAIT WITH RASPBERRY COULIS

JOSEF TEUSCHLER
Four Seasons Resort
Nevis

SERVES 4

Towering icy parfaits are made of lime custard and whipped cream disks alternating with thin discs of pure chocolate. The tart raspberry coulis is the perfect counterpoint. If the stacked preparation seems daunting, try just the parfait, frozen in scoops and served with a lacing of chocolate and raspberry sauces. Stack them half as high, and serve twice as many!

LIME PARFAIT

½	cup sugar
½	cup milk
6	egg yolks
½	cup fresh lime juice
	Zest of 1 lime
1	cup heavy (whipping) cream

CHOCOLATE DISKS

12	ounces bittersweet chocolate, chopped

RASPBERRY COULIS

1	cup fresh raspberries
¼	cup confectioners' sugar
1	teaspoon fresh lemon juice

GARNISH

½	cup Crème Anglaise (see page 234)
	Shaved white chocolate
	Confectioners' sugar
	Fresh raspberries
	Mint sprigs

❀| TO MAKE THE PARFAIT: In the top of a double boiler over simmering water combine the sugar, milk, yolks, lime juice, and zest. Heat, whisking constantly, until the mixture doubles in volume and reaches 160°F. Immediately set the pan in a large bowl filled with ice to chill, whisking constantly as it cools. When cooled below room temperature, remove from the ice bath and set aside.

❀| In a large deep bowl whip the cream to soft peaks. Gently fold the whipped cream into the lime custard. Line a 13 x 9-inch baking pan with plastic wrap or aluminum foil. Spread the parfait one half to three-quarters of an inch deep in the pan and freeze for at least 3 hours.

❀| TO MAKE THE CHOCOLATE DISKS: Cover a sheet pan with heavy flexible plastic or aluminum foil. In the top of a double boiler over gently simmering water melt the chocolate and heat to 100 F. Remove from the heat and cool to 90°F. Pour the chocolate out on the prepared sheet and spread to ⅛ inch thick. Refrigerate for 4 to 5 minutes. While still slightly soft, cut out sixteen 3-inch discs with a cookie cutter. Peel the extra chocolate away, leaving the disks. The extra chocolate may be remelted and used again.

❀| TO MAKE THE COULIS: In the bowl of a blender or food processor combine the ingredients and purée. Strain through a fine-mesh sieve, pressing on the pulp to extract all the juice. Place in a squeeze bottle and chill.

❀ | To ASSEMBLE AND GARNISH THE DESSERT: Cut sixteen 2½-inch discs out of the frozen parfait with a cookie or biscuit cutter. Set a chocolate disk in the center of each dessert plate. Squeeze 3 circles of coulis evenly spaced around each disk. Squeeze a smaller circle of crème anglaise on the inside edge of each coulis circle, and draw through the crème anglaise with the point of a knife, creating a swirled design in the coulis. Stack a disk of parfait on each chocolate disk, pressing down lightly, then top with a chocolate disk. Build each dessert with 4 chocolate and 4 parfait discs, starting with chocolate and ending with parfait. Sprinkle white chocolate shavings on top of the parfaits and around the parfaits on the plates; dust lightly with confectioners' sugar. Garnish with raspberries and mint sprigs.

CHOCOLATE FLOATING ISLANDS WITH TROPICAL FRUITS

ROGER WILES

Half Moon Bay Club
Montego Bay, Jamaica

SERVES 4

Chocolate cubes hidden inside the floating islands melt as the islands are cooked. Sage is a creative, surprising, and delicious touch for this dessert. The beautiful presentation of fruits includes the otheiti apple, an unusual tropical fruit resembling a cross between a pear, a coconut, and a rose in flavor. If you can't find it—and you probably can't, outside the Caribbean—substitute mango or other tropical fruit.

SAGE INFUSION

1	leaf fresh sage, cut into chiffonade
⅓	cup coconut water
⅓	cup coconut cream
1	teaspoon brown sugar

FRIED GREEN BANANA STRIPS

2	green bananas, peeled and grated
½	cup canola oil

SAGE SAUCE

1	egg
1	teaspoon brown sugar
¼	cup cream
2	tablespoons milk
	Sage Infusion (recipe above)

FLOATING ISLANDS

1	egg white
1	teaspoon sugar
2	ounces semi-sweet chocolate, cut into ½-inch cubes

TROPICAL FRUIT GARNISH

1	otheiti apple, peeled, cored, and cut into ½-inch balls or julienned
1	naseberry, peeled and cut into ½-inch balls or julienned
1	papaya, peeled, seeded, and cut into ½-inch balls or julienned
½	cup sun-dried pineapple, cut into ½-inch balls or julienned
4	sage leaves
12	large coconut shavings, toasted

❀ | TO MAKE THE INFUSION: Place the ingredients in a small saucepan over medium heat and warm until nearly boiling. Remove from the heat and set aside to steep.

❀ | TO MAKE THE BANANA STRIPS: In a deep frying pan or sauté pan heat the oil to 350°F. On a work surface, spread out a long, narrow, thin strip of grated banana and press together with the back of a spatula. Lift the banana strip with the spatula and slide into the hot oil. Fry just until golden, about 30 seconds; turn and fry 15 more seconds. Remove and drain on paper towels; the strips may be shaped and curved while they are still very warm, and will retain the shape when cooled.

❀ | To make the sage sauce: Whisk the ingredients together over low heat until the mixture coats the back of a spoon. Do not allow it to become too warm or the egg will curdle; lift the pan from the heat periodically to allow it to cool slightly before continuing to cook.

❀ | To make the floating islands: Bring a large pot of water to a boil over medium-high heat. Reduce the heat to medium. In the bowl of an electric mixer beat the egg white at high speed until frothy, then add the sugar. Continue beating at high speed until stiff peaks form. Scoop a very large spoonful of meringue, and place the chocolate cube in the center of the top. Cover with another large spoonful of meringue, encasing the chocolate cube. Gently slide the meringue into the simmering water and cook for 30 seconds. Turn with a long-handled slotted spoon and cook another 30 seconds. It will puff slightly when it is done. Remove and drain on paper towels. Roll the floating islands in toasted coconut.

❀ | To serve: Place a pool of sage sauce in the center of each plate. Place a floating island across the sauce. Garnish the plate with tropical fruit, a sage leaf, coconut shavings, and a fried green banana strip. Cut the floating island open to release the chocolate.

FLOATING ISLAND HISPANIOLA

PHILIPPE MONGEREAU

Casa de Campo
Dominican Republic

SERVES 8

The use of vegetables in desserts is unusual to Americans, but many cultures make use of the sugars in vegetables to create dessert dishes. These floating islands are adrift in a sea of red, or kidney, bean purée scented with cinnamon, allspice, and vanilla. It is a sauce that is usually made for Easter on the island; the floating islands are a classic French preparation. Begin the day before: The dried beans must soak for 24 hours.

RED BEAN SAUCE

1	pound dried red (kidney) beans
1	fresh coconut, split (see page 240)
1	vanilla bean, split
3	whole allspice
1	stick cinnamon, snapped in half
2	cups plus 1 cup milk
⅓	cup sugar
½	cup coconut liqueur

FLOATING ISLANDS

4	egg whites
	Pinch of cream of tartar (if not using a copper bowl)
1	cup plus 2 tablespoons sugar

PRESENTATION

¼	cup coconut liqueur

❈ | To PREPARE THE SAUCE: Soak the red beans in water to cover for 24 hours. Drain. Open the coconut, drain and reserve the liquid inside for another use, and split the coconut into 8 sections. In a large pot place the red beans with one half of the vanilla bean, 3 allspice, half of the cinnamon stick, and 1 section of the coconut. Add water to cover by 2 to 3 inches and bring to a boil; reduce heat and simmer until the beans have completely softened, 1½ to 2 hours. Drain the beans, discard the spices, and purée with 2 cups of the milk in a blender or food processor until they are a creamy consistency. Press the mixture through a fine-mesh sieve. Place the red beans and remaining half of the spices, 1 cup of the milk, and the sugar in a covered pot over low heat and simmer for 1 hour, whisking occasionally to keep the mixture from sticking. Add more milk if necessary to keep the mixture from getting too dry and sticking to the pot. Toward the end of the hour, stir in the coconut liqueur. Remove from heat.

❈ | To MAKE THE FLOATING ISLANDS: In a deep bowl beat the egg whites and cream of tartar on high speed until stiff. Beat in the sugar a little at a time, beating until the mixture forms a stiff meringue. In a large saucepan bring several inches of water to a boil. Reduce the heat and let the water simmer. Dip a large spoon into cold water, then scoop a large spoonful of meringue from the bowl. Using another large spoon, shape the meringue into an oval quenelle shape and drop into the simmering water. Turn after 30 seconds and cook another 30 seconds on the other side. Remove with a slotted spoon or skimmer and set on a wire rack that is covered with a cloth to dry. You may cook several at a time, but do not let them touch.

🦋 | To serve: Remove the spices from the bean sauce. Spoon the sauce into the bottom of 8 large soup bowls. Place 3 floating islands in each. Shave long strips of fresh coconut over the floating islands. Spoon a little coconut liqueur over each.

Crème Brûlée with Sautéed Exotic Fruits

ALAIN LAURENT
**Malliouhana Hotel
Anguilla**

SERVES 6

Fruit is sautéed in brown sugar and orange liqueur (or rum), then molded with crème brûlée for a rich but simple dessert filled with island flavor. The recipe can be simplified by serving just the fruit sauté with ice cream or whipped cream; the sauté can be adjusted for seasonal availability of fresh fruits.

CRÈME BRÛLÉE

1	quart heavy (whipping) cream
2	vanilla beans, split
½	cup sugar
8	egg yolks
¼	cup brown sugar, packed

FRUIT SAUTÉ

2	pineapples, diced
2	mangoes, diced

4	tablespoons unsalted butter
2	bananas, diced
6	kiwi, diced
1	cup brown sugar, packed
2	ounces (¼ cup) dry white wine
2	ounces (¼ cup) orange liqueur, rum, or liqueur of choice

GARNISH

6	mint sprigs

🦋 | To make the crème brûlée: Preheat the oven to 350°F. Put the cream in a saucepan over medium-high heat. Scrape the vanilla bean seeds into the cream, then add the pods. Add the sugar and bring the mixture to a boil. In a small bowl whisk together the egg yolks and brown sugar. Temper the egg yolks by adding a spoonful of the hot cream mixture to the egg yolks and stirring to warm to yolks, then pour the egg mixture into the hot cream, whisking to mix. Strain through a fine-mesh sieve into a heatproof baking dish in a bain marie: Set the baking dish in a larger baking pan and pour warm water into the baking pan to cover halfway up the sides of the baking dish. Cover loosely with aluminum foil. Bake for 1 hour to 1 hour and 30 minutes or until the middle of the crème brûlée moves only slightly. Remove from the oven and set aside to cool; chill in the refrigerator.

❋| To MAKE THE FRUIT SAUTÉ: In a small sauté pan or skillet over medium-high heat sauté the pineapple and mango in butter for 2 minutes. Add the banana and kiwi and sauté for 1 minute. Caramelize the fruit: Add the brown sugar, cooking until the sugar has melted and coats the fruit. Add the white wine and drizzle with liqueur. Remove from the heat and keep warm.

❋| To SERVE: If using the broiler to brown the desserts, heat the broiler to the highest setting. Place a ring mold in the center of a plate. Spoon caramelized fruit into the mold, pressing down gently to fill halfway. Spoon chilled crème brûlée into a piping bag fitted with a large plain tip and pipe into the mold. Repeat with the remaining dishes. Sprinkle sugar on top of the crème brûlées and brown under the broiler or by using a small kitchen torch. Remove the molds and garnish with mint sprigs.

Exotic Fruit Gratin with Old Rum

Patrick Gateau

The Carl Gustav Hotel
St.-Barthélemey

SERVES 4

This simple Caribbean dessert offers a wonderful combination of flavors, textures, and temperatures. The apple fountains are extraordinary.

Apple Fountains

	Juice of 1 lemon
1	cup water
1	very crisp large golden apple
1	very crisp large red apple

Pastry Cream

½	cup heavy (whipping) cream
1	cup half-and-half
½	teaspoon vanilla extract
½	cup sugar
¼	cup cornstarch
2	egg yolks

Gratin

6	egg whites
½	cup pastry cream (above)
4	tablespoons Myers's Old Rum
1	cup diced pineapple
1	cup diced papaya
1	cup diced bananas
1	cup diced mango
1	cup diced kiwi

Garnish

4	large strawberries, thinly sliced

❀ | TO MAKE THE APPLE FOUNTAINS: In a small bowl mix the lemon juice and water. Quarter both apples, leaving the core intact. Dip the pieces in the lemon water. Lay each apple quarter flat on one side, flesh down; skin will be facing up along one side. Using a very sharp serrated knife held at a 45° angle, place the knife ⅛ inch from the edge of the apple. Slice down to ⅛ inch from the bottom of the apple, being careful to slice all the way through the apple quarter. Turn the apple quarter to the other side, still skin side up, and cut down in the same way to meet where the first cut ended, removing the apple center. Repeat these steps until the remaining apple center is too small to slice (you should have 5 to 6 apple slices when completed). Apple slices will lie on top of each other, each slice overlapping the one beneath it, attached by thin strips. Brush with the lemon-water mixture.

❀ | TO PREPARE THE PASTRY CREAM: In a medium saucepan heat the cream, half-and-half, and vanilla until very hot but not boiling. In a medium mixing bowl mix the sugar and cornstarch. Whisk in the egg yolks. Slowly pour one-half of the cream mixture into the egg mixture, stirring constantly. Pour this mixture back into the saucepan, gently whisking to blend with the cream mixture remaining in the saucepan. Heat, stirring constantly, until the mixture thickens, about 2 minutes. Scrape into a bowl and cover with plastic wrap to prevent a skin from forming. Let cool to room temperature.

❀ | TO PREPARE THE GRATIN: In a small mixing bowl beat the egg whites until stiff, then gently fold in the pastry cream and rum.

❀ | TO ASSEMBLE: Heat the broiler to the highest setting. Place the oven rack 5 inches beneath the broiler. In a medium mixing bowl toss the fruit together. Divide the fruit equally between 4 ovenproof soup bowls. Spread ½ cup of gratin mixture over the fruit in each soup bowl. Set the bowls beneath the broiler until the top of the dessert is browned, about 5 minutes. Remove from heat. Place the bowls on serving plates and slide the apple fountains between the rim of the bowl and the plate edge to hold in place. Garnish with strawberry slices and serve immediately.

FRUIT AND CEREAL SALAD WITH LEMON CREAM IN A WHITE CHOCOLATE CRUST

MICHEL CICHE
La Samanna
St. Martin

SERVES 4

Crunchy whole wheat kernels are mixed with apple, pineapple, and sweet corn for a refreshing salad that is topped with lemon cream and white chocolate. The lemon curd and whole wheat kernels must be prepared the day before, and the chocolate circles can be made and stored in the refrigerator, so last-minute preparation can be kept to a minimum.

SALAD

4	tablespoons whole wheat kernels
½	cup water
1	Granny Smith apple, diced
½	fresh pineapple, diced
½	cup sweet corn kernels (1 ear of corn) (frozen or canned whole kernel corn may be substituted)

LEMON CREAM

	Juice and zest of 10 lemons
13	eggs
8	egg yolks
3	cups sugar

1	pound (2 cups) unsalted butter, cut into pieces
½	cup heavy (whipping) cream
½	cup sour cream

WHITE CHOCOLATE CRUST

14	ounces white chocolate, chopped

GARNISH

Guava Coulis (see page 234)
Strawberry Coulis (see page 234)
Banana Coulis (see page 234)

❀| To MAKE THE SALAD: Soak the whole wheat kernels in water overnight in the refrigerator. The next day, wash and drain. Add ½ cup of cold salted water to the kernels in a saucepan, and bring to a boil. Reduce the heat to medium and simmer for 10 minutes. Strain through a sieve and chill. Chill the apple, pineapple, and corn kernels.

❀| To MAKE THE LEMON CREAM: In the top of a double boiler over simmering water combine the lemon juice, zest, eggs, egg yolks, and sugar, stirring with a wooden spoon until thickened and translucent. Take off the heat and whisk in the butter, 1 piece at a time. Cover with plastic wrap and chill overnight. The next day, beat the whipped cream to soft peaks. Fold in the sour cream and whipped cream. Cover with plastic wrap and chill.

❀| To MAKE THE CHOCOLATE CRUST: In the top of a double boiler over barely simmering water, melt the white chocolate; be careful not to let any water drop into the chocolate or it will seize. Wrap plastic wrap tightly over a flat work surface and spread the chocolate out ⅛ inch thick with a spatula. When firm, cut into eight 3-inch circles.

❀| To MAKE THE GARNISH: Combine the strained coulises and place in a squeeze bottle. Chill. Take ½ cup of apple dice and ½ cup of pineapple dice from the salad ingredients and cut into finer dice for garnish.

❀| To SERVE: In a large bowl mix the salad ingredients together. Lay a white chocolate circle in the center of each chilled plate. Place a 3-inch ring mold over each circle and fill halfway with salad, gently pressing down. Spoon lemon cream on top of the salad. Remove the ring, lay another chocolate circle on top, and garnish with coulis and small diced fruit.

SPONGE CAKE WITH SAUTÉED BANANAS AND SPICED RUM BUTTER

DAVID KENDRICK

Kendrick's
St. Croix U.S. Virgin Islands

SERVES 4

SPONGE CAKE

7	eggs
5	egg yolks
1⅓	cups (6 ounces) confectioners' sugar
2	cups flour

CARAMELIZED BANANAS

2	large bananas

¼	cup firmly packed dark brown sugar
½	cup spiced rum
½	cup (1 stick) unsalted butter
1	cup heavy (whipping) cream
	Zest of 1 lime, cut into narrow strips

❀ | TO MAKE THE SPONGE CAKE: Preheat the oven to 350°F. Spray a sheet pan with vegetable oil, cover with parchment paper, and spray again. Dust with flour. Beat the eggs and sugar on high speed for 4 to 5 minutes, until thickened and light in color. Gently fold in the flour. Pour into the prepared pan and bake for 12 to 15 minutes, until the center springs back when touched and a toothpick inserted comes out clean. Remove and cool.

❀ | TO MAKE THE CARAMELIZED BANANAS: Slice the bananas diagonally into long ovals ¼ inch thick. In a large sauté pan heat the brown sugar and spiced rum together over medium heat. Avert your face and ignite the rum with a long match; shake the pan until the flames die down, then add the banana pieces. Toss to coat. Stir in the butter.

❀ | TO SERVE: Whip the cream until it stands in soft peaks. Cut the cake into 12 circles. Place a cake round on each plate. Top with bananas and sauce. Cover with another cake round and top with more bananas and sauce. Top with a final cake round and pour the remaining sauce over the desserts. Pipe whipped cream on the tops and sprinkle with lime zest strips.

Virgin Gorda Coconut Layer Cake

John Rhymer
Little Dix Bay Resort
Virgin Gorda, British Virgin Islands

MAKES ONE 9-INCH LAYER CAKE; SERVES 8

This beautiful layer cake is unforgettable for both its taste and its presentation. An intense flavor boost comes from the toasted coconut flakes. The coconut cream can be either fresh or canned.

3   cups coconut flakes (for instructions on handling fresh coconuts, see page 240)

SPONGE CAKE

    Unsalted butter, softened
    All-purpose flour for dusting
6   whole eggs, room temperature
8   egg yolks, room temperature
1¼   cups sugar
1   cup all-purpose flour
1   cup cornstarch
½   teaspoon vanilla extract
5   tablespoons unsalted butter, melted

PASTRY CREAM

1   cup milk
1   teaspoon vanilla extract
2   egg yolks
⅓   cup sugar
2   tablespoons all-purpose flour
1   tablespoon cornstarch

ICING

2½   cups heavy (whipping) cream
½   cup sugar

PRICKLY PEAR COULIS

1   cup prickly pear juice, canned or fresh
⅓   cup sugar

FILLING

¼   cup coconut cream
1   cup Pastry Cream (above)
1   cup toasted coconut flakes (above)

GARNISH

2   cups toasted coconut flakes (above)
12   maraschino cherries, stems on
    Prickly Pear Coulis (above)
2   mangoes, skinned, pitted, and sliced
8   sprigs mint

❋ | TO TOAST THE COCONUT: Preheat the oven to 350°F. Spread coconut flakes in a thin single layer on a baking sheet. Toast in the oven for 7 to 9 minutes until golden brown.

❋ | TO MAKE THE SPONGE CAKE: Preheat the oven to 350°F. Cut 1 round of parchment paper to fit the bottom of a round 9-inch springform cake pan. Brush the cake pan evenly with softened butter, then line the cake pan with the parchment. Dust with flour, tapping out the excess.

❋ | Place the eggs, egg yolks, and sugar in the large bowl of an electric mixer. Whip on high speed until light and fluffy, 3 to 4 minutes. In a small bowl sift together the flour and cornstarch. Gently fold this mixture into the egg-sugar mixture. Fold in the vanilla and butter. Pour the batter into the prepared cake pan and bake for 30 to 35 minutes, until the blade of a small knife or a toothpick inserted in the center of the cake comes out clean. Remove from the oven and let sit for 10 minutes, then turn out onto a wire rack and cool to room temperature.

❀| TO PREPARE THE PASTRY CREAM: In a heavy-bottomed saucepan combine the milk and vanilla and bring to a boil. In a heatproof bowl combine the egg yolks and sugar and beat until thick and pale yellow. Whisk in the flour and cornstarch. Whisk in the hot milk and return the mixture to the saucepan. Bring to a boil over medium-high heat, whisking constantly. Reduce the heat and simmer 5 minutes, whisking constantly to reach all parts of the pan. Pour the cream into a shallow dish and film with butter to prevent a skin from forming. Let cool.

❀| TO MAKE THE ICING: In a medium mixing bowl whip the cream, gradually adding the sugar. Beat cream and sugar until stiff peaks form. Set aside in the refrigerator.

❀| TO PREPARE THE PRICKLY PEAR COULIS: In a medium saucepan combine the prickly pear juice and sugar. Cook over low heat until the mixture becomes syrupy. Remove from the heat and let cool to room temperature.

❀| TO ASSEMBLE: Using a sharp serrated knife, remove the crusts from the top and sides of the cake. Slice the cake evenly into 3 thin layers. Using a pastry brush, lightly dab the top surface of the bottom layer with ⅛ cup of coconut cream, following with ½ cup of the pastry cream spread in a thin layer. Top the pastry cream with ½ cup of toasted coconut flakes. Place the middle cake layer on top and press down slightly to anchor. Dab with coconut cream and spread with pastry cream; sprinkle with coconut flakes. Add the top cake layer, making sure all 3 layers are centered and even with each other; press down gently to anchor. Frost the entire cake with the whipped icing, reserving 1 cup. Using your hands, press toasted coconut flakes onto the sides of the cake. Sprinkle toasted coconut flakes on the center of the cake in a circle, leaving the outer edge open. Place the reserved icing in a pastry bag fitted with a medium fluted tip and pipe rosettes around the open area of the top, making a double circle of rosettes. Garnish the rosettes with maraschino cherries.

❀| TO SERVE: Cut the cake into slices. On dessert plates, pipe prickly pear coulis in a swirled or zigzag design on one side. Place a cake slice next to the coulis and garnish with mango slices and fresh mint.

Passion Fruit Chiboust with Exotic Fruit Sauté

PATRICK LASSAQUE
The Ritz-Carlton Cancún
Cancún, Mexico

SERVES 4

Light frozen passion fruit mousse sits atop molds of tropical fruit in a pool of orange-passion fruit sauce. The chiboust gets a broiled topping, like a crème brûlée, for this dish; to simplify, a dollop of whipped cream could crown each instead. The unusual garnish is a patchwork formed of torn phyllo dough.

PASSION FRUIT CHIBOUST

¼	gelatin packet
1	tablespoon cold water
¾	cup Passion Fruit Purée (see page 234)
¼	cup heavy (whipping) cream
4	egg yolks
2	teaspoons cornstarch
¾	cup sugar
¼	cup water
4	egg whites

EXOTIC FRUIT SAUTÉ

1	banana, split lengthwise
⅛	cup (2 tablespoons) firmly packed brown sugar
¼	cup water
½	mango, peeled, pitted, and diced
1	guava, peeled, seeded, and cut into julienne

| ⅛ | cup (2 tablespoons) sugar |
| ½ | teaspoon pectin |

PHYLLO PATCHWORK GARNISH

2	tablespoons unsalted butter
2	tablespoons Mango Purée (see page 234)
1	sheet phyllo dough

ORANGE-PASSION FRUIT SAUCE

⅔	cup Passion Fruit Purée (see page 234)
½	cup orange juice concentrate
¼	cup white sugar
⅛	teaspoon pectin
¼	cup firmly packed brown sugar
½	cup Blackberry or Strawberry Purée (see page 234)

❀ | TO MAKE THE CHIBOUST: Dissolve the gelatin in the cold water. In a heavy pan over medium heat bring the passion fruit purée and heavy cream to a boil. In a small bowl mix the egg yolks and cornstarch. Whisk in a large spoonful of the cream mixture to temper the eggs, then slowly pour the egg mixture back into the cream and purée, whisking constantly. Cook until thickened, whisking gently, about 1 minute. Remove from the heat and stir in the gelatin mixture. In a heavy pan over medium-high heat cook the sugar and water until they thicken into a clear syrup. Remove from the heat. In a deep bowl beat the egg whites until soft peaks begin to form, then slowly pour in the sugar syrup while beating until the sugar is incorporated and a shiny meringue (Italian meringue) has formed. Fold half the pastry cream into the meringue, then fold in the remaining pastry cream. Place 4 ring molds on a baking sheet or flat plate and fill with chiboust, smoothing the tops. Freeze for 2 to 4 hours.

❀| TO MAKE THE EXOTIC FRUIT SAUTÉ: Cut each banana slice in half and scoop out the center pulp and seeds. Dice the remaining banana. Put the brown sugar and water in a nonstick skillet over medium heat and stir to melt. Add the fruit, toss to coat, and sauté for 1 minute. Mix the sugar and pectin and add to the fruit mixture. Cook 30 seconds. Remove from the heat and let cool slightly. Place 4 ring molds on a baking sheet or flat plate and spoon the fruit mixture into the molds, pressing down slightly. Refrigerate for 2 to 4 hours.

❀| TO MAKE THE PHYLLO PATCHWORK GARNISH: Preheat the oven to 375°F. Butter a baking sheet. Blend the butter with the mango purée. Tear the phyllo sheet into large ragged pieces. Lay a piece of phyllo on the prepared sheet and brush with the butter mixture. Lay another piece near it, overlapping a little, and brush with the butter mixture. Continue placing pieces of phyllo irregularly over the baking sheet, overlapping them until the sheet is covered, brushing each with the butter mixture as it is placed. Bake for 5 minutes, or until golden. Let cool, lift, and break into irregular pieces.

❀| TO MAKE THE SAUCE: Mix the passion fruit purée with the orange juice concentrate and bring to a boil over medium-high heat. Mix the sugar with the pectin and stir into the purée mixture. Boil for 1 minute, remove from heat, and let cool. Chill in the refrigerator.

❀| TO SERVE: Preheat the broiler to its highest setting. Unmold the chibousts and trim with a cookie cutter to make slightly smaller than the fruit molds. Place 4 dessert plates on a baking sheet. Pool each plate with orange-passion fruit sauce. Place one fruit mold in the center of each plate and lift off the molds. Top each with a chiboust. Put a tablespoon of brown sugar on the top of each chiboust and broil just until the sugar melts; alternatively, melt the sugar with a small kitchen torch. Place the blackberry or strawberry purée in a squeeze bottle and place dots of purée around the orange-passion fruit sauce. Pull through the dots with a toothpick or the point of a sharp knife, drawing a comma shape to the outside of the sauce, to create a design. Place 3 pieces of phyllo patchwork on each plate.

ALMOND STICKS (KRANSEKAGE)

BENT RASMUSSEN
Top Hat
St. Croix, U.S. Virgin Islands

MAKES 2 DOZEN

Chef Rasmussen says this tasty recipe can be made into different forms, like cornucopias, rings, petit fours, and sticks. These almond sticks traditionally appear at anniversaries, birthdays, and weddings in Denmark.

2	pounds, 3 ounces almond paste	1	egg yolk
2	cups (1 pound) sugar	1	teaspoon cold water
6	egg whites	1	cup hazelnuts, sliced and toasted
1	pound nougat		

❀ | Line 2 baking sheets with parchment paper. Mix the almond paste and sugar together with the hook or paddle attachment of a mixer, then gradually add the egg whites. Divide the dough between 2 pastry bags, one fitted with a large round tip, and one with a large round tip with one flat side. Place the nougat in a pastry bag fitted with a medium round tip. Pipe strips of dough across the prepared pan, side to side, with the flat-sided tip, keeping the flat side up. Pipe a strip of nougat along the top of each pastry strip. Chill 15 minutes. Using the round-tip bag, pipe the pastry dough along the top of each strip, covering the nougat. Chill for 15 minutes.

❀ | Preheat the oven to 425°F. In a small bowl gently beat the egg yolk and water together to blend. Take the pastry from the refrigerator and gently press the strips down with your hands, sealing in the nougat. Brush the tops with the egg wash and sprinkle with hazelnuts. Bake for 8 to 10 minutes, until golden. Remove from the oven and cut into 3-inch segments, slicing on the diagonal. Let cool.

SWEET YUCA FRITTERS

ALFREDO AYALA

Chayote Restaurant
San Juan, Puerto Rico

SERVES 4

The yuca, or cassava, provides the sweet starch for this dish. The fritters could be served with other fruits, but the mango and rum add a distinctively "island" note to the dish.

MANGOES AND RUM

4   ripe mangoes, peeled, seeded, and sliced into thick strips
½   cup dark Puerto Rican rum
¼   cup Spanish sweet anisette
¼   cup chopped fresh tarragon leaves

YUCA FRITTERS

2   pounds yuca (cassava), peeled and grated very fine

¼   cup (½ stick) soft unsalted butter
1   whole egg
2   egg yolks
1   teaspoon baking powder
2   tablespoons sugar
    Pinch of salt
1   teaspoon anise seed

Vegetable oil for frying

❀| TO PREPARE THE MANGOES: In a medium bowl combine the mangoes, rum, and anisette. Cover and refrigerate for 3 to 4 hours.

❀| TO MAKE THE FRITTERS: In a large bowl mix the yuca and butter and add the eggs and egg yolks. Whisk together gently. Add the remaining ingredients and blend. Cover and refrigerate for 30 minutes.

❀| TO SERVE: In a deep frying pan over medium-high heat, heat 2 inches of oil to 350°F. Using a large soup spoon, drop spoonfuls of batter into the oil and fry until golden brown on all sides. Remove with a slotted spoon and drain on paper towels. Stir the tarragon leaves into the mangoes and put the mangoes on a serving plate. Garnish with flowers. Pass a bowl of fritters.

The Unnameable Dessert

Cecile Briaud

Le Chanticlair
St. Martin

SERVES 4

Frozen balls of rich chocolate ganache are tucked into beignets that are fried and placed into tuiles. With the touch of a fork, the melted ganache pours out. The dessert is served with crème anglaise and ice cream. Begin a day ahead, as the ganache balls must freeze solid.

GANACHE BALLS

10	ounces dark chocolate, roughly chopped
1	cup heavy (whipping) cream

BATTER

4	egg whites
2	tablespoons sugar
1¼	cups all-purpose flour
	Pinch of salt
1	tablespoon oil
1	large egg
⅔	cup cold beer

TUILE DOUGH

3	egg whites
½	cup sugar
¾	cup plus 1 tablespoon flour
¼	cup butter, melted
1	teaspoon vanilla extract
1	quart vegetable oil for deep frying
1	cup all-purpose flour
	Crème Anglaise (see page 234)
4	scoops vanilla ice cream
4	sprigs of mint
	Cocoa powder for dusting

❈ | To make the ganache: In a small mixing bowl set over a saucepan of hot water melt the chocolate. Stir in the cream. Pour into a heatproof shallow pan and refrigerate at least 2 hours. Line a baking sheet with waxed paper. Using a small melon baller, make small chocolate balls and place them on the prepared sheet. Freeze for 6 hours.

❈ | To make the beignet batter: Beat together the egg whites until foamy. Add the sugar and beat until the sugar is dissolved and firm peaks form. Combine the flour, salt, oil, and egg in a separate bowl, blending until smooth. Slowly add the cold beer. Fold in the egg white mixture to form a soft batter. Set the mixture aside for at least 1 hour.

❈ | To make the tuiles: In the bowl of an electric mixer beat the egg whites, sugar, and flour together. Stir until the mixture is smooth. Melt the butter over low heat. Very slowly, pour the melted butter into the batter, beating slowly to incorporate it completely. Stir in the vanilla extract. Set aside for at least 2 hours. When ready to bake, preheat the oven to 400°F. Use your hands to smear very thin 5-inch circles of dough on a Teflon baking sheet; do not let the circles touch. Dip your fingers in cold water between smears. Bake 5 minutes. Quickly lift 1 hot circle and place it in a ramekin; place a slightly smaller ramekin inside, shaping the dough into a cup. Leave 10 seconds and unmold. Repeat with remaining circles. If the tuiles begin to stiffen, place them back in the warm oven for a few moments until they become pliable. Set the molded tuile cups aside. The cooled tuile cups may be sealed tightly in plastic and stored overnight.

※| TO MAKE THE BEIGNETS: Heat the oil in a deep fryer to 350°F. Take the frozen chocolate balls from the freezer. Place the flour in a shallow bowl. Roll the chocolate balls in the flour, then spear them with a fork and dip in the batter, coating completely. Drop them into the hot fat and fry for 30 seconds, then roll them on the other side and fry 30 seconds more. They should be golden brown. Remove with a slotted spoon and drain on paper towels.

※| TO SERVE: Fill the bottom of large soup plates with crème anglaise. Center a tuile cup on each plate. Put 1 scoop of vanilla ice cream in each cup. Arrange 5 to 6 chocolate beignets on top of the ice cream in each cup and garnish the tops with mint sprigs. Sprinkle the rims of the plates with cocoa powder.

CARAMELIZED APPLE PIE WITH MANGO ICE CREAM AND FRESH FRUIT

KEITH GRIFFIN

**Lantana's
Grand Cayman**

SERVES 4

This unusual apple pie is cooked right on the serving plate, so be sure the plates you plan to use can withstand the heat. The apple slices are arranged on the plate, topped with thick caramel, and sealed under puff pastry. Chef Griffin uses mango ice cream, but you may also use any compatible flavor, such as cinnamon, vanilla, or praline.

CARAMEL SAUCE
½   cup sugar
½   cup heavy (whipping) cream

    Clarified butter for brushing
2   medium Granny Smith apples, peeled, cored, and sliced thinly
4   tablespoons Caramel Sauce (see above)
1   egg yolk

4   6-inch puff pastry rounds, rolled ⅛ inch thick
4   tablespoons sugar

4   scoops Mango Ice Cream
1   cup mixed fruits, such as star fruit, strawberries, and blackberries
    Confectioners' sugar for dusting
4   sprigs of mint

❀ | TO MAKE THE CARAMEL SAUCE: In a Teflon pan melt the sugar over medium heat, stirring occasionally with a wooden spoon. Lift off the heat, stir in the heavy cream, and return to the heat. Cook until it bubbles and pulls away from the edge of the pan. Pour the caramel into a heatproof bowl and chill, preferably overnight.

❀ | Heat the oven to 400°F. With a pastry brush, grease the bottom of 4 large heatproof dinner plates with clarified butter. Arrange the apple slices in a swirled circle on each plate and place a large spoonful of caramel sauce over the center. Brush a little egg yolk around the edges of the plate. Place a pastry circle over the apples and, with your fingertips, lightly press the edges onto the plate to seal. Repeat with the remaining plates. Brush the tops with the remaining egg yolk, sprinkle with sugar, and bake for 8 to 10 minutes or until golden brown.

❀ | Place a large scoop of ice cream directly on top of each pie. Scatter fruit over the pies and dust with confectioners' sugar. Top with mint sprigs.

CRISPY FEUILLANTINES WITH FRESH STRAWBERRIES AND CARAMEL ICE CREAM

CECILE BRIAUD

Le Chanticlair
St. Martin

SERVES 4

Caramel ice cream is layered between pastry triangles crisped with sugar and almonds. Strawberries and a berry coulis surround the pastry. For a simple version for the family, try the coulis by itself over ice cream.

RED FRUITS COULIS

1	cup strawberries, hulled
1	cup raspberries
¼	cup sugar
	Juice of ½ lemon
¾	cup water

SIMPLE SYRUP

1	cup sugar
½	cup water
1	cup sliced almonds

STRAWBERRIES

1½	cups strawberries, hulled and roughly chopped
1	cup sugar
	Juice of ½ lemon
8	sheets rice paper or phyllo dough
2	cups caramel ice cream
	Confectioners' sugar for dusting
4	mint sprigs

To MAKE THE RED FRUITS COULIS: Combine all ingredients in a saucepan and bring to a boil. Lower the heat to medium-low and simmer for 10 minutes. Press through a fine-mesh sieve and refrigerate at least 6 hours, or overnight.

To MAKE THE SIMPLE SYRUP: In a saucepan combine the sugar and water and bring to a boil. Cook for 5 minutes. Remove from the heat and let cool to room temperature.

To CARAMELIZE THE ALMONDS: Preheat the oven to 400°F. Spread one-fourth of the almonds on a teflon baking sheet and roast for 5 minutes. Remove and set aside in a bowl to cool. Toss the remaining almonds with ½ cup of the simple syrup, then spread them in a single layer on a Teflon baking sheet. Bake for 5 minutes, or until lightly colored. Remove from the oven and spread the almonds out on a cold work surface. Let cool, stirring them occasionally to make sure they do not stick.

To PREPARE THE STRAWBERRIES: Toss the strawberries, sugar, and lemon juice together in a bowl. Cover with plastic wrap and chill in the refrigerator.

To MAKE THE PASTRY TRIANGLES: Preheat the oven to 400°F. Cut the dough into 16 triangles. Place them on a Teflon baking sheet. Brush the triangles with simple syrup, flip them over, and brush the other side with simple syrup. Slice the toasted almonds and sprinkle on the triangles. Bake 5 minutes, or until the triangles are golden. Quickly remove the triangles with a spatula and cool on a clean work surface.

❀ | TO ASSEMBLE: Place a triangle in the center of each dessert plate. Place pieces of strawberries around the plate and spoon some of the fruit coulis on the strawberries. Sprinkle caramelized almonds on the strawberries. Top the triangle with a small scoop of caramel ice cream, then top with another triangle, turning the longest point at an angle to the first triangle. Top with another scoop of ice cream, another triangle, and another small scoop of ice cream. Dust the final triangle with confectioners' sugar and place on the top. Garnish with a sprig of mint.

TURTLE BAY'S CHOCOLATE-BANANA TART

ANDREW COMEY

Caneel Bay Resort
St. John, U.S. Virgin Islands

SERVES 8

A filling that includes bananas and chocolate is tucked into pastry molds. When finished, the tarts are topped with white chocolate ice cream. Serve the tarts warm from the oven.

WHITE CHOCOLATE ICE CREAM

5	egg yolks
1	cup sugar
3	cups light cream
14	ounces white chocolate, chopped
1½	cups heavy (whipping) cream

SWEET DOUGH

½	cup (1 stick) unsalted butter
¾	cup confectioners' sugar
2	eggs
2	cups all-purpose flour
2	teaspoons vanilla extract

FILLING

3	bananas
4	ounces white chocolate, chopped
4	ounces unsweetened chocolate, chopped
½	cup corn syrup
1	cup sugar
4	eggs
½	cup (1 stick) butter, melted

GARNISH

2	large bananas, cut into thin strips
8	large strawberries
½	cup berries (blackberries, raspberries, or blueberries, or a mixture)
1	cup Caramel Sauce (see page 239)

❀ | TO PREPARE THE WHITE CHOCOLATE ICE CREAM: Whisk together the egg yolks and sugar until pale yellow in color. In a heavy medium saucepan over medium-high heat, bring the light cream to a boil. Whisking gently, slowly pour one-fourth of the hot cream into the egg mixture, then pour the egg-hot cream mixture back into the saucepan of hot cream and stir to blend. Cook over low heat until it thickens and coats the back of a spoon.

❀ | Place the white chocolate in a heatproof bowl and pour the hot egg-cream mixture over the chocolate. Let stand for 2 minutes, then stir to blend completely. Stir in the heavy cream and let the mixture cool to room temperature. Follow the manufacturer's directions on your ice cream machine to freeze the mixture.

❀ | TO PREPARE THE DOUGH: In a medium bowl cream the butter and sugar until fluffy. Stir in the eggs and mix well. Add the flour and vanilla and blend until just combined. Refrigerate until firm. Roll the dough out ⅛ inch thick. Cut circles from the dough and line eight 4-inch tart molds, pressing into place with your fingers.

❀│ Preheat the oven to 350°F. Peel and chop the bananas into large pieces, and divide the pieces among the molds. Divide the white chocolate among the molds and sprinkle over the bananas. In the top of a double boiler set over barely simmering water melt the chocolate. In a medium bowl stir together the corn syrup, sugar, and eggs. Add the butter to the chocolate, then slowly pour into the egg mixture, stirring until blended. Pour the chocolate filling over the bananas and white chocolate, filling the molds to the top. Bake for 20 minutes, or until set. Remove from oven and let cool for 20 to 30 minutes.

❀│ To SERVE: Unmold each tart and cut a large wedge from one side. Place 1 tart and wedge together on each plate, with the wedge slightly separated from the tart. Place 3 banana strips on each plate. Place berries at one end of the banana strips. Place the caramel sauce in a squeeze bottle and drizzle 3 bands of sauce on each plate. Place a scoop of ice cream on the bananas, which will keep the ice cream from sliding on the plate.

BANANA-CHOCOLATE TART WITH HAZELNUT SAUCE

PATRICK LASSAQUE
The Ritz-Carlton Cancún
Cancún, Mexico

SERVES 6

Caramelized banana slices are hidden beneath the rich chocolate filling of this dessert. The flavors are further intensified by the hazelnut crust and a garnish of praline crème anglaise.

SWEET DOUGH TART SHELLS

½   cup unsalted butter at room temperature
½   cup confectioners' sugar
⅓   cup hazelnut powder
1   egg
2   cups unbleached all-purpose flour

CHOCOLATE FILLING

7   ounces semisweet chocolate, melted
¾   cup plus 2 tablespoons (7 ounces) milk
½   cup sugar
¼   cup cocoa powder
6   tablespoons unsalted butter at room
        temperature

CARAMELIZED BANANAS

2   tablespoons water
4   tablespoons firmly packed brown sugar
2   bananas, sliced ¼ inch thick

PRALINE CRÈME ANGLAISE

4   egg yolks
¼   cup plus 2 tablespoons sugar
7   tablespoons (3½ ounces) milk
10   ounces heavy (whipping) cream
½   cup praline paste

CHOCOLATE SAUCE

3½   ounces heavy (whipping) cream
1   tablespoon sugar
1½   ounces bittersweet chocolate, chopped

GARNISH

½   cup Chocolate Sauce (above)
½   cup Praline Crème Anglaise (above)
    Cocoa powder for dusting
    Chocolate shavings

❈| TO MAKE THE TART SHELLS: In the bowl of an electric mixer combine the butter and confectioners' sugar. Whip together, then add the hazelnut powder and beat until mixed. Add the egg and beat again until the mixture is light and fluffy. Add the flour all at once, mixing by hand just until the mixture holds together. Form the dough into a ball, wrap in plastic wrap, and chill at least 2 hours before rolling out for the tart shells.

❈| Preheat the oven to 350°F. Roll the dough to ⅛-inch thickness, using a small amount of flour to keep the dough from sticking to the work surface and rolling pin. For 4-inch tart rings, cut 6-inch circles from the dough. Carefully press each circle into a tart ring, removing excess dough around the top edge. Using plastic bags filled with rice, press one bag into each tart ring to weigh down the dough. Remove the rice bags and place the tart shells on a baking sheet. Bake for 8 to 10 minutes, until the shells are light golden brown. Remove from the oven and set aside to cool.

❀ | To MAKE THE CHOCOLATE FILLING: Place the melted chocolate in a warmed heatproof bowl. In a large pan warm the milk, then add the sugar and cocoa. Bring to a boil over medium heat, stirring constantly. Strain through a fine-mesh sieve over the melted chocolate and stir to blend. Add the butter and stir until the butter is completely melted and the mixture is smooth and shiny.

❀ | To MAKE THE CARAMELIZED BANANAS: In a medium skillet over medium-high heat, stir the water and brown sugar to blend. Add the banana slices and cook until slightly softened, 30 to 45 seconds.

❀ | To ASSEMBLE THE TARTS: Make a single layer of banana slices in the bottom of each tart shell. Pour the chocolate filling over the banana slices to fill the shells. Refrigerate for 15 minutes.

❀ | To MAKE THE PRALINE CRÈME ANGLAISE: In a small mixing bowl beat the egg yolks and add the sugar. In a large skillet mix the milk with the cream and bring to a boil over medium heat. Stir in the egg yolk mixture and the praline paste, and cook until the mixture coats the back of the spoon, stirring constantly. Remove from the heat and pour this mixture into a bowl that is placed in a larger bowl filled with ice water to quickly chill the sauce. Place the sauce in a squeeze bottle.

❀ | To MAKE THE CHOCOLATE SAUCE: In a medium skillet over medium heat, mix the cream with the sugar and bring to a boil. Put the chocolate in a heatproof bowl and pour the cream mixture over it. Let sit for 1 minute, then gently stir until smooth. Put the sauce in a squeeze bottle.

❀ | To SERVE: Place a tart to one side of each serving plate. Decorate one side of each plate with swirls of chocolate sauce and praline crème anglaise. Dust the other side of the plate with cocoa powder. Decorate with chocolate shavings.

HAZELNUT NAPOLEON FILLED WITH CHOCOLATE-KAHLUA MOUSSE AND PASSION FRUIT GRANITE

JOSEF TEUSCHLER

Four Seasons Resort Nevis
Nevis

MAKES 13 NAPOLEONS

These are traditional napoleons, made of of hazelnut meringue sponge layered with chocolate-kahlua mousse and iced with dark and white chocolate. The passion fruit granite and lace cookie baskets are optional; the dessert is elegant without them. There's an extra bonus: cutting the napoleon strip into triangles leaves two tiny triangles on each end, just right for sampling!

PASSION FRUIT GRANITE

1	cup sugar
1	cup water
½	cup dry white wine
2	cups Passion Fruit Purée (see page 234)

HAZELNUT MERINGUE SPONGE

16	egg whites
2½	cups sugar
2½	cups ground hazelnuts

CHOCOLATE-KAHLUA MOUSSE

1½	packets unflavored gelatin
⅓	cup cold water
1	pound semi-sweet chocolate, chopped
7	egg yolks
¾	cup confectioners' sugar
½	cup kahlua liqueur
1½	cups heavy (whipping) cream

4	ounces semisweet chocolate, chopped
1	ounce white chocolate, chopped

LACE COOKIE BASKETS

6	ounces (1½ sticks) unsalted butter
⅔	cup sugar
¾	cup corn syrup
2	tablespoons orange juice
1	cup plus 2 tablespoons unsifted flour

CHOCOLATE GARNISH

8	ounces bittersweet chocolate, chopped
12	strawberries
12	kumquats, sliced
6	passion fruit, quartered
	Confectioners' sugar for dusting
1½	cups Mango Purée (see page 234)

✣ | TO MAKE THE GRANITE: In a saucepan bring the sugar and water to a boil over medium-high heat. Remove from the heat and let cool to room temperature. Stir in the white wine and passion fruit purée. Pour into a shallow layer in a 2-inch-deep metal baking pan and freeze until slushy. Stir with a fork and let freeze again. Stir again with a fork, and let freeze again.

✣ | TO MAKE THE SPONGE: Preheat the oven to 350°F. Line two 14 x 16-inch sheet pans with parchment paper. Beat the egg whites until foamy, then add the sugar gradually while beating until stiff, glossy peaks form. Fold in the ground hazelnuts. Spread out ¾ inch thick on the prepared pan. Bake for 10 minutes or until crisp. Remove from the oven and let cool. The meringue will flatten slightly.

✿ | To MAKE THE MOUSSE: Dissolve the gelatin in the cold water. Melt the 1 pound of chocolate in the top of a double boiler over barely simmering water. In a medium bowl beat the egg yolks and sugar until light. Fold the chocolate into the egg mixture. Add the gelatin and stir until completely dissolved. Stir in the kahlua. Beat the cream until soft peaks form. Gently fold the cream into the chocolate mixture.

✿ | To ASSEMBLE THE NAPOLEON: Place a large wire rack in a large baking sheet. In separate small pans melt the 4 ounces of semisweet chocolate and 1 ounce of white chocolate held over barely simmering water. Place the white chocolate in a small squeeze bottle. Gently lift the meringue sponge out of the pans and place on a work surface. Cut each meringue sponge crosswise into 3 equal pieces (pieces will measure approximately 5¼ x 14 inches). Trim the sponge so that all pieces are the same size. Begin with a layer of sponge placed on the wire rack; spread a layer of mousse on the sponge, covering edge to edge. Top with another piece of sponge, and spread with another layer of mousse. Continue until you have 6 layers of sponge and 5 layers of mousse. Gently press together. Ladle the melted semisweet chocolate over the top layer of sponge, letting it run down the sides. Spread smooth with a spatula. Working diagonally from one corner across the top of the glaze to the opposite corner, draw lines across the top of the napoleon with the white chocolate. Pull across the lines at right angles with a toothpick or sharp knife, spacing the pulls about 3 inches apart. Then pull back in the opposite direction between the first pulls, forming a feathered design. Refrigerate to set.

✿ | To MAKE THE COOKIE BASKETS: Preheat the oven to 400°F. Grease and flour a baking sheet. Cream the butter and sugar together until light. Stir in the corn syrup, orange juice, and flour. Drop the batter on the prepared sheet by rounded teaspoonfuls and spread into a circle with the back of the spoon. Bake for 4 to 6 minutes until the edges of the cookies are lightly browned. Remove from the oven and immediately press down over the bottoms of inverted small cups or glasses to form into baskets. If the cookies become too cool to form, rewarm by placing them back in the oven.

✿ | To MAKE THE CHOCOLATE GARNISHES: In the top of a double boiler melt the chocolate over simmering water. Spread heavy plastic on a work area. Pour the chocolate on the plastic and spread it out just under ¼ inch thick. Let cool until the surface just loses its gloss, then cut through the chocolate in abstract S-shaped curves, making 12 long thin curving pieces. Peel the extra chocolate away from the garnishes, and chill the garnishes to set. The extra chocolate may be remelted and reused.

✿ | To SERVE: Cut the napoleons into triangles: Measure 2-inch intervals down one long side of the strip. Measure in 1 inch from the end of the other side of the strip and then again measure 2-inch intervals, ending with 1 inch left over. Using a very sharp knife or an electric knife, cut diagonally from mark to mark, creating 13 triangles. Clean the knife blade between each cut. With a small sharp knife, slice the strawberries almost all the way through from the tip up to the green top, leaving the top attached; fan out. Slice the kumquats crosswise into circles. Quarter the passion fruit. Dust the plates with confectioners' sugar. Draw a zigzag of mango purée on each serving plate. Stand one napoleon point up on each serving plate. Place a cookie basket on each plate, anchoring it in the coulis. Place 2 passion fruit quarters on each plate. Garnish each plate with kumquat slices, a chocolate garnish, mint leaf, and strawberry fan. Stir the granite again with a fork and fill the cookie cups with a scoop of granite.

PITHIVIERS

PIERRE CASTAGNE
Le Perroquet
St. Maarten

SERVES 6 TO 8

Pithiviers is named after the town of Pithiviers in France, where its swirled design and almond filling are a signature. It is made with puff pastry, which must be kept cold while you are working with it. If it begins to lose its stiffness, chill it for 15 to 20 minutes before continuing. Chill the filling as well before assembling the pithiviers, and work in a cool room. The good news is that good puff pastry dough is available in the freezer section of most large groceries.

FRANGIPANE FILLING

2¼	cups (4½ sticks) unsalted butter
1½	cups sugar
4	whole eggs
¾	cup all-purpose flour
2	cups almond powder
3	tablespoons rum

PASTRY

2	12-inch circles of puff pastry, rolled ⅛ inch thick
1	egg
1	teaspoon water

❊ | TO PREPARE THE FRANGIPANE FILLING: In the bowl of an electric mixer or food processor, cream the butter and sugar until the mixture is light and fluffy. Beat in the eggs 1 at a time, and beat for another 3 minutes. Add the flour and beat to incorporate completely. Add the almond powder, and beat to incorporate completely. Add the rum and beat for 30 more seconds. Chill for 30 minutes.

❊ | TO MAKE THE PITHIVIERS: Line a baking sheet with parchment paper. Place 1 of the pastry circles on the baking sheet. Mound the filling in the center. Brush the edge around the filling with cold water, and cover the filling with the second circle of pastry. Press the edges together to seal.

❊ | Cover the mound formed by the filling with an inverted bowl or cake pan that allows about ½ inch of the pastry to peek out all around. Using a small knife, cut 1½-inch scallops all around the dough. Press down firmly with the bowl or cake pan to seal, and refrigerate for 20 minutes. The pithiviers may be frozen at this point, then taken from the freezer at a later date; begin working on it as soon as the knife will penetrate the dough.

❊ | Just before baking, slightly beat the egg with the water. Preheat the oven to 450°F. Butter a 4-inch circle of aluminum foil, twist it into a narrow cone, and cut off the bottom to create a chimney. Brush the top of the pithiviers with egg glaze. Cut a small hole in the center of the top and insert the chimney. Brush the pithiviers with a second coating of egg glaze. With the point of a small sharp knife, begin at the chimney and cut a spiral line around the filling and out to meet one of the indentations of the scallops. Cut through the glaze and slightly into the dough. Repeat all the way around the pithiviers.

❀| Place immediately in the oven and bake for 25 to 30 minutes, until the pastry is puffed and golden brown. If it is getting too brown on top, lay a piece of parchment or foil loosely over the top. Remove from the oven and remove the funnel.

❀| Heat the broiler to very high, or use a small blowtorch. Dust the top with confectioners' sugar. Place the pithiviers under the broiler until the sugar melts into a shiny coating. Or, quickly toast the sugar with a small blowtorch. Cool the pithiviers on a rack.

TIRAMISU

ERNESTO GARRIGOS
Virgilio's
St. Thomas, U.S. Virgin Islands

MAKES 30

This popular dessert "pick me up" layers ladyfingers soaked in strong coffee with cream. Chef Garrego tops his with a layer of chocolate, and a dollop of whipped cream. The tiramisu must be well chilled to hold its shape when cut.

3	packets unflavored gelatin
¾	cup cold water
3	cups heavy (whipping) cream
3	tablespoons kahlua or other coffee-flavored liqueur
3	cups Mascarpone cheese
3	ladyfingers
2	cups strong black coffee

GANACHE

1	pound bittersweet chocolate, chopped
1¼	cups heavy (whipping) cream
1	cup heavy (whipping) cream
¼	cup sugar
	Ground cinnamon for sprinkling

❀ | To MAKE THE CREAM: Dissolve the gelatin in the cold water and let stand for 5 minutes. In a large bowl combine the gelatin, cream, kahlua, and Mascarpone and whisk together gently to blend, then whip to form soft peaks.

❀ | To MAKE THE TIRAMISU: Line a 9 x 13-inch rectangular baking dish or pan with parchment paper. Dip each ladyfinger in the coffee, then place in the pan, lining the bottom of the pan completely with a layer of ladyfingers. Spread one-third of the cream over the ladyfingers. Dip and place a second layer of ladyfingers. Spread with one-third of the cream. Dip and place the third and final layer of ladyfingers, and spread with the remaining cream. Refrigerate until chilled.

❀ | To MAKE THE GANACHE: In a double boiler over simmering water melt 12 ounces of the chocolate. Gently stir the cream into the chocolate. Remove the chocolate from the heat, pour into a heat-proof bowl, and stir in the remaining chopped chocolate. Set aside to cool; when the chocolate is at room temperature, put it in the refrigerator for 5 minutes.

❀ | To FINISH THE TIRAMISU: Take the tiramisu and ganache out of the refrigerator, and gently spread the thickening chocolate over the tiramisu. Smooth the top, cover with plastic wrap, and refrigerate until firm, at least 2 hours.

❀ | To SERVE: In the deep bowl of an electric mixer, beat the cream until soft peaks form. Slowly add the sugar while beating, then beat to firm peaks. Cut the tiramisu into 2-inch squares. Place a square on a serving plate and sprinkle with cinnamon. Top with a dollop of whipped cream.

Cognac-poached Plums with Chocolate Truffle and Champagne Granite

Kyle Kingrey

Villa Madeleine
St. Croix, U.S. Virgin Islands

SERVES 4

Luscious cognac-poached plum slices combine with a champagne granite-filled tuile cup and dense chocolate truffle for this beautiful dessert plate.

Champagne Granite

1½	cups water
¾	cup sugar
1½	cups champagne

Chocolate Truffles

12	ounces unsweetened chocolate bits
2	egg yolks
½	ounce cognac

Chocolate Garnish

4	ounces bittersweet chocolate, chopped

Plums and Plum Sauce

2	large ripe plums, split in half and pitted
1	cup cognac
½	cup sugar
1	tablespoon water
1	teaspoon arrowroot
3	teaspoons cold water
4	Tuile Cups (recipe follows)
4	chocolate truffle candies

❀ | To make the granite: In a medium pan over medium-low heat stir together the water, sugar, and half the champagne. Simmer for 3 minutes, remove from the heat, and let stand to cool to room temperature. Add the remaining champagne and stir to blend. Cool, then freeze in a shallow metal pan or baking dish, stirring the mixture with a fork every 30 minutes as it freezes. The crystals will be coarse.

❀ | To make the truffles: Melt the chocolate in the top of a double boiler over barely simmering water. Gently whisk in the yolks, then the cognac. Remove from the heat and let cool to room temperature. Roll tablespoon-size pieces into balls. Set aside in a cool, dry place.

❀ | To make the chocolate garnish: Spread heavy plastic, foil, or parchment paper on a baking sheet. In the top of a double boiler melt the chocolate over barely simmering water. Remove from the heat and place in a squeeze bottle. Draw 12-inch-long squiggles with the chocolate on the prepared baking sheet. Let cool, then refrigerate until firm.

❀ | To make the plums and sauce: In a saucepan combine the ingredients and bring to a boil over medium-high heat. Reduce the heat to medium-low and simmer until tender, 8 to 10 minutes. Remove the pan from the heat and lift out the plums with a slotted spoon. Set aside. Dissolve the arrowroot in the 3 teaspoons of cold water and stir into the poaching liquid to thicken. Place in a squeeze bottle.

❀| TO SERVE: Slice each plum piece in half. For each dessert plate, cut a plum quarter into 4 slivers and arrange like petals across one side of the plate. Put a dot of plum syrup on the other side of the plate, and anchor a tuile cup in the syrup. Put another large dot of plum syrup next to the cup, and place a truffle on it. Place a chocolate squiggle garnish diagonally across the center of the plate, dividing the plum slices from the tuile and truffle. Take the granite out of the freezer and let soften slightly. Just before serving, stir the granite one final time and place a scoop in each tuile.

TUILE CUPS

(MAKES 8)

½	cup (1 stick) unsalted butter, at room temperature	1	egg, beaten
¾	cup sugar	2	egg whites, slightly beaten
1⅓	cups cake flour	1	teaspoon vanilla extract

❀| Preheat the oven to 325°F. Butter and lightly flour 2 baking sheets. In a medium bowl cream the butter and sugar together. Gradually stir in the cake flour until smooth. Stir in the egg, egg whites, and vanilla. Spread on the prepared pan in 8-inch circles, 4 inches apart. Bake for 10 to 12 minutes, until the edges are browned and the centers are cooked through. Remove from the oven and immediately press down gently over inverted cups or bowls, forming into cups; if the tuiles become brittle, rewarm for a few moments in the oven to soften. Let cool to crisp. Extra cups may be put in an airtight container when cold and stored up to 2 days.

Strawberry Brulée Napoleon

Kyle Kingrey

Villa Madeleine
St. Croix, U.S.V.I.

SERVES 4

Slices of baked cream are stacked between crisp phyllo with strawberries and topped with brown sugar which is melted over the strawberries. Melting the top of any brulee is tricky: if you make creme brulee often, invest in a small cooking torch. Otherwise, use the highest setting on your broiler and place the dessert as close to the heat as possible for as short a time as possible.

BAKED CREAM

    Milk
2   vanilla beans, split
2   eggs
    Sugar

PHYLLO CRISPS

4   sheets of phyllo

½   cup (1 stick) unsalted butter, melted
    Sugar for dusting

2   pints strawberries, hulled and halved
¾   cup firmly packed brown sugar
4   mint sprigs
4   Tuile Palms (recipe follows)
1   cup Strawberry Coulis (see page 234)

❀ | TO MAKE THE BAKED CREAM: Place a large baking pan of water on the bottom rack of the oven. Preheat the oven to 350 F. Put the milk in a deep heavy pan over medium-high heat. Scrape the seeds from the vanilla bean pods into the milk, then drop the pods into the milk. Bring the milk just to the boiling point and remove from heat. Set aside. In a large heat-proof bowl, whisk the eggs and sugar together to blend. Pour the milk into the eggs through a strainer, the immediately whisk the egg mixture to blend and cool it. Pour into a large square pan so that the cream mixture is about ½-inch thick. Bake on the upper rack of the oven, above the water bath, for 4 minutes, until firm. Remove from oven and let cool to room temperature; cover with plastic wrap and refrigerate.

❀ | TO MAKE THE PHYLLO CRISPS: Preheat the oven to 375 F. Line a baking pan with parchment paper. Spread a sheet of phyllo dough on a flat work surface and top with another sheet of phyllo. Spread with melted butter and sprinkle with a coating of sugar. Top with two more sheets of phyllo and gently press them together. Brush the top sheet with more butter and sugar. Cut into 20 squares. With a wide spatula, lift the phyllo squares and place them in the prepared pan. Dust liberally with more sugar. Bake 4 - 5 minutes, until crisp and lightly browned. Remove from oven and let cool.

❀ | TO SERVE: Preheat the broiler to highest setting, or use a small kitchen torch. Place the brulee squares on a baking sheet. Place four strawberry halves on top of each square. Top each with a tablespoon of brown sugar. Melt the sugar with a torch, or place as close as possible to the broiler and melt the sugar, removing immediately. Place the strawberry coulis in a squeeze bottle and draw a rough square on each dessert plate using two lines for each side. Place a piece of phyllo crisp in the center of each. Put a brulée square on top of each phyllo crisp. Top with a second layer of phyllo crisps and brulée squares. Garnish the dishes with more strawberries and a mint leaf. Lean a palm tuile against each stack.

TUILE PALMS

(MAKES 8)

½	cup (1 stick) unsalted butter, at room temperature	1	egg, beaten
¾	cup sugar	2	egg whites, slightly beaten
1⅓	cups cake flour	1	teaspoon vanilla extract

❀ | Preheat the oven to 325°F. Trace a palm tree shape on a thin piece of cardboard or stiff plastic and cut out to form a stencil. Butter and lightly flour 2 baking sheets. In a medium bowl, cream the butter and sugar together. Gradually stir in the cake flour until smooth. Stir in the egg, egg whites, and vanilla. Place the stencil on the pan and spread a thin layer of dough across the stencil, smoothing with the back of a spoon. Lift the stencil, clean, and repeat, about 4 inches apart. Bake for 8 to 10 minutes, until the edges are browned and the centers are cooked through. Remove from oven and let cool to crisp. Extra tuiles may be put in an airtight container when cold and stored up to 2 days.

THE CHEFS

Thierry Alix
La Samanna, St. Martin

Executive chef Theirry Alix draws inspiration for the innovative cuisine at La Samanna from his world travels. Chef Alix's cooking is based in traditional French cuisine that has been accented with native Caribbean and Creole spices.

Before working at La Samanna, Chef Alix served as Executive Chef at The Plantation Club, an exclusive resort in Seychelles, and as executive chef at the prestigious Camino Real in Mexico. He began his career in Normandy, France as an apprentice. He received his degree from Hotel de Cheval Blanc in Vire, France.

Alfredo N. Ayala
Chayote Restaurant, San Juan, Puerto Rico

Alfredo Ayala is the chef-owner of Chayote Restaurant. He trained with Eric Ripert, chef of Le Bernardin Restaurant in New York, and spent two months in France at Joel Robuchon's Restaurant JAMIN.

Since living in Puerto Rico, Chef Alaya has been involved in several fine restaurants, including Su Casa Restaurant in the Hyatt Dorado Beach, Chayote Restaurant, Yukiyu Restaurant and Sushi Bar, and Ali-Oli Resaurant.

Janice Barber
The White House Inn, St. Kitts, West Indies

In 1988 Janice Barber and her husband, after changing both career and lifestyle, bought The White House, an old Plantation house in St. Kitts. The White House Inn was opened in 1990 and Janice began to cook for guests of the Inn using only the information from books and TV programs as her guide.

After six sucessful years of cooking at The White House Inn, Janice opened The Georgian House in Basseterre, the capital of St. Kitts. Both inns offer fine dining in 18th century houses.

Stéphane Bois
Village St. Jean, St. Barts

Chef Stéphane Bois has worked at many fine restaurants in Paris, as well as the Caribbean. He started as an apprentice in 1983 at Restaurant Olympe, a 2-star restaurant in Paris, and then became chef de partie at Restaurant Lucas Carton, a 3-star restaurant. While in Paris he moved to the position of second de cuisine at Bains Douches, Palace, and Piscine d'Eliny, and then chef de cuisine at Comptoire. Chef Bois moved to St. Barthélémy as second de cuisine at Restaurant Hibiscus, and then Restaurant Captain Monbars. In 1991 he became the chef de cuisine at Restaurant Maya's, and then worked at the Mayotte Océan Indien.'

Chef Bois is currently working at Le Patio, at Village St. Jean.

Kevin Boxx
The Ritz-Carlton St. Thomas, U.S. Virgin Islands

Kevin Boxx began his career pursuing an engineering and math degree until his infatuation and fascination with baking wooed him out of the classroom and into the kitchen. It is with a keen architectural eye that Kevin masterminds whimsical concoctions with detailed flair.

Kevin performed externships at The Ritz-Carlton Amelia Island and The Ritz-Carlton, San Francisco before graduating from the New England Culinary School in Essex, Vermont. He joined the pastry team at The Ritz-Carlton Amelia Island and was promoted to pastry chef ten months later. His artistic desserts helped The Grill win the prestigious AAA Five Diamond Award in 1995 and 1996, making it one of only two Five Diamond restaurants in the state. In 1996, Chef Boxx joined The Ritz-Carlton, St. Thomas as the pastry chef.

Cecile Briaud
Chanteclair Restarant, St. Martin

Cecile Briaud is the chef-owner of the Chanteclair Restaurant. She trained at the Hotel and Catering High School in La Rochelle earning her BTS Catering, BTH Cooking, and CAP Service. She gained experience at the Le Crillion, Le Concorde Lafayette, the Flo Prestige Laboratory and the Fauchon Patisserie, all in Paris.

Chef Briaud's professional experiences include Chef of Le Cottage Restaurant in Grand Case, Second chef at the Chez Martime Rstaurant in Grand Case, Chef De Partie at the Le Carre Des feuillants in Paris, Aide to the pastry chef at the Hotel Le Crillon in Paris, and Aide to the chef at the Le Martinez Hotel, La Palme d' Or in Cannes.

Richard Buttafuso
The Sugar Mill, British Virgin Islands

Chef Rick Buttafuso was born in Connecticut. Following high school, he worked for an inn in Vermont and then moved on to a famous local Jewish delicatessan where he worked intermittently throughout college. After a one year course in the Connecticut Culinary Arts Program, Rick enrolled at the Culinary Institute of America to increase his knowledge of European cuisine with a heavy emphasis on French food. He interned at the Beverly Hilton Hotel as pastry chef.

Chef Buttafuso then joined Lucians restaurant as sous chef, learning many Italian dishes at this well respected restaurant. Continuing the European theme, he moved to Deer Island Gate Restaurant, again as sous chef, gaining experience in German cuisine.

In 1993 he joined the Sugar Mill team in the British Virgin Islands as executive chef at age 24.

Pierre Castagne
Le Perroquet, St. Maarten, Netherlands
Pierre Castagne is the chef-owner of Le Perroquet Restaurant. He trained at Relais de la Belle Aurore and Hotelschool Rue Jean Merderie, both in Paris. Since 1964 Castagne has been a member of La Chaine des Rotisseurs, L'Ordre dos Coteaux de Champagne, and Commanderie des Cordon Bleus de France-Dijon.

Chef Castagne has gained experience at many fine restaurants including Chez Drouant, Chez Maxime, and Au Fouguets in Paris. He has been chef de cuisine at Royal Champagne in Epernay, TEN-BEL Resort at Tenerife Canary Islands in Spain, Le Bistroquet at The Hauge, and Do Hoefslag in Zeist, Netherlands. He has also been manager as well as chef de cuisine at Alt Munchen in Lome, Togo, and La Grenouille in St. Maarten.

Michel Chiche
Hotel La Samana, St. Martin
Chef Michel Chiche has been the Pastry Chef at Hotel La Samana since 1992. There he is responsible for the creation of their fabulous pastries and sugar sculptures.

Chef Chiche studied at Hottellerie College in Nice, France. He apprenticed at Capa Patisserie in Nice, France. He has recieved personal training from Michel Richard since he bagan his career. Before coming to Hotel La Samana, Chef Chiche worked at several well recognized restaurants and hotels including the five-star Beverly Hills Hotel.

Andrew F. Comey
Caneel Bay Resort, St. John
Chef Andrew Comey is the Pastry Chef at Caneel Bay Resort where he is responsible for the design and creation of the pastries served to guests of the resort.

Chef Comey was trained at the Culinary Institute of America in Hyde Park, New York. He then went to the International Pastry Arts Center in Elmsford, New York where he studied with Albert Kumin. He began his career at Branches Restaurant in North Branch, New Jersey.

From there he went to the Headquarters Plaza Hotel in Morristown, New Jersey, then Atlanta, Georgia, at the Hyatt Regency Atlanta and the Capitol City Club. He moved to Maryland and worked at the Center Club in Baltimore and the Historic Inns of Annapolis in Annapolis.

Jeremie Cruz
Cassave Restaurant, Puerto Rico
Jeremie Cruz was born and raised on the beautiful tropical island of Puerto Rico. Since childhood he was interested in learning to cook. At the age of 17 he started working at a bakeshop in Ceiba, Puerto Rico. At the age of 18 he became a prep cook at Isabela's Restaurant, a Mediterranean restaurant at El Conquistador. Two months later her was promoted to Commis I. Within eight months he was promoted once again and granted a scholarship to The Culinary Institue of America.

Mark Ehrler
The Ritz-Carlton Cancun, Mexico
It's not unusual to see Marc Ehrler, the executive chef at The Ritz-Carlton Cancun, arrive at the local marketplace riding his customized Harley Davidson. A thoroughly modern chef, this native of Provence, France brings innovation and creativity to his interpretation of traditional and regional cuisine.

At The Ritz-Carlton, Chef Ehrler works with a highly trained team of culinary experts to plan menus and create dishes at The Cafe, The Club Grill, Fantino, and The Caribe Bar and Grill. He came to The Ritz-Carlton Cancun in 1995 after garnering rave reviews at San Ysidro Ranch in Santa Barbara, California and La Sammana on St. Maarten.

Philippa Esposito
Le Bistro, St. Johns, Antigua
Philippa Esposito is the proprietor-patisserie chef of Le Bistro, the first authentic French restaurant in Antigua. Le Bistro is situated five minutes from the sea in the countryside in Hodges Bay.

Before coming to Le Bistro, Philippa Espisito trained at the Park Hotel in Brunnen, Switzerland, as well as working at Noah's Ark in Oxford, England and Columbo's Restaurant, an Italian restaurant in Antigua, as the proprietor-patisserie chef.

Philip Fitzpatrick
Villa Madeleine, St. Croix
Chef Philip Fitzpatrick started out in New York at Panza's Restaurant in Saratoga Springs, and worked his way up to executive chef while there. He then worked at the Queensbury Hotel, the Parkwood Restaurant, and then Sheraton Hotel and Conference Center and Siro's in Saratoga Springs. In 1998, Chef Fitzpatrick moved to St. Croix as the executive chef of Villa Madeleine, where he

has created a new concept and a menu of Island-influenced American cuisine.

Christopher George Fulcher
Old Stone Farmhouse, St. Thomas

Chef Fulcher has been in the restaurant business for thirteen years. He studies at Southeast Institute of Culinary Arts in St. Augustine, Florida where he completed the apprentice program in 1994.

Before becoming executive chef at the Old Stone Farmhouse, Chef Fulcher was the executive chef at La Scala on St. Thomas and at Paridiso on St. John.

The Old Stone Farmhouse was once the hub of a 250-acre sugar plantation over 2 centuries, having withstood countless assaults by wind, fire, and storms (including Hurricane Hugo). The Old Stone Farmhouse offers the nostalgia of a by gone era and gourmet cuisine at its best.

Martin Frost
Four Seasons Resort, Nevis

A native of London, Chef Martin Frost discovered his passion for cooking when he was 12, working in his father's seafood restaurant. He studied at the Westminster Hotel School, earning several medals in culinary competition. Early in his career he worked in London at the Inter-Continental Hotel and at the Park Tower Hotel. He then signed on with Four Seasons-Regent Hotels and Resorts and worked at the Four Seasons Hotel London.

From London to Toronto, and on to San Francisco at Four Seasons-Regent hotels, Frost's creativity and talent drew acclaim. In San Francisco he headed the kitchens at the famed Four Seasons Clift Hotel.

Frost now directs two gourmet restaurants, the 24-hour room service, and the Cabana restaurant at the Four Seasons Resort, Nevis, with a team of 40.

Ernesto Garrigos
Virgilio's, St. Thomas, U.S. Virgin Islands

Chef Ernesto Garrigos is the executive chef at Virgilio's, responsible for all kitchen operations and menu design. He has assisted Virgilio de Mare, the owner of Virgilio's, in redesigning the kitchen in the restaurant. Prior to arriving in St. Thomas, Chef Garrigos was the executive chef at the 4-star Virgilio's Restaurant in Los Angeles.

As an apprentice, Chef Garrigos the sous chef under Salvatorie Cabsallo, a chef from Sicily Palermo, Italy, and the pantry chef under Antonio Orlando, a chef from Naples, Italy, making all homemade pasta, and his duties included garde manager, and roundsman.

Patrick Gateau
The Carl Gustav, St. Barthélemy, French West Indes

Patrick Gateau was born in Paris. He learned to discriminate fine tastes even as a child, the son of parents who were butchers and skilled in the art of charcuterie. He

apprenticed, then began his career at Hotel de Crillon, an Michelin four-star hotel and a Gault Millau selection. He continued at the Hotel de Paris in Moulins, and the Toque Royale in Casino d'Evian. Gateau moved to Monte Carlo to work at Bec Rouge, and to Beaune to work at Cheval Noir, his first position as sous chef. He moved to Chateau d"Artigny in Montbazon, and then the Site du Cap Chabian at Port Camargue. The step across the ocean to St. Barthélemy is long in miles only; St. Barts is French in language and culinary tradition. At The Carl Gustav, Patrick Gateau has arrived at the position of Chef de Cuisine, responsible for all of the provisioning and preparation, and for the restaurant personnel.

Patrick Gauducheau
Le Bistro, St. Johns, Antigua

Patrick Gauducheau is the chef de cuisine at Le Bistro, a gourmet French restaurant with Caribbean traditions. The menus change twice yearly, and are served impeccably in an elegant tropical setting. One of Antigua's most frequented restaurants, Le Bistro has been recommended very highly by Gourmet and many Caribbean gastronomic guides.

Chef Gauducheau has held positions at many fine retaurants and resorts, including The Hotel Restaurant Le Nive Bleu, Golf Hotel, and Hotel Conte Vevey in Switzerland; the Cable Beach Hotel, The French Quarter Restaurant, and the Hodges Club in Antigua; and The Reading Room in Saratoga, New York.

Keith Griffin
Lantana's, Grand Cayman

Keith Griffin is the Head Chef at Lantana's Restaurant. He attended the City & Guilds of London Institute focusing on cooking for the catering industry. He apprenticed at the Athenaeum Hotel in London and went on to become the 2nd Commis on grill station at the Inn on the Park Hotel in London. He has also held positions at the Fourways Inn Restaurant as the Chef de Partie Garde Manager, Grand Pavillion Hotel as the Chef Garde Manager, and L'Escargot Restaurant as Sous Chef, then Head Chef.

Lantana's, under the guidance of Griffin has been feautured in *Gourmet*, *Bon Appetit*, and *Brides* magazines.

Rolston Hector
St. James's Club, Antigua

Chef Rolston Hector began his career in the hospitality industry in 1982 when he became pastry cook at the Jolly Beach Resort. In 1984 he moved to the St. James's Club, also as pastry cook. Two years later he was promoted to the position of supervisor of the pastry department, and promoted again in 1988 to assistant pastry chef. In 1990 St. James's Club selected Hector to attend the Culinary Institute of America to complete courses in professional baking and decorations. In 1991 Chef Hector became the pastry chef.

Peggy Hughes
Cinnamon Reef Resort, Little Harbour, Anguilla

Peggy Hughes is currently working with executive chef Vernon Hughes at Cinnamon Reef Resort where she was hired as pastry chef in 1994. Through her study of Home Economics in high school, she found a desire to be a pastry chef. She left school to work at The Mariners Hotel as a kitchen assistant. She was trained by the many of the chefs there until she was able to move up to take a chef's position.

Vernon Hughes
Cinnamon Reef Resort, Little Harbour, Anguilla

Vernon Hughes is the Executive chef at Cinnamon Reef Resort. He began working at Cinnamon Reef Resort as a dishwasher, but because of his hard work and willingness to learn the sous and executive chefs began to take an interest in him. He was given small cooking responsibilities and began to read cookbooks that gave him new ideas on food preparation.

David Kendrick
Kendrick's Restaurant, St. Croix

Chef David Kendrick's culinary interest was first sparked when he went to work for the International Food Corporation of California in 1974. To broaden his experience, he moved to the east coast of Florida, and then on to the U.S. Virgin Islands where he cooked at several fine restaurants before realizing his dream of having his own restaurant. Kendrick's Restaurant was first opened in 1986 in an eighteenth century greathouse in the heart of Christiansted, St. Croix. David, with his wife and partner Jane, currently own and operate their successful restaurant at its new location in downtown Christiansted.

Roy Khoo
The Ritz Carlton St. Thomas

Born in Penang, Malaysia, Chef Khoo started out with his family in the catering business, delivering food on a bicycle.

He joined the Golden Sands Beach Resort in Penang as a kitchen artist, mainly doing ice sculptures and tallow work.

His first break came when he was offered a job as assistant chef garde manager in Bermuda at the Southampton Princess in 1987. After three months, the garde manager chef left and Khoo was promoted, where he stayed for three and a half years.

In 1990, he joined The Ritz-Carlton Buckhead in Atlanta as assistant garde manager chef, where he won best of show in food competition. After a year, he joined The Ritz-Carlton Amelia Island, Florida as an opening

team member and garde manager chef. In his six years there, he headed all areas of the kitchen as café, banquet chef, and finally executive sous chef.

Chef Khoo is the executive chef of The Ritz-Carlton St. Thomas.

Kyle Kingrey
Villa Madeleine, St. Croix

Chef Kyle Kingrey began as an apprentice at Beno's Cabin in Beaver Creek, Colorado. He moved to Asheville, North Carolina to work at Magnolia's, and then the Asheville Downtown City Club, participating in creating upscale gourmet cuisine. Chef Kingrey has been the executive chef at Indian Cove in South Hampton, New York, Mountain Air Country Club in Burnsville, North Carolina, and Siro's, a fine dining restaurant open only during the Saratoga horse racing season. Kingrey became the consulting chef at Diva Cantinetta in Saratoga Springs to train staff, and then chef de cuisine at Star Boggs in West Hampton Beach in New York before moving to St. Croix to work at Villa Madeleine on Teague Bay.

Patrick Lassaque
The Ritz-Carlton Cancun, Mexico

Patrick Lassaque is the Pastry Chef at The Ritz-Carlton Cancun. He earned his Certificate of Professional Aptitude in pastry, Certificate of Professional Aptitude in kitchen and Diploma of Professional Studies at Lycee Hotelier of Marselille, France.

Chef Lassaque has been employed at Pastry Boutique, Hotel Rosalp, Hotel residence La Pinede. He has been pastry assistant in Le Louis XV at the Hotel de Paris, and Restaurant Le Chantecler at the Hotel Negresco. He has been pastry chef at Le Manior De Paris, and the Hotel Manapany Cottage. He has also been in charge of the Window on the World pastry at The London Hilton on Park Lane.

Alain Laurent
Malliouhana Hotel, Anguilla

Alain Laurent is currently Head Chef at Malliouhana Hotel. He discovered his talent for cooking at an early age and went to France's School of Countryside Tourism to develop his talent. His first apprenticehsip ,at the age of16, was with Master Chef Louis Le Roy. Laurent was then recommended to la Bonne Auberge by Louis Le Roy where he met Jo Rostang, France's internationally-acclaimed Michelin three star and top rated Gault & Millau restaurateur. Through his association with Jo Rostang, Laurent was brought to Malliouhana Hotel where he continues to create unique dishes.

Hubert Lorenz
Caneel Bay Resort, St. John

Chef Hubert Lorenz is the Executive Chef at Caneel Bay

Resort where he was hired to oversee the reorganization of the kitchen prior to the grand re-opening after the resort was aquired by the Rosewood Hotel Group. He is now responsible for a staff of seventy-five.

Chef Lorenz recieved his Master's Degree in Culinary Arts at the Hotel School in Heidelberg, Germany. From there he held various positions in hotels and restaurants throughout Germany and Switzerland. He then moved to the Hotel Queen Elizabeth in Montreal. In 1979 he went to work for ITT Sheraton, first in Cairo, then Hong Kong, and the Sheraton Utama Hotel in Brunei, where theme parties were organized for the Sultan, his family, and visiting dignitaries. In 1984 Chef Lorenz went to work for Hyatt Hotels and Resorts in Bangkok, then Acapulco, Bali, Newport Beach in California, and Lake Tahoe in Nevada.

Michael Madsen
Divi Resort & Casino, St. Croix
Chef Michael Madsen began his apprenticeship at La Cocotte Restaurant, at the Hotel Richmond in Copenhagen, Denmark, first as chef apprentice and then waiter apprentice. He graduated with honors from the Hotel and Restaurant Management School of Copenhagen, Denmark. He then went to the Hotel Kong Frederik in Copenhagen as the chef de partie, in charge of banquet facilities and the seafood and shellfish station.

From 1983 to 1986, Chef Madsen was the executive chef for the Ambassador of Denmark to the United States in Washington, D.C. He then became the executive sous chef at Garden Gourmet, a restaurant featuring contemporary American and classic French cuisine.

As an owner and chef of his own catering company, Scandinavian Cuisine, Chef Michael Madsen had among his many notable clients the U.S. Department of State, the Smithsonian Institution, CBS, PBS, and foreign embassies.

Chef Madsen is currently at Divi Carina Bay Hotel and Casino in St. Croix.

George McKirdy
Aquarela, Isla Verde, Puerto Rico
Pastry Chef George McKirdy learned his craft with several of the nation's finest dessert makers. Prior to arriving at Aquarela, he was an integral part of the successful launching of tte much acclaimed Tribeca Grill, the restaurant housed within Robert DeNiro's Tribeca Film Center.

Chef McKirdy has prepared desserts commissoined for many of New York's most elite and prestigious celebrations, including Nelson Mandela's historic first visit to New York City, as well as fund-raisers for President Clinton. As consulting pastry chef for The Myriad Restaurant Group, McKirdy has produced innovative dessert menus for fine restaurants such as Nobu, TriBakery, The Grill at Reebok Sports Club in New York, and Pine Island Grill.

Philippe Mongereau
Casa de Rio, Dominican Republic
Philippe Mongereau is the chef-manager at Casa de Rio, a gourmet restaurant at Casa de Campo Hotel & Resort. Mongereau is a graduate of Mederic Restaurant & Hotel School in Paris, and took specialzed courses in Cuisine "sous-vide." He has held positions at Ma Maison Restaurant in Los Angeles, Royal Monceau Hotel, La Tour D'Argent, and La Maison Blanche in Paris, and Le Relais St. James in Bordeaux.

Chef Mongereau has been nominated for "Special Chef of the Year" by the New York James Beard Foundation, represented Casa de Campo for the Inernational Wine Association, organized the culinary aspect for the *Casa de Campo Cookbook*, helped organize and prepare the gastronomic festival "Meeting of the Two Worlds, 1992", and represented Casa de Campo in various cities in Japan.

Benoit Pepin
Little Dix Bay, Virgin Gorda, British Virgin Islands
As the executive chef at Little Dix Bay, Benoit Pepin is in charge of creating a wide variety of fresh light fare for guests at three dining rooms and a deli cafe. Pavilion, the most formal of the three restaurants, has a refreshing open-air ambiance and serves freshly caught island seafood, international favorites, and Caribbean specialties with a French flair.

The bi-level Sugar Mill Restaurant is set in the ruins of the stone sugar mill of an ancient Caribbean plantation. Chef Pepin draws inspiration for this menu from Italy.

The casual Beach Grill serves fresh, simple dishes such as grilled burgers, cool salads, and light desserts.

Ivor Peters
The Sugar Mill, British Virgin Islands
Chef Igor Peters was born in St. Vincent. He developed an interest in cooking and baking at a very young age by assisting his mother in the kitchen. In 1987 he left St. Vincent and took to sea as third cook on a Windjammer sailing ship. In 1990 he moved to the British Virgin Islands and began working at the Sugar Mill Hotel and Restaurant on Tortola. When the restaurant offered him an opportunity to further his education at the Culinary Institute of America, he enrolled in some summer courses. During this time he decided to specialize in desserts.

Ramesh M. Pillai
El Conquistador, Puerto Rico
Through the years Ramesh Pillai has been fortunate to work with hotels throughout Europe, India and the Caribbean. Among his long list of hotel openings are Taj Coromandel in Madras, India; Chola Sheraton in Madras; Hotel le Belage, Los Angeles; Grand Hyatt, Washington,

D.C.; and The Hyatt Regency in Aruba, Netherlands.

Born in Tamil Nad, a small town on the southern tip of India, Pillai attended Culinary University in Madras. According to Pillai, it is "the blending of ancient spices with modern Caribbean flair, incorporating the tastes and colors so important to Indian cuisine."

Bent Rasmussen
Top Hat Restaurant, St. Croix

Chef Bent Rasmussen was born in Denmark. He became an apprentice in a small, exclusive restaurant in Copenhagen, working and going to culinary school to achieve his chef's diploma. He spent the required two years in the Danish Navy as a chef in the Officers Mess on a small fort ouside Copenhagen. He then went to Italy for six months, to learn Italian cooking, and then on to Los Angeles, where he worked in Restaurant Scandia in Hollywood. In 1964-65 he was part of the chef team at the Danish Pavillion at the World's Fair in New York, and in the winter when the fair was closed he spent three months doing a promotion for Danish food in the Virgin Islands. He fell in love with the Islands, and returned to work as head chef at the Buccaneer Hotel in St. Croix. In 1967 he and his wife, Hanne, opened their first restaurant, The Top Hat Restaurant. .

John Rhymer
Little Dix Bay Resort, Virgin Gorda, British Virgin Islands

A native of Virgin Gorda, Chef Rhymer started out as a breakfast cook, and then went to the Culinary Institute of America. He graduated as a pastry chef, and returned to Virgin Gorda to work at Little Dix Bay.

Douglas Rodriguez
Aquarella, San Juan, Puerto Rico

Douglas Rodriguez is the Executive Chef and owner of Aquarella in San Juan, Puero Rico as well as Patria in New York, NY. His natural affinity for food became apparent when at 14 he obtained a job in a Miami Beach kitchen. He attended Johnson and Wales University in Providence, Rhode Island and then apprenticed at several South Florida hotels.

Chef Rodriguez recieved the Chefs of America Award in 1991, and the Culinary Master of North America in 1994. He was nominated Rising Star Chef by the James Beard Foundation three times and was awarded the coveted honor in 1996.

Keith Scheible
St. James Club, St. Johns, Antigua

Prior to his position at St. James Club, Keith Scheible has worked at the Jumby Bay Island Resort in Antigua, the China Grill Restaurant in New York City, and River Station Restaurant in Poughdeepsie, New York.

Chef Scheible is a graduate of The Culinary Institute of America.

Norma Shirley
Norma at the Wharfside, St. James, Jamaica

Trained as a nurse, Norma Shirley lived in Sweden, Scotland, England, New York, and Massachusetts before returning to Jamaica to settle 18 miles from where she was born.

Praised by many magazines, Shirley has been described by *Caribbean Travel and Life* as creating "her own little gourmet enclave that reflects her international lifestyle and impeccable taste." *Food & Wine* magazine characterized her as "Jamaica's Julia Child," and she has been featured in *Bon Appetit*, as well.

Chef Shirley works with traditional Jamaican dishes and local ingredients to create a refined, contemporary cuisine.

Dayn Smith
Stingray Cafe, El Conquistador, Puerto Rico

Chef Dayn Smith is the chef/owner of Stingray Cafe and Ballyhoo Bar and Grill at the El Conquistador Resort and Country Club, along with his wife, Nancy Moon. Prior to the inception of Stingray Cafe, Chef Smith had been the executive chef of El Conquistador. His passion for cooking has joyfully returned him to the line, which he works virtually every night at Stingray.

Chef Smith graduated from the Culinary Institute of America with honors, then traveled to Europe to train at the reknown Le Beau Rivage Palace in Lausanne, Switzerland as Chef de Partie Tournant. He has been chef of La Fontain (the gourmet room) of the Westin Detroit Plaza; executive chef ot the United Nations Plaza Hotel; the St. Moritz Hotel, owned and operated by Donald Trump; and the Condado Plaza Hotel and Casino. Chef Smith is on the board of directors of the Caribbean Culinary Federation.

Troy Smith
Necker Island

Chef Smith worked in various hotels and restaurants across Australia before coming to work on Necker Island. He has received many awards for his culinary abilities.

Necker Island began as the private retreat of airline mogul Richard Branson. Composed of a breezy main house, two Balinese cottages, tennis courts, a gym, and a meditation temple, the island can accomodate up to twelve couples at any given time.

Joseph Teuschler
Four Seasons Resort, Nevis

Chef Joseph Teuschler began his career working in a bakery at the age of 13. By the time he was 15, he had entered a formal apprenticeship. Upon completion, he went to work at the Hotel Central in Lech, Austria. From there he was off across the continent, working at the Arlberg and Almhof Schneider hotels in his native Austria, and at the Hotel Maison Blanche in Leukerbad, Switzerland. Moving to Toronto, he began his career with Four Seasons-Regent Hotels and Resorts.

Teushler moved to the Four Seasons Resort Nevis as the assistant pastry chef.

Chef Teushler is now at the Four Seasons Hotel Atlanta as the pastry chef. He manages all pastries, cakes, ice cream, sorbets, chocolates, and breads for the hotel.

Jeffery K. Vigilla
The Ritz-Carlton Cancun, Mexico

As the executive sous chef of The Ritz-Carlton Cancun, Mexico, Jeffery Vigilla is responsible for all restaurant kitchen operations and banquet facilities. He has been involved in menu development throughout the culinary division.

Prior to his position at The Ritz-Carlton Cancun, Vigilla worked at the The Ritz-Carltons in Seoul, Korea; Kapalua, Hawaii; and San Francisco; as well as other fine hotels in Hawaii. He was selected in 1993 to represent The Ritz-Carlton Hotel Company in Monte Carlo for a stage at the Hotel de Paris under Michelin 3-star Chef Alain Ducasse.

Ottmar Weber
Ottmar's Restaurant, Grand Cayman

Ottmar Weber began his career with an apprenticeship as a confectioner by attending the Professional School for Bakers and Confectioners in Dortmund, West Germany, where he was born. He apprenticed under the watchful eye of Maitre de cuisine Cornelius van Sprang, and then the director of Dortmund Hotel and Management School. After passing his chef's exam, Chef Ottmar attended an additional year in management school and practiced his trade at Hotel Petersburg in Bonn and the five-star Hotel Breidenbader Hof in Dusseldorf. He then took the postion as sous chef at the famous Grand Hotel Bad Ragaz in Switzerland.

Chef Ottmar then worked at the Hotel Riviera Dei Fiori on the Italian Riviera, the Divan Hotel in Izmir, Turkey, the Bull Hotel in Long Melford, England, and the Coral Beach and Tennis Club in Bermuda.

Finally Chef Ottmar traveled to what would be his permanent home, the beautiful island of Grand Cayman in the Cayman Islands. He accepted the position of chef de cuisine at the Caribbean Club. One year later, Robert and Jeanne Brenton reopened Petra Plantation as the Grand Old House Restaurant. With Chef Ottmar's culinary skills and the Brenton's eye for detail, Grand Old House soon became a well-known name in the Caribbean as well as the United States and Europe.

In June of 1985, Chef Ottmar opened Ottmar's Restaurant in Grand Cayman. Here he excercises his vast experience with international cuisine and cooking styles.

Roger William Wiles
Half Moon Bay Club, Jamaica

Roger William Wiles is the Executive Chef at the Half Moon Beach Club. He has been Executive Chef at Royal Antiguan, Ramada; St. James Club, Antigua; Royal Bahamian, Nassau; Fourways Inn, Bermuda; and Inn on the Park, London. He has also been Sous Chef at Al' Ecu de France and Chef Patron at Own Restarant.

Chef Wiles has been selected to represent Jamaica as a member of the National Culinary Team to compete at the "Taste of the Caribbean" competition, and upgraded to "Master Craftsman" of the Cookery and Food Association.

Scott Williams
Necker Island

Chef Scott Williams recieved training at Wolluston Comprehensive and Northampton College of Further Education. He began his career at the Falcon Hotel in Northanse, England. Since then he has worked at the Capitol Hotel in London, Hambleton Hall in Leicestershire, The Feathers Hotel in Woodstock in Oxon, The Criterion in Picadilly in London, and Quaqliano's Restaurants in London.

Glossary

A

ACHIOTE: Annatto, the dark, brick-red seeds from the annatto tree that are often made into a paste; these are especially popular in the Yucatán for adding color and an earthy flavor to food. They must be soaked in water overnight before grinding, or you can bring them to a simmer, let them soak for an hour, and then grind them.

ADOBO: A meat or poultry seasoning that includes salt, pepper, garlic, oregano, olive oil, and vinegar.

AHI: The Hawaiian name for both yellowfin and bigeye tuna. Often served as sashimi (Japanese-style raw fish).

ALMOND PASTE: A thick paste made of finely ground almonds, sugar, and water. Almond paste can be formed into sheets or molded into shapes. It is similar to marzipan, but marzipan is made from almond paste, confectioners' sugar, flavoring, and sometimes egg white.

ANAHEIM CHILI: Long green narrow chili used often in Southwest cuisines.

ANISE: Two types of unrelated spices that impart a licorice flavor to food: European or green anise is in the form of small seeds from a bush related to parsley, and star, badian, or Chinese anise takes the form of small brown star-shaped pods. In Southwestern cooking the European type is used, although the two can be interchanged.

ANNATO: See achiote.

ARBORIO RICE: Imported Italian rice with a short, fat grain and high starch content that makes it ideal for risotto.

AVOCADO: A light- to dark-skinned fruit, roughly the shape of a pear, with creamy light green flesh. The pale green flesh is eaten as a vegetable, dip, garnish, or butter substitute. The skin of the avocado may be smooth and green or dark and rough; a ripe avocado should be soft when touched, but not mushy unless it is to be mashed. Do not allow the flesh of any avocado to be exposed to air or it will turn brown. Sprinkle cut surfaces with lemon juice or acidulated water, and for dips such as guacamole, press plastic wrap directly onto the surface of the food until ready to serve.

B

BALSAMIC VINEGAR: Imported from Italy and prized for its mild, almost sweet flavor, balsamic vinegar is made from unfermented grape juice that has been aged for at least ten years. Balsamic vinegar may be used in sauces and salad dressings, and as a topping for fresh fruit.

BAY LEAVES: Flavorful leaves of the laurel tree, used as a seasoning in many dishes. The leaves should always be removed before serving.

BEANS, BLACK: Also called frijoles negros, or turtle beans, these small black kidney-shaped beans are from the Yucatán and central Mexico and have a smoky mushroom flavor stronger than pinto beans. They are used for black bean soup, and have a black-purplish cast when cooked.

C

CALABAZA: A pumpkin-like squash popular throughout the Caribbean as well as Central and South America. Also called a West Indian pumpkin, it is round and can range in size from as large as a watermelon to as small as a cantaloupe. The flesh is a brilliant orange, and the flavor is similar to butternut squash. The seeds are crisp and very good toasted.

CALALOO: A leafy green vegetable similar in taste and texture to spinach. It is an important ingredient in Caribbean cooking, especially in calaloo soup. May also be used in salads, as a garnish, or as an accompanying vegetable.

CAPERS: The small picked flower buds of a shrub thought to have originated in the Orient or the Sahara region. Mexican capers are large; large Italian capers are widely available and may be substituted.

CASSAVA: Also called manioc and yuca, the cassava is a root that ranges from 6 to 12 inches in length and from 2 to 3 inches in diameter. It has a tough brown skin and a crisp, white flesh. There are many varieties, but only two main categories, sweet and bitter. The bitter cassava is poisonous unless cooked. Cassava is available year-round in Caribbean and Latin American markets.

CELERY ROOT: Available September through May, celeriac is a brown, gnarled root prized for its flavor, which is more intene than celery. It should be placed in acidulated water after peeling to prevent discoloration. It can be eaten raw in salads, or braised, sautéed, or boiled and pureed. Store, wrapped in plastic, in the refrigerator for seven to ten days.

CHAYOTE SQUASH: Also called mirliton or christophene, chayote was originally a staple of the Mayas and the Aztecs. The pear-shaped gourd with pale green furrowed skin is grown in the southern states, from California to Florida. Widely available in supermarkets, chayote may be stored in the refrigerator, wrapped in plastic, for up to 30 days. It can be boiled, sautéed, baked and stuffed, or used raw in salads.

CHERIMOYA: a heart-shaped fruit sometimes referred to as a custard apple. The taste combines the flavors of pineapple, mango, banana, and pineapple. Ripe cherimoyas are dull brownish-green.

CHILI PASTE: A thick chili sauce produced and used in many Asian cuisines such as Thai, Vietnamese, Indonesian, and Filipino. It is made of chilis, onions, sugar, and tamarind.

CHOCOLATE

Unsweetened: Also referred to as baking or bitter chocolate, this is the purest of all cooking chocolates. A hardened chocolate liquor (which is the essence of the cocoa bean, not an alcohol), it contains no sugar and is usually packaged in a bar or eight blocks weighing 1 ounce each. Unsweetened chocolate must contain 50 to 58 percent cocoa butter.

Bittersweet: This chocolate is slightly sweetened with sugar, in amounts that vary depending on the manufacturer. It must contain 35 percent chocolate liquor and is used whenever an intense chocolate taste is desired. Bittersweet chocolate may be used interchangeably with semisweet chocolate in cooking and baking.

Semisweet: Sweetened with sugar, semisweet chocolate, unlike bittersweet, may have flavorings such as vanilla added to it. It is available in bar form as well as in chips and pieces.

Milk: A mild-flavored chocolate used primarily for candy bars but rarely (except for milk chocolate chips) in cooking. It may have as little as 10 percent chocolate liquor, but must contain 1 percent milk solids.

Unsweetened cocoa powder: Powdered chocolate that has had a portion of the cocoa butter removed.

Dutch process cocoa powder: Cocoa powder that has been treated to reduce its acidity. It has a more mellow flavor than regular cocoa, but it burns at a lower temperature.

White chocolate: Ivory in color, white chocolate is technically not chocolate at all: It is made from cocoa butter, sugar, and flavoring. It is difficult to work with, and should be used only in recipes that are specifically designed for it.

CHRISTOPHENE: See chayote squash.

CILANTRO: A pungent flat-leaf herb resembling parsley; also called fresh coriander or Chinese parsley. The flavor is pungently sweet, and the scent has been compared to that or orange or lemon peel; a combination of caraway and cumin, or honey. Look for crisp, green, unwilted leaves. Although much less interesting, parsley may be substituted.

CINNAMON: The inner bark from shoots of a tree called Cinnamomum zeylanicum. Cinnamon was originally imported from Spain and Mexico, where it continues to be heavily used; however, the Mexican variety of cinnamon, originally from Sri Lanka, is a lighter brown, is softer in texture, and has a milder taste than the American variety.

CLARIFIED BUTTER: Butter from which the milk solids and water have been removed, leaving pure butterfat that can be heated to a higher temperature without smoking or scorching.

CLOVES: Originally from the Spice Islands and now grown in Madagascar and Zanzibar, supposedly all clove trees are descended from one tree saved when Frenchman Pierre Poivre's collection was destroyed by members of Louis XV's court for political reasons. Cloves are a labor-intensive and expensive spice, as clove buds must be hand-picked from the trees just before they are ready to bloom. Ground cloves will impart a brown shade along with their flavor.

COCONUT MILK: A liquid extracted from shredded coconut meat by soaking it with hot water and straining. Available in cans from Southeast Asia.

CONCH: A shellfish native to the warm waters of the Caribbean and used in the cuisine of south Florida. Conch meat must be tenderized by being pounded before it is cooked.

CORIANDER: The seed of cilantro, or Chinese parsley. See cilantro.

CRAB MEAT: The crab meat called for in Cajun seafood recipes is lump crab meat from the blue crab. Lump meat distinguishes the large pieces of white body meat from flaked crab meat, or small pieces of dark and white body meat from the body and claws. Crab meat is sold fresh, frozen, pasteurized, and canned.

CRAWFISH: Variously known as crawfish, crayfish, mudbugs, and crawdaddies, these fresh-water crustaceans resemble little lobsters, and are sold fresh and frozen, whole and raw, or whole and cooked. Tails are also sold blanched and peeled, and blanched, peeled, and frozen.

CULANTRO: The Spanish term for long coriander, an herb of the parsley family similar to coriander, with a stronger taste. *

CUMIN: Seeds from pods of the indigenous and plentiful Southwestern cumin plant. Used whole and ground, they are mixed with ground chilies to make commercial chili powder, and are also used in curry powder. If a recipe calls for ground red chilies and cumin, do not add additional cumin if substituting chili powder.

F

FLAT-LEAF (ITALIAN) PARSLEY: A variety of parsley with large leaves and a stronger, more pungent flavor than curly-leaf parsley.

FOIE GRAS: The oversized liver of force-fed geese or ducks, foie gras is considered one of the most luxurious of foods. Fresh foie gras should be soaked in tepid water for 1 hour. Then it should be patted dry, the lobes gently separated, and any connecting tubes and visible blood vessels removed and discarded.

FRISÉE: A green with decorative curley edges, frisée is used in salads and as a garnish.

G

GANACHE: A filling or coating made from heavy cream and chocolate. It is also used to make chocolate truffles.

GINGER: Fresh ginger is a brown, fibrous, knobby rhizome. It keeps for long periods of time. To use, peel the brown outside skin and slice, chop, or puree. It will keep indefinitely placed in a jar with sherry and refrigerated.

GOAT CHEESE: Called chèvre in French, goat cheese ranges in flavor from mild and tangy in its fresh form to sharp when it is aged.

GREEN PAPAYA: The unripe form of the papaya, usually shredded and used in salads and stir-fries in Southeast Asian cuisines.

GRITS: Ground white hominy, eaten as a cereal that is similar in texture to pudding.

H

HARICOTS VERTS: Tender, long, and very thin green beans used in French cuisine and now becoming popular in America. They are available in specialty produce markets. Baby Blue Lake beans may be substituted.

J

JÍCAMA: A bulbous, turniplike root vegetable with a taste similar to a very mild and slightly sweet radish. Jícama is crisp and white with a thick brown skin. Choose jícamas that are small, firm, and not visibly damaged. Peel both the brown skin and the woody layer underneath, and use raw or slightly cooked as a vegetable. Fresh water chestnuts have a similar flavor. Available in Asian and Latino markets.

K

KIWI: Kiwis hide their sweet green flesh in a fuzzy brown skin. Select fruit with few imperfections in the skin, and no very soft bruised spots. Peel the kiwi and slice; the seeds are edible.

KOSHER SALT: Also known as coarse salt or pickling salt, kosher salt is pure refined rock salt that does not contain magnesium carbonate. It is less salty than table salt and has larger grains. Use 1/2 to 1 teaspoon of table salt for each tablespoon of kosher salt specified.

L

LANGOUSTINES: A shellfish that resembles a tiny lobster or crayfish, usually 5 to 6 inches long from claw to end of tail, and orange in color.

LEMONGRASS: Long greenish stalks with a pungent lemony flavor. Also called citronella. Substitute grated lemon zest.

LOBSTER: The American, Atlantic, or Maine lobster is a crustacean with a jointed body and two large pincer claws. The larger claw is used for crushing and the smaller one is used for catching its prey. The spiny, or rock, lobster, found in warmer waters from South Africa to the eastern Pacific, lacks the large claws of its northern relative.

M

MAHIMAHI: Also called dolphinfish, with a firm pink flesh. Best fresh, but often available frozen. A standard in island restaurants and markets. Substitute snapper, catfish, or halibut.

MALANGA: A vegetable closely related to the taro root, also called yautia, cocoyam, and Japanese potato. It is about the shape of a regular white potato, resembling an overgrown gladiola bulb because the outside skin is brown and somewhat hairy.

MANGO: Gold and green tropical fruit available in many supermarkets. A ripe mango has a smooth yellow to red skin and smells sweet, with the pale to bright orange-yellow flesh tender to the touch and having a very pleasant but complex taste, simultaneously sweet and tart. A fibrous but gracefully shaped fruit, the mango looks something like a smooth, elongated curved disk or partial kidney bean that is 5 to 6 inches long and 3 to 4 inches wide. The skin should be peeled and the flesh cut away from the stone in strips. Substitute fresh peaches or papaya. Available fresh June through September in the tropics.

MASA: A cornmeal dough used to make tortillas and tamales.

MASCARPONE: A soft, fresh Italian cheese with a high fat content used primarily in desserts and for cheese tortas. If it is not available, combining equal parts of cream cheese and unsalted butter will produce a similar product.

MESCLUN: a mixture of young, small salad greens commonly found in most supermarkets and specialty produce markets. Commonly included are arugula, dandelion, frisée, oak leaf, and radicchio. Choose greens with crisp leaves and no signs of wilting.

MISO: A soybean paste made by salting and fermenting soybeans and rice. Shiro miso, or white miso, is the mildest of several different types. Available shrink-wrapped, and in cans and jars, in Asian markets. Can be stored for months in a refrigerator.

MUSHROOMS

Morels: These spring mushrooms are about 1 inch long with a tall, hollow, pitted cap. The colors range from grey to brown to black, depending on where they are found. Their flavor is rich, nutty, and meaty when cooked, and they should never be eaten raw. Morels are also available dried.

Portobello mushrooms: Huge mushrooms with caps from 3 to 6 inches in diameter. The brown gills underneath the cap should be cut away before the mushrooms are cooked or they will give a dark brown color to the dish.

Shiitake mushrooms: Although they originated in Japan and Korea, shiitake mushrooms are now cultivated in the U.S. They have a meaty flavor and texture and average from three to six inches in diameter. Widely available year-round both fresh and dried, the fresh ones tend to be expensive. They are most plentiful in spring and fall.

N

NASEBERRY: An oval, brown fruit similar in size to kiwi. It has a thin smooth skin, and yellow to light brown flesh, and becomes soft and juicy when ripe. The flavor is similar to that of a pear.

NORI: Sheets of dried and compressed seaweed used in making rolled sushi. Available in Japanese markets.

O

OREGANO: Also called wild, bastard, or dwarf marjoram, oregano is used to season many foods, especially sauces and soups. Though similar to marjoram, oregano plants grow wild in the Southwest and are shorter, heartier, huskier, and more potent than marjoram. The best substitute for oregano is marjoram or, if preferred, sage.

P

PAPAYA: An attractive fruit with shiny round black seeds surrounded by bright orange or pink flesh. It is tender to the touch, shaped like a gourd or a large, elongated pear, and has a mottled yellow-green skin. Papayas are available year-round. They have a sweet, musky flavor with a slight citrus tang and are used primarily for dessert. They must be ripe when used or they will be bitter and acid. The skion of the papaya contains a natural enzyme that tenderizes meat, and is frequently included in marinades for that reason. In Hawaii, the most common papaya used is the solo papaya, a tropical fruit with a yellow flesh, black seeds, and a perfumey scent. Other types are larger, and may have pink flesh; all are suitable for island recipes. Also see green papaya.

PARCHMENT PAPER: A white heat-resistant paper sold in rolls at cookware stores. It is used in cooking to line baking pans and baking sheets, to cook foods en papillote, and to loosely cover delicate foods like fish fillets during poaching.

PASSION FRUIT: A small yellow, purple, or brown oval fruit of the passion fruit vine. The "passion" in passion fruit comes from the fact that its flower resembles a Maltese cross and refers to Christ's crucifixion, not to aphrodesiac qualities. The flavor is delicate but somewhat sharp, and perfumelike. Passion fruit is a natural substitute for lemon juice. Passion fruit concentrate can be found in the frozen juice section of many markets. Substitute oranges.

PEPPERS (CHILIS): Indigenous to South American and culti-aved by the Incas and Aztecs, chilis were used as a sea-soning and spread north through Mexico City to the Pueblo Indians in New Mexico. In lore, chilies are credit-ed with everything from increasing sexual potency to aid-ing digestion. We do know they are high in vitamins A and C, and cause a secretion in the stomach that may aid in digestion. Chilies may be named for their use, appear-ance, flavor, creator, or potency. Chili potency is commer-cially rated from 1 (for the weakest) to 120 (for the strongest), with jalapeños rated at 15. When shopping, look for firm, unblemished, and fairly straight chilies with smooth skinds. Dried chilies should be free from mold and unbroken.

Anaheim: Also called California, California greens, chiles verdes, or, when canned, mild green chilies, Anaheim chilies are dark green, about 7 inches long, $1^{1/2}$ inches wide, and mild to hot in flavor. When the chilies ripen completely in the fall, they turn red and are sweet-er and milder. Their large size makes Anaheim chilies ideal for stuffing.

Cayenne: Also called finger or ginnie peppers, cayenne chilies are long (3 to 8 inches) and slender. The bright green chilies turn red when ripe and are very hot. Cayennes are usually dried and ground; the powder may be used interchangeably with pure red New Mexico chili powder. Cayenne pepper is a staple in Louisiana cuisine.

Jalapeño: A fairly small, dark green hot chili approxi-mately 2 inches long and 1 inch wide. One of the most widely available fresh chilies. Serrano is a common sub-stitution, although the heat from jalapeños is immediate while the serrano provides more of an afterburn. Jalapeños can vary in the level of hotness, and those with striations on the skin are older and usually hotter. It's bet-ter to start with less than the required amount, and add to suit personal taste.

Poblano: A shiny dark green chili pepper, about three inches wide and five inches long, poblanos are mild to hot. They are widely availabe fresh in supermarkets, and are also sold canned. They are the chili used in chiles relleños. When used in sauces, they may be interchanged with Anaheim chilies, though the flavor will be different. In their dried form, they are known as ancho peppers.

Scotch bonnet (habañero): The hottest of all chilies, these tiny crinkled red or yellow peppers are available in supermarkets and specialty produce markets.

Thai: Very powerful chilies that are about 1 inch long, slender, and dark green or deep red. Cayennes or pequíns may be substituted.

PHYLLO (FILO) DOUGH: This tissue-paper-thin pastry is made from a flour and water dough. Phyllo sheets are used in layers, and brushed with butter or oil before baking. They are widely available in packages in the frozen section of supermarkets.

PINEAPPLE: Fresh pineapples are covered with a prickly brown skin, and topped with sharp, pointed leaves. To select a fresh ripe pineapple, give the tiny center leaves at the top a light tug: The leaves will easily pluck out of a ripe pineapple. Fresh pineapple contains an enzyme which will break down protein; rinse well and add as close to serving time as possible when using in dishes contain-ing gelatin.

PLANTAINS: Similar to a banana in both shape and texture, plantains are a member of the same family. The green skin will develop black spots as it ripens, and the slightly pink flesh must be cooked to be edible. Most commonly sliced thin and fried.

PLUM (ROMA) TOMATOES: Small plum-sized red tomatoes fre-quently used in Italian cuisine because their thick, meaty flesh is excellent for drying and for making sauces. Regular red tomatoes may be substituted.

POLENTA: Coarsely ground yellow or white cornmeal. Polenta is traditoinally combined with stock or water and cooked slowly until thick. It may be served creamy, or it may be chilled, cut into shapes, and grilled.

PUFF PASTRY: Flaky pastry that rises up to ten times its orig-inal height when baked. It is made from flour, water, but-ter, and salt. The distinctive flakiness results from adding the butter during a series of at least six rollings, turnings, and foldings that trap layers of butter and air between the layers of the pastry; when baked, the butter melts and the air expands as steam, puffing up the pastry. It can be pre-pared at home, or purchased frozen.

Q

QUINOA: Tiny and bead-shaped, ivory-colored quinoa looks like rice and expands to four times its original size. The flavor is delicate, almost bland, and is similar to couscous. It is available packaged as a grain and in several forms of pasta, and can be used in any way suitable for rice. It can be found in health food stores and some supermarkets.

R

RICE PAPER: Thin sheets of noodles made from rice flour and water. Soften the sheets in water before wrapping food with them.

RICE WINE VINEGAR: A light vinegar made from fermented rice.

S

SAFFRON: Saffron is the most expensive food in the world. It is made up of the dried stigmas of the Crocus sativus, which are laboriously hand-picked from each flower. One acre of crocus plants produces about four-four pounds of saffron. Saffron is used both as a flavoring and to impart its characteristic yellow color to food. It takes only a few threads to achieve the desired flavor and color.

SAKE: Clear Japanese rice wine. Other strong clear liquors, such as tequila or vodka, can be substituted.

SHIITAKE MUSHROOMS: The second most widely cultivated mushroom in the world, medium to large with umbrella-shaped, flopped tan to dark brown caps with edges that tend to roll under. Shiitakes have a woodsy, smoky flavor. Can be purchased fresh or dried in Asian groceries. To reconstitute the dried variety, soak in warm water for 30 minutes before using. Stem both fresh and dried shi-itakes.

SOY SAUCE: A dark salty liquid made from soybeans, flour, salt, and water. Dark soy sauce is stronger than light soy sauce. A staple in most Asian cuisines.

SOY SOP: A fruit native of the Americas, common through-out South America and the Caribbean. Usually heart-shaped and 6 to 12 inches in length with soft, thorny green skin. The flesh is creamy in color and has black seeds. It is not sour, rather sweet and musky.

STAR ANISE: Brownish seeds with eight points that taste like licorice.

STAR FRUIT: A waxy, light green fruit; also called carambo-la. Cut in cross section, it reveals a five-pointed star shape. Trim the points off the stars if the points are too dark for your taste.

T

TAMARIND: A brown, bean-shaped pod from the tamarind tree. The fruit is sweet-sour, and is made into sauces, candy, and pastes.
Thai basil: A green and red variety of basil. Substitute fresh sweet basil.

THAI CHILI PASTE: A slightly sweet, thick, hot bottledpaste of garlic, vinegar, and chilies. Sriracha is a brand name.

THAI CURRY PASTE: Yellow, red, and green curry pastes used in many Thai and Southeast Asian sauces. Yellow is gen-erally the mildest and green the hottest. Thai ginger:

V

VANILLA BEANS: The pods of a relative of the orchid, vanilla beans are green and have no flavor when picked, they are then cured by a process of sweating and drying. Once cured, the long, wrinkled black beans are either bundled whole for export or processed into extract.

W

WAKAME: A deep green, edible seaweed popular in Japanese and other Asian countries used like a vegetable in soups and simmered dishes, as well as occasionally in salads. The browner versions are more strongly flavored.

Y

YAMS: A sweet root vegetable similar in appearance to the sweet potato, but with pointed ends and a subdued yel-low-orange color. Though Dioscorea sativa is the most popular commercial type, the darker variety called yam-pee, or cush-cush (D. trifida) grows in the southern U.S. and Mexico and produces clusters of smaller, tastier yams. Yams are often candied. They should be firm, unwithered, and umblemished when purchased.

YAUTIA: see malanga.

YUCA: A plant native to Latin America and the Southwest. The petals, fruit, and root can all be eaten, and the root is also used as a thickener for soups and stews.

Z

ZEST: The thin, brightly colored outer part of citrus rind. It contains volatile oils, making it ideal for use as a flavor-ing.

Basic Recipes

Clarified Butter

Melt butter over low heat, then cover and refrigerate it. Once the fat has hardened, scoop it off, being careful to leave the bottom layer of milk solids. Cover the clarified butter and refrigerate for up to 2 weeks.

If you don't have time to let the butter chill, melt the butter gently so that the milk solids settle on the bottom of the pan, forming a creamy white sediment. Carefully pour off the clear yellow butter, and discard the milk solids or add them to soup or sauce.

Crème Anglaise
Makes 2 cups

4   egg yolks
⅓   sugar
1½   cups milk, heated
1   vanilla bean, split in half lengthwise, or 2 teaspoons vanilla extract
1   tablespoon butter, at room temperature (optional)

In a medium heavy saucepan whisk the egg yolks over low heat until they are pale in color. Whisk in the sugar 1 tablespoon at a time, then whisk until the mixture reaches the consistency of cake batter.

Whisk in the milk and vanilla bean, if using, then stir continuously with a wooden spoon until the custard coats the spoon and a line drawn down the back of the spoon remains visible. Remove the pan from the heat and stir in the vanilla extract, if using, or remove vanilla bean pods.

If the custard is to be chilled, press a sheet of plastic wrap directly onto the surface to prevent a skin from forming, or dot the top with bits of optional butter. Chill the custard for up to 2 days.

Note: If the custard begins to overheat and the egg yolks are forming lumps, remove it immediately from the heat and whisk briskly to cool the mixture. Push the custard through a fine mesh sieve with the back of a spoon to remove the lumps. If it has not sufficiently thickened, return it to heat to complete cooking.

Cooked Fruit Purée or Sauce
Makes 2 cups

4   cups fresh berries or fruit
¼   cup sugar (or to taste)
¼   cup water
2   tablespoons raspberry liqueur (or eau-de-vie) (optional)
1   tablespoon fresh lemon juice (or more to taste)
½   teaspoon ground cinnamon (or more to taste)

Put the berries in a large sauté pan or skillet with the sugar, water, and optional liqueur or eau-de vie. Cook over medium heat for 15 minutes, or until the fruit is soft enough to mash with a spoon and most of the liquid has evaporated. Add the lemon juice and cinnamon, then taste and adjust the flavor with additional sugar, lemon juice, or cinnamon as needed.

Transfer the mixture to a blender or food processor and purée until smooth. Strain the fruit through a fine-mesh sieve, cover, and refrigerate until cold, about 2 hours; this should be a very thick purée. It may be used as an ingredient in another recipe, or by itself as a sauce.

VARIATIONS: Plum, Prune, Apple, or Pear Purée or Sauce: Substitute 12 chopped pitted large plums or dried prunes, or 8 peeled, cored, and chopped large apples or pears for the berries.

Uncooked Fruit Purée (Coulis)
Makes about 2 cups

4   cups fresh berries (or 2 cups diced fresh fruit)
2   tablespoons sugar or more to taste
1   teaspoon fresh lemon juice

Purée the berries or fruit in a blender or food processor. Strain the purée through a fine-mesh sieve. Stir in the sugar and lemon juice. Adjust the amount of sugar if necessary. Cover and refrigerate until needed. This purée may be used as an ingredient in another recipe, or by itself as a sauce.

Peppers

HANDLING BELL PEPPERS AND CHILIS

Bell peppers now come in a rainbow of colors, and there are literally hundreds of varieties of chilies. Here are some general rules common to all:

Handling fresh chilies: Precautions should be exercised in handling fresh hot chilies, since they contain potent oils. Either wear rubber gloves, or wash your hands thoroughly with soap and hot water after handling chilies. Never touch your skin until you've washed your hands. Also, wash the knife and cutting board in hot soapy water. Do not handle hot chilies under running water, since that spreads the oil vapors upward to your eyes.

Seeding and deribbing: Either cut out the ribs and seeds with a paring knife, or cut away the flesh, leaving a skeleton of ribs and seeds to discard. For the second method, cut a slice off the bottom of the pepper or chili so that it will stand up on the cutting board. Holding the pepper or chili with your free hand, slice its natural curvature in sections. You will be left with all the flesh and none of the seeds and ribs. The flesh may now be cut as indicated in the recipe.

Roasting and peeling: Cut a small slit near the stem end of each whole pepper or chili to ensure that it will not explode. Roast the peppers or chilies in one of the following ways:

For a large number of peppers or chilies, and to retain the most texture, lower them gently into 375°F (almost smoking) oil and fry until the skin blisters. Turn them with tongs when one side is blistered, since they will float to the surface of the oil. This method is also the most effective if the vegetables are not perfectly shaped, since it is difficult to get the heat from the broiler into the folds of peppers and some chilies.

Place the peppers or chilies 6 inches from the preheated broiler, turning them with tongs until all surfaces are charred.

Place the peppers or chilies on the cooking rack of a hot charcoal or gas grill and turn them until the skin is charred.

Place a wire cake rack over a gas or electric burner set at the highest temperature and turn the peppers or chilies with tongs until all surfaces are charred.

Place the peppers or chilies on a rack on a baking sheet in a preheated 550°F oven until they are totally blistered. Use this method only for a sauce or a recipe in which the peppers or chilies are to be puréed.

Cool the peppers or chilies by one of the following methods:

Place them in ice water. This stops the cooking action immediately and cools them enough to peel them within 1 minute. The peppers or chilies will stay relatively firm.

Place the peppers or chilies in a paper bag, close it, and let them cool. This also effectively separates the flesh from the skin, but it will be about 20 minutes before they are cool enough to handle, and they will soften somewhat during that time.

Finally, pull the skin off and remove the seeds.

CHICKEN STOCK
Makes 12 cups

6	quarts water
5	pounds chicken bones, skin, and trimmings
2	carrots, peeled and cut into chunks
1	large onion, halved
3	garlic cloves, halved
3	celery stalks, halved
3	fresh thyme sprigs, or 1 teaspoon dried thyme
6	fresh parsley sprigs
3	bay leaves
12	black peppercorns

In a large stockpot combine the water and the chicken bones, skin, and trimmings. Bring to a boil, then reduce the heat to a simmer, skimming off the foam that rises for the first 10 to 15 minutes. Cook for 1 hour, then add the remaining ingredients. Increase the heat to bring the liquid to a boil, reduce heat to low, and simmer the stock for 3 hours.

Strain the stock through a fine-mesh sieve and let cool to room temperature, then refrigerate. Remove and discard the congealed layer of fat on the surface. Store in the refrigerator up to 3 days. To keep longer, bring the stock to a boil every 3 days, or freeze it for up to 3 months.

To clarify the stock: Let the stock cool until lukewarm. Blend 3 egg whites together and pour into the warm stock; as the whites coagulate and rise they will trap bits still floating in the stock. When the egg whites have risen to the top and the stock is clear, skim the eggs off the top with a slotted spoon. Repeat the process if necessary to obtain clear stock.

VEAL OR BEEF STOCK
Makes 12 cups

8   pounds veal or beef bones and trimmings
2   onions, halved
2   carrots, peeled and cut into chunks
2   celery stalks, halved
3   garlic cloves, halved
8   quarts water
3   fresh thyme sprigs, or 1 teaspoon dried thyme
6   fresh parsley sprigs
2   bay leaves
12 black peppercorns

Preheat the oven to 400°F. Put the bones and trimmings in a roasting pan and roast until they are browned, about 45 minutes, turning occasionally. Add the vegetables to the pan and roast 20 minutes longer or until the vegetables are browned. Pour off any fat.

Place the bones and vegetables in a large stockpot. Add 1 quart of the water to the pan and place on the stove over high heat. Stir to scrape up the brown bits, clinging to the bottom of the pan. Pour this liquid into the stockpot with the remaining 7 quarts of water and the herbs and spices. Bring to a boil, then reduce the heat to a simmer, skimming off the foam that rises for the first 10 to 15 minutes. Simmer for 5 to 6 hours.

Strain the stock through a fine-mesh sieve and discard the solids. Let cool, then refrigerate. Remove and discard the congealed layer of fat on the surface. Store the stock in the refrigerator up to 3 days. To keep longer, bring the stock to a boil every 3 days or freeze it for up to 3 months.

FISH STOCK
Makes 12 cups

4   quarts water
1   cup dry white wine
4   pounds fish trimmings such as skin, bones, and heads
2   tablespoons fresh lemon juice
1   onion, halved
2   celery stalks, halved
4   fresh parsley sprigs
2   fresh thyme sprigs, or 1 teaspoon dried thyme
2   bay leaves
6   black peppercorns

In a large stockpot bring the water and wine to a boil. Rinse all the fish trimmings under cold running water, add to the stockpot, and return to a boil.

Reduce the heat to a simmer, skimming off the foam that rises for the first 10 to 15 minutes. Simmer for 1 hour.

Add the remaining ingredients to the pot. Bring the mixture to a boil, then reduce the heat and simmer for 1 hour and 30 minutes to 2 hours. Strain the stock through a fine-mesh sieve, pressing on the solids with the back of a large spoon. Discard the solids. Let cool, then cover and refrigerate up to 3 days. To keep longer, bring the stock of a boil every 3 days, or freeze it for up to 3 months.

Shrimp or lobster stock: Follow the preceding recipe, using 4 pounds shrimp shells or lobsster shells in place of the fish trimmings.

VEGETABLE STOCK
Makes 12 cups

4   large leeks, carefully washed
2   large carrots, peeled and sliced
4   large celery stalks, sliced
4   large yellow onions, sliced
5   garlic cloves
6   fresh parsley sprigs
4   fresh thyme sprigs, or 1 teaspoon dried thyme
2   bay leaves
16 cups water
½   teaspoon white peppercorns
1   teaspoon black peppercorns
    Salt to taste

Place all the ingredients except the salt in a large stockpot. Slowly bring the liquid to a boil over medium heat, reduce heat to a simmer, and cook, partially covered for 1 hour and 30 minutes. Strain through a fine-mesh sieve, pressing the liquid from the solids with the back of a large spoon. Let cool, then cover and refrigerate for up to 3 days. To keep longer, bring to a boil every 3 days or freeze for up to 3 months.

LAMB STOCK

3   pounds lamb trimmings (bones, skin, fat, and/or anything else you can trim away) and meat
4   quarts (16 cups) water
1   onion, halved
1   carrot, peeled and halved
2   celery stalks, including leaves, cut into sections
3   fresh thyme sprigs, or 1 teaspoon dried thyme
3   fresh parsley sprigs
6   black peppercorns

Preheat the oven to 450°F. Put the trimmings and meat in a shallow roasting pan and roast for 30 minutes, or until browned.

Bring the water to a boil over high heat. Add the trimmings and meat to the water and reduce the heat to medium. When the water comes back to a boil, skim frequently until the scum stops rising, then add the remaining ingredients and simmer, uncovered, for at least 6 hours. Add additional water if the stock level falls below the level of the ingredients.

Strain the stock and discard the solids. Let the stock cool to room temperature, then refrigerate. remove and discard the congealed fat layer from the top. Store in the refrigerator for up to 3 days. To keep longer, bring to a boil every 3 days or refrigerate for up to 3 months.

Rich Stock: Multiply the amount of rich stock specified in the recipe by 1½, and pour that amount of the kind of stock specified into a small saucepan. Bring to a boil over high heat. Cook the stock to reduce it by one third. If the stock was not salt-free, add a few slices of raw potato or some uncooked rice before reducing the stock; the starchy substance will absorb much of the salt.

LAMB, VEAL, OR BEEF DEMI-GLACE
Makes 2 cups

Demi-glace is unsalted meat stock that has been degreased and then reduced over medium low heat until it becomes rich and syrupy. The concentrated flavor adds richness and depth to sauces and stews. Traditional demi-glace is thickened with flour and must simmer gently with much tending, but this quick version is lighter and can be made more quickly because it is thickened at the end with arrowroot or cornstarch.

2	tablespoons vegetable oil
1	large onion, diced
2	celery stalks, diced
1	carrot, peeled and sliced
½	cup diced ham
3	tablespoons tomato paste
1	fresh thyme sprig
1	bay leaf
6	peppercorns
10	cups Lamb, Veal, or Beef stock (see page xxx)
½	cup Madeira
2	to 3 teaspoons arrowroot or cornstarch mixed with 2 tablespoons cold water
	Salt and freshly ground black pepper to taste
1	tablespoon unsalted butter

In a large saucepan heat the oil over medium heat. Stir in the onion, celery, carrot, and ham. Cover and cook over low heat for 10 minutes. Uncover the pan and stir in the tomato paste, thyme, bay leaf, and peppercorns. Whisk in the stock and Madiera, and bring to a boil over high heat.

Once the mixture has started to boil, reduce heat to medium high and cook the sauce to reduce to 2 cups. Depending on the rate at which the liquid is boiling, this may take anywhere from 30 minutes to 1 hour. Strain the liquid through a fine-mesh sieve into a 2-cup measuring cup. If it has not reduced enough, pour the liquid back into the pan and keep boiling. If it has reduced too much, add enough water to make 2 cups.

Pour the liquid back into the pan and bring it back to a simmer. Whisk in the arrowroot or cornstarch mixture 1 teaspoon at a time, returning the sauce to a simmer after each addition, until the sauce reaches the desired consistency. Add salt and pepper. If using the sauce immediately, swirl in the butter. If not serving immediately, do not whisk in the butter, but remove the pan from heat and place dots of butter on the surface of the sauce to prevent a skin from forming. Whisk in the butter when reheating the sauce. To store, cover and refrigerate for up to 5 days or freeze for up to 3 months.

TOMATOES

To peel and seed tomatoes: Cut out the core of the tomato. With a knife, make an X on the bottom of the tomato. Plunge the tomato into boiling water for exactly 10 seconds. Remove with a slotted spoon and plunge into a bowl of cold water, then drain. Peel off the skin. Cut the tomato in half crosswise. Squeeze and shake the tomato gently over a bowl or sink to remove the seeds. Any clinging seeds may be removed with the tip of a paring knife or your fingers.

BALSAMIC GLAZE

1	cup balsamic vinegar
⅓	cup sugar

To make the glaze: Mix the vinegar and sugar together in a saucepan and cook over medium-low heat until the mixture is reduced by one fourth. Let cool.

BALSAMIC SYRUP

½   cup balsamic vinegar

Warm the balsamic vinegar over low heat and simmer until it is reduced and syrupy, 15 - 20 minutes. Serve warm.

Fried Vegetable Garnishes

FLASH-FRIED PARSLEY
(also for ginger, basil, and other herbs)

Flash-frying parsley in very hot oil produces brittle-crisp dark green parsley leaves for garnishes. Any similar thin-leaved herb may be substituted for the parsley; ginger may also be cut in flat strips or in very small julienne and flash-fried. Be very careful with the oil as you are working at very high temperature.

1   bunch fresh parsley, stemmed
    Flour for dusting
    Vegetable oil for deep-frying
    Salt and finely ground pepper (optional)

Thoroughly wash and dry the parsley. Heat 4 inches of vegetable oil to 375 F in a saucepan or deep fat fryer. Very lightly dust the parsley with flour, shaking off all excess to leave just the barest coating. Drop a handful of parsley into the hot oil and fry for 30 seconds, or until just crisp. Drain on a paper towel to absorb excess oil. Optional: season with salt and pepper.

FRIED VEGETABLE CHIPS OR STRIPS

Vegetables can be cut in any variety of slices and strips and fried for attractive garnishes. Don't crowd the vegetables in the fryer and let the oil reach full temperature between each batch so that the vegetables are crisp. Try slices and discs of potato, yam, beetroot, parsnip, carrot, plantain, and other firm vegetables and fruits; try ⅛-inch fine julienne of leeks, onion, or any of the previously mentioned vegetables. Quantities vary depending on what you are doing with the fried vegetables and how much you need to make; allow enough flour to very lightly dust the surface of the vegetables, and enough oil to immerse the vegetables fully.

Vegetable pieces (discs, slices, strips, sticks)
All-purpose flour for dusting
Vegetable oil for frying

In a deep fryer or deep saucepan, heat the oil to 350 to 360°F, or until a breadcrumb immediately sizzles and comes to the top when dropped in. Dust the vegetable pieces with flour, shaking off all but the thinest coating. Fry a handful at a time for 30 seconds, until they have floated to the top and crisped. Remove with a slotted spoon, and drain on paper towels. Repeat until all the pieces have been fried.

FRIED SPIRAL OR SHOESTRING VEGETABLES

Curly crisp fried vegetable spirals or shoestrings piled high over appetizers and entrees are a delight to the eye, and interesting to eat. These clever garnishes are basically firm vegetables, cut very very thin in strips or spirals, and flash-fried until crisp but not browned. The secret lies in not crowding the vegetables into the hot oil, and keeping the oil very hot.

For garnish, use about one potato, beet, carrot, or similar firm vegetable per serving. Peel the vegetable and cut into spiral slices on a spiral slicing machine, or by hand on or mandolin or other slicer into shoestrings. Heat the oil to 350 or 360°F, or until a breadcrumb immediately sizzles and comes to the top when dropped in. Toss the vegetables lightly with the flour in a paper bag, dusting off excess: you want just enough to slightly dry the surface of the vegetable. Put a handfull of the spirals or shoestrings into the oil and let fry for 15 to 20 seconds, just until slightly crisp but not browned. Remove and drain on paper towels. Repeat with the remaining spirals or shoestrings, letting the oil return to temperature between additions.

VEGETABLE CUPS OR BASKETS

Attractive cups and baskets can be made by cutting long, very thin strips of vegetables, then overlapping and frying them. Carrots, plantains, parsnips—any vegetable you can cut into long thin strips can be used.

One vegetable per basket
Vegetable oil for frying

Peel the vegetables and cut into very thin lengthwise slices, ⅛-inch thick. In a large skillet over medium-high heat, heat 2 inches of oil to 350°F, or until a breadcrumb immediately sizzles and comes to the top when dropped in. On a work surface, crisscross two slices, pressing at the center. crisscross them with four more slices to create a "star," pressing together at the center each time more slices are added. Using a large spatula, drop into the hot oil. Fry the vegetable "star," turning once, until lightly browned and crisp, about 3 to 4 minutes. Invert a cup or small bowl and lay a paper towel over the bottom. Remove vegetable "star" from the oil with a slotted spoon and lay over the inverted cup or bowl, pressing the sides down around the cup. Let stand until cooled, then remove and set aside on more paper towels. Repeat this process with the remaining plantains to complete 3 more cups.

TO TOURNER VEGETABLES

This term refers to the classic French technique of cutting hard vegetables such as carrots and potatoes ionto elegant ovals less than 1 inch in length with a sharp paring knife. The vegetables were cut into these uniform sizes and shapes to cook quickly and uniformly. To master the craft, cut a vegetable into a rectangle slightly larger than the desired size of the finished tourneed vegetable, and then cut away the corners to form an oval. Vegetables cut into chunks or dice of the same size will cook in the same amount of time as tourneed vegetables and are, of course, far simpler to prepare for home dining.

VEGETABLE CURLS

To curl carrots, beets, and radishes for garnish, grate or pare the cleaned vegetable in long thin strips and immediately place the strips in ice water. To curl green onions (scallions), with a small sharp knife, cut in half lengthwise through the bulb. Trim the stems 4 to 5 inches above the bulb. Cut the green stems into lengthwise strips, leaving attached at the bulb, and place in ice water.

PLANTAIN CHIPS

3 plantains, peeled and thinly sliced
½ cup butter
   Salt to taste

In a skillet melt half of the butter and sauté the plantain slices a few at a time until golden brown. Add more butter as needed. Salt and lightly serve.

GARLIC BUTTER
Makes 2 cups

1 tablespoon garlic powder
3 minced fresh cloves garlic
   Juice of 1 lemon
1 pound (4 sticks) salted butter

In the bowl of a food processor or mixer combine all of the ingredients. Beat until smooth, about 4 minutes. Pack into molds or a glass container with a lid, and refrigerate. Keeps up to 1 week.

CARAMEL SAUCE
Makes 2 cups

1½ cups sugar
½ cup water
3 tablespoons butter
1 cup heavy (whipping) cream, heated
½ teaspoon vanilla extract

In a heavy medium saucepan combine the sugar and water and bring to a simmer over medium heat, swirling occasionally. Cover, increase the heat to medium high, and cook for 2 minutes or until the liquid gives off large thick bubbles. Uncover and cook, swirling the syrup, until it turns golden brown.

Remove the pan from the heat and stir in the butter with a wooden spoon. Add the cream, stirring constantly, then add the vanilla. Return the pan to low heat and stir constantly until any lumps have melted and the syrup is smooth. Serve warm over ice cream or cake, or pour into a jar, cover, and refrigerate for up to 1 week.

CHOCOLATE SAUCE
Makes 4 cups

1 cup sugar
2 cups half and half
8 ounces bittersweet chocolate, chopped
8 ounces unsweetened chocolate, chopped

In a large, heavy saucepan heat the sugar and half-and-half over medium-low heat until hot but not boiling. Add the chocolate and stir until the chocolate is melted and the mixture is smooth. Serve warm, or pour into a jar, cover, and refrigerate for up to 1 week.

ICE CREAM BASE
Makes 3 cups

2   cups heavy (whipping) cream
½   cup half and half
8   egg yolks
1   cup sugar

In a medium saucepan over medium-high heat bring the cream and half and half to a boil. Meanwhile, beat the egg yolks with the sugar in a medium bowl until light and fluffy, 6 to 8 minutes. Stir some of the hot cream iinto the egg yolks, then add the egg yolks to the hot cream mixture. Cook over medium heat for 8 minutes, or until the mixture begins to boil and is thick enough to coat a spoon. Remove from the heat. Cover and chill.

OPENING COCONUTS

Puncture one of the "eyes" of the coconut with a sharp, pointed tool such as an icepick. Pour out the liquid, then crack the coconut by hitting it with a hammer in the middle, where the shell is widest. Continue around the nut until you have cracked the shell in a circle around the middle and can separate the two halves. Pry the meat out of the shell with a sharp, heavy knife. Or, heat the coconut in a pre-heated 350° oven for 15 minutes, then let sit until cool emough to handle. Wrap the coconut in a kitchen towel and crack it into pieces with a hammer.

SHAVING COCONUT

Break the meat into small pieces, peel off the brown papery inner covering, and grate the meat with the large holes of a box grater or use a vegetable peel-er to create shavings. Coconut may also be shred-ded in a food processor using the shredding disk or chopped finely with the steel blade.

GRINDING COCONUT

Break the meat into small pieces, peel off the brown papery inner covering, and grate the meat with the small holes of a box grater or cut the meat into ½-inch cubes using a heavy, sharp knife, and grind in a food processor using the pulse button.

Index